3rd Edition Extra

with business skills lessons and self-assessment

Intermediate

MARKET LEADER

Business English Course Book

with MyEnglishLab

David Cotton David Falvey Simon Kent

FT Publishing
FINANCIAL TIMES

GLOBAL SCALE
of English

Contents

Introduction

What is *Market Leader*, and who is it for?

Market Leader is a multi-level business English course for businesspeople and students of business English. It has been developed in association with the *Financial Times*, one of the leading sources of business information in the world. It consists of 12 units based on topics of great interest to everyone involved in international business.

This third edition of the Intermediate level features completely updated content and a significantly enhanced range of authentic resource material, reflecting the latest trends in the business world. If you are in business, the course will greatly improve your ability to communicate in English in a wide range of business situations. If you are a student of business, the course will develop the communication skills you need to succeed in business and will enlarge your knowledge of the business world. Everybody studying this course will become more fluent and confident in using the language of business and should increase their career prospects.

The authors

David Falvey (left) has over 25 years' teaching and managerial experience in the UK, Japan and Hong Kong. He has also worked as a teacher trainer at the British Council in Tokyo, and was Head of the English Language Centre and Principal Lecturer at London Metropolitan University.

David Cotton (centre) has over 45 years' experience teaching and training in EFL, ESP and English for Business, and is the author of numerous business English titles, including *Agenda*, *World of Business*, *International Business Topics* and *Keys to Management*. He is also one of the authors of the best-selling *Business Class*. He was previously a Senior Lecturer at London Metropolitan University.

Simon Kent (right) has over 25 years' teaching experience, including three years as an in-company trainer in Berlin at the time of German reunification. He has spent the majority of his career to date in higher education in the UK where he has taught on and directed programmes of business, general and academic English.

What is in the units?

STARTING UP

You are offered a variety of interesting activities in which you discuss the topic of the unit and exchange ideas about it.

VOCABULARY

You will learn important new words and phrases which you can use when you carry out the tasks in the unit. You can find definitions and examples, and listen to the pronunciation of new vocabulary in the i-Glossary feature on the DVD-ROM. A good business dictionary, such as the *Longman Business English Dictionary*, will also help you to increase your business vocabulary.

READING

You will read authentic articles on a variety of topics from the *Financial Times* and other newspapers and books on business. You will develop your reading skills and learn essential business vocabulary. You will also be able to discuss the ideas and issues in the articles.

LISTENING

You will hear authentic interviews with businesspeople and a variety of scripted recordings. You will develop listening skills such as listening for information and note-taking. You can also watch the interviews on the DVD-ROM.

LANGUAGE REVIEW

This section focuses on common problem areas at intermediate level. You will become more accurate in your use of language. Each unit contains a Language review box which provides a review of key grammar items.

SKILLS

You will develop essential business communication skills, such as making presentations, taking part in meetings, negotiating, telephoning, and using English in social situations. Each Skills section contains a Useful language box, which provides you with the language you need to carry out the realistic business tasks in the book.

CASE STUDY

The Case studies are linked to the business topics of each unit. They are based on realistic business problems or situations and allow you to use the language and communication skills you have developed while working through the unit. They give you the opportunity to practise your speaking skills in realistic business situations. Each Case study ends with a writing task. After you've finished the Case study, you can watch a consultant discussing the issues it raises on the DVD-ROM.

WORKING ACROSS CULTURES

These four units focus on different aspects of international communication. They help to raise your awareness of potential problems or misunderstandings that may arise when doing business with people from different cultures.

REVISION UNITS

Market Leader Intermediate third edition also contains four revision units, each based on material covered in the preceding three Course Book units. Each revision unit is designed so that it can be completed in one session or on a unit-by-unit basis.

EXTRA BUSINESS SKILLS

The new Business Skills lessons offer the learner a task-based, integrated skills approach to the development of core business skills such as Presentations, Negotiations, Meetings, and Small Talk. These lessons appear at the end of every three units and incorporate performance review, suggestions for professional development and goal setting. They are based on the Global Scale of English Learning Objectives for Professional English. These objectives are signposted at the top of each new lesson in the Student's book and the carefully scaffolded activities are crafted around each objective, creating a clear sense of direction and progression in a learning environment where learners can reflect on their achievement at the end of the lesson.

Brands

'Products are made in the factory, but brands are made in the mind.'
Walter Landor (1913–1995), branding pioneer

STARTING UP

A   **Work with a partner. List some of your favourite brands. Then answer these questions.**

1   Do you / Would you buy any of the following brands? Why? / Why not?

Coca-Cola	Ikea	Microsoft	Tesco	Chanel
IBM	General Electric	Virgin	Nokia	Kellogg's
Toyota	Google	Intel	Samsung	Ford
McDonald's	Mercedes-Benz	Disney	Marlboro	China Mobile

2   Which of the brands above do you think feature in the top-ten Interbrand list in both 1999 and 2007? (Check your answer on page 134. Are you surprised?)

3   Pick some of the brands above which interest you. What image and qualities does each one have? Use these words and phrases to help you.

value for money	upmarket	timeless	well-made	classic
durable	inexpensive	cool	reliable	stylish
fashionable	sexy	sophisticated	fun	

4   How loyal are you to the brands you have chosen? For example, when you buy jeans, do you always buy Levi's? Why do people buy brands?

5   Why do you think some people dislike brands?

B   CD1.1 **Listen to two speakers talking about brands. What reasons does each person give for liking or disliking brands? Which person do you agree with?**

VOCABULARY
Brand management

A **Match these word partnerships to their meanings.**

brand

1 loyalty   a) the title given to a product by the company that makes it
2 image   b) using an existing name on another type of product
3 stretching   c) the ideas and beliefs people have about a brand
4 awareness   d) the tendency to always buy a particular brand
5 name   e) how familiar people are with a brand (or its logo and slogan)

product

6 launch   f) the set of products made by a company
7 lifecycle   g) the use of a well-known person to advertise products
8 range   h) when products are used in films or TV programmes
9 placement   i) the introduction of a product to the market
10 endorsement   j) the length of time people continue to buy a product

market

11 leader   k) the percentage of sales a company has
12 research   l) customers of a similar age, income level or social group
13 share   m) the best-selling product or brand in a market
14 challenger   n) information about what consumers want or need
15 segment   o) the second best-selling product or brand in a market

B **Complete these sentences with word partnerships from Exercise A.**

brand

1 No one recognises our logo or slogan. We need to spend more on advertising to raise  *brand awareness*.

2 Consumers who always buy Sony when they need a new TV are showing ....

3 A fashion designer who launches his or her own perfume is an example of ....

4 The .... of Mercedes-Benz is such that its products are seen as safe, reliable, luxurious, well made and expensive.

product

5 George Clooney advertising Nespresso is an example of ....

6 A .... consists of introduction, growth, maturity and decline.

7 Tesco's wide .... means that it appeals to all sectors of the UK market.

8 The use of Aston Martin cars and Sony computers in James Bond films are examples of ....

market

9 Microsoft is the .... in computer software.

10 In countries with ageing populations, the over-60s age group is becoming an increasingly important ....

11 Pepsi is the .... in carbonated soft drinks.

12 Focus groups and consumer surveys are ways of conducting ....

C **Discuss these questions.**

1 What are the advantages and disadvantages for companies of product endorsements?

2 How can companies create brand loyalty?

3 Can you give any examples of successful or unsuccessful brand stretching?

4 Think of a cheap or expensive idea for a product launch.

5 What other market segments can you identify (e.g. young singles).

6 What action can companies take if they start to lose market share?

See the DVD-ROM for the i-Glossary.

7

Chris Cleaver

Watch the interview on the **DVD-ROM.**

LISTENING
Successful brands

A ◀)) CD1.2 **Chris Cleaver is Managing Director, Business Brands at Dragon Brands. Listen to the first part of the interview and tick the points that he makes.**

A brand ...

1 helps people to become familiar with a product.
2 gives a product an identity.
3 increases the sales of a product or service.
4 enables the target consumer to decide if they want the product or not.

B ◀)) CD1.3 **Listen to the second part of the interview and answer the question.**

What is the main function of a brand?

C ◀)) CD1.4 **Listen to the final part. In which two ways has Chris Cleaver's company helped Nokia?**

D **Think of three brands you really like and discuss what 'appealing and persuasive' ideas they communicate to you.**

READING
Building luxury brands

A **What is the brand image of Dior?**

B **Skim the article on the opposite page quickly and say which of the following points are mentioned:**

1 The high profit margins on bags
2 Investing in markets that may take some time to grow
3 People are ready to pay a lot of money for very high-quality things because they are beautiful.
4 Building customer loyalty through ready-to-wear

C **Read the article and complete the notes in the maps below. Then correct the ten mistakes.**

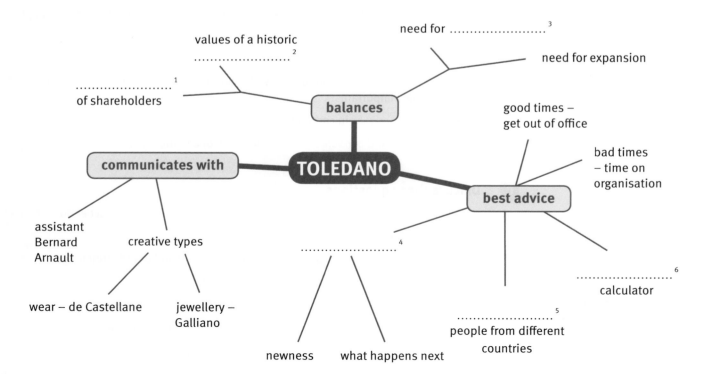

FT

Restless pursuer of luxury's future

by Vanessa Friedman

Sydney Toledano (Dior's Chief Executive) is one of the longest-serving chief executives in the luxury industry. As the industry goes global, he must balance the demands of shareholders and the values of a historic label, the need for exclusivity and the need for expansion.

He routinely communicates with his demanding boss, Bernard Arnault, main shareholder of Christian Dior, and a number of creative types, including Dior's clothes designer John Galliano and jewellery designer Victoire de Castellane.

'The best advice I ever got was that, when times are bad, you need to get out of the office; when things are good, you can spend time on the organisation,' says Mr Toledano, who travels almost every week to one of Dior's 224 stores round the world. 'You have to look for newness, look for what is happening next. Forget the calculator. Understand the people from different countries and what they want.'

It was by spending time in China in the 1980s, for example, when he worked at the French leather-goods house Lancel, that Mr Toledano first realised China would one day be prime territory for luxury.

'I met some factory owners, and they were working so hard, but then they would bring you to a restaurant and it was clear they wanted to enjoy life,' he says. 'And I thought: one day these people are going to have money and they are going to spend it.'

A few years later, Bernard Arnault contacted him. 'The interview took 15 minutes. He knew exactly what he wanted,' says Mr Toledano: to take a small couture house he had bought out of bankruptcy and build it into the biggest luxury group in the world. Mr Arnault has used Dior to create LVMH (Louis Vuitton Moët Hennessy, the world's largest luxury group).

'Christian Dior can double in five years,' he says. 'There may be difficult times coming, but if you look at the Middle East, China, even Europe, I believe there is growth coming, and we have to develop our network and perfect our supply chain.'

The next wave of luxury buyers is now in the new territories: the Middle East, Russia, Hong Kong and South Korea.

Sydney Toledano, CEO Dior

Mr Toledano believes not only that a brand should go to its customers but that it should anticipate their needs and invest early in markets that may not show real growth for up to six years.

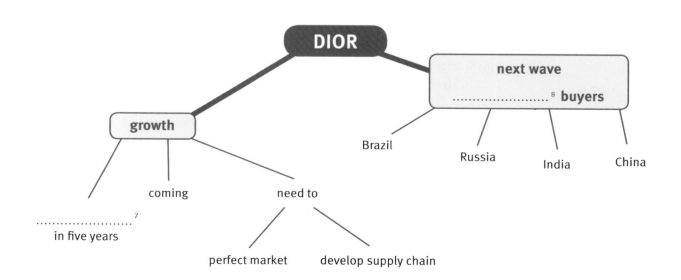

LANGUAGE REVIEW
Present simple and present continuous

The present simple and the present continuous have several uses.

- We use the present simple to give factual information, for example about company activities.
  *Christian Dior Couture **makes** luxury, ready-to-wear fashion.*
  *Dior Homme **targets** the male consumer.*

- We use the present simple to talk about routine activities or habits.
  *Toledano routinely **communicates** with his demanding boss.*
  *Toledano **travels** every week to one of Dior's 224 stores.*

- We use the present continuous to talk about ongoing situations and projects.
  *Fashion house Christian Dior **is** now **selling** baby bottles.*

- We use the present continuous to talk about temporary situations.
  *Dior **is** currently **looking** to recruit a marketing director for the UK and Ireland.*

➡ *Grammar reference* page 146

A **Which of the time expressions below do we usually use with the present simple? Which do we usually use with the present continuous? Which are used with both?**

usually	this year	every day	now
often	nowadays	once a month	currently
at the moment	these days		

B **Complete these sentences with the present simple or the present continuous form of the verbs in brackets.**

1 a) At the moment, eBay .... (work) with brand owners to remove fake items.

   b) eBay .... now (spend) $20m a year analysing suspicious sales.

2 a) Louis Vuitton usually .... (sell) its products through authentic Louis Vuitton boutiques.

   b) At the moment, Louis Vuitton .... (negotiate) with Hubert de Givenchy.

3 a) Both Apple and BlackBerry .... (launch) important new products this year.

   b) These days, a lot of people .... (have) a BlackBerry.

C **Complete this text with the present simple or the present continuous form of the verbs in brackets.**

The Google brand ....[1] (grow) rapidly. According to the Millward Brown Brandz report, it ....[2] (hold) first place in the list of top 100 brands. In fact, the IT field ....[3] (dominate) the top-ten corporate brands. Google ....[4] (operate) websites at many international domains, the most popular being www.google.com, and ....[5] (generate) revenue by providing effective advertising opportunities. Google always ....[6] (focus) on the user, and consumers usually ....[7] (see) Google as quite trustworthy.

Nowadays, companies ....[8] (begin) to recognise that brands are amongst their most valuable assets. They understand that brands ....[9] (become) ever more powerful in driving business growth. Strong brands ....[10] (generate) superior returns and protect businesses from risk. Google currently ....[11] (hold) the top position, but it has to keep innovating if it wants to remain number one. BlackBerry and Apple are the two fastest-growing brands in the top 100, and China Mobile ....[12] (grow) steadily, too.

SKILLS

Taking part in meetings

A ◀)) CD1.5 **Four marketing executives at a sports sponsorship agency are talking about finding a new sport for their client, a well-known media company to sponsor. Listen to the conversation and answer the questions.**

1   Why does the client want to change the sport they sponsor?

2   Which four sports do the executives consider?

3   Which sport does Mario suggest? Why does he suggest it?

4   What must David do before he contacts Larry Harrington's agent?

B ◀)) CD1.5 **Listen again and complete the extract.**

Joy   Well, there are several possibilities. .... [1] ice hockey? It's an incredibly fast, exciting sport, it's very popular in America and in a lot of European countries.

David   OK, that's a possibility. .... [2], Natasha? Would ice hockey be a good choice?

Natasha   Mmm, ... [3]. It's not really an international sport, is it? Not in the same way as baseball, for example, or ... tennis.

David   .... [4] – baseball's got a lot more international appeal, and it's a sport that's got a good image. I don't know about tennis – I'm not sure it would be suitable. Mario, ... [5]?

Mario   .... [6], motor racing would be perfect for our client. It's fast, exciting, and the TV coverage of Formula One races is excellent. They would get a lot of exposure, it will really strengthen their image.

David   That's a great idea, Mario. .... [7] get in touch with Larry Harrington's agency and see if he's interested? Harrington's young, exciting – he'd probably jump at the chance to work with our client. They're a perfect match. But first I must check with our client and make sure they're happy with our choice.

C **Which of the phrases in Exercise B are:**

1   asking for opinions?

2   giving opinions?

3   agreeing or disagreeing?

4   making suggestions?

D **Role-play this situation.**

Jeanne de Brion is a jewellery company in Boston, USA. A year ago, it launched a line of jewellery with the brand name 'Cecile'. This is the name of the French designer who created the collection. Unfortunately, the Cecile line has not achieved its sales targets. Three directors of the company meet to discuss how to improve sales.

Work in groups of three. Read your role cards, study the Useful language box and then role-play the discussion.

Student A: Turn to page 134.   Student C: Turn to page 143.
Student B: Turn to page 140.

USEFUL LANGUAGE

ASKING FOR OPINIONS	GIVING OPINIONS	AGREEING	DISAGREEING	MAKING SUGGESTIONS
How do you feel about that?	I think / I don't think that's a good idea.	That's true.	I see / know what you mean, but I think there's a problem.	I think we should reduce our prices.
What do you think?	In my opinion, we need new products.	I agree.		How about a special promotion?
What's your view?		Absolutely.	I'm not so sure.	Why don't we talk to the big stores?
		Exactly.	Maybe, but that's not enough.	Maybe / Perhaps we could offer incentives.
		I think so, too.		

HUDSON CORPORATION

A luxury luggage manufacturer is facing increased competition from cheaper imports. It must decide how to protect its brand and create new markets for its products.

Background

Hudson Corporation, based in New Jersey, USA, makes top-of-the-range luggage and travel accessories. It is a well-known brand name in the USA. Its suitcases and bags are associated with high quality, traditional design and craftsmanship. Hudson emphasises in its advertising that its products are 'made in America'. Recently, the company's market share in the USA has decreased. One reason for this has been the increased competition from Asian companies selling similar products at much lower prices.

A year ago, the management decided to boost sales by entering the European market, focusing initially on Switzerland, Germany, France and Italy. They set up a branch office and warehouse facility in Zurich, which would be the base for their European expansion.

What problems do you think Hudson will face on entering the European market? Make a list of your ideas.

Market research

Hudson recently set up a series of focus groups to find out how consumers perceived the company's brand in the USA.

Which of the findings do you think may have contributed to the company's lower market share in its home market?

Do you think Hudson's luggage and bags are:	% of people answering 'yes'
expensive?	72
exclusive?	56
value for money?	48
good quality?	82
old-fashioned?	68
exciting?	15
innovative?	18

◀》 **CD1.6** Four of Hudson's American managers are talking about the problems they could face in Europe. **Listen and make notes on the key points.**

MARKETING STRATEGIES FOR EUROPE – OPTIONS

Reposition the brand

Sell Hudson suitcases and bags at medium price ranges. Manufacture the products in a country where labour costs are low, e.g. India or China. Do *not* promote the products as 'Made in America'. Use a high-volume, low-cost strategy for Hudson's core products.

Develop the Hudson brand

Promote the Hudson products as an exclusive brand and keep the 'Made in America' tag. Sell the products in the higher price ranges. Use product placement in films and television to support the brand. Hire a famous, sophisticated, influential man and woman to endorse the products. Two well-known French film stars have shown interest in endorsing a new range.

Hire a top designer

Employ a top designer to produce a new range of smaller suitcases and shoulder bags aimed at businesspeople travelling in Europe and at rich, younger, fashion-conscious buyers. Sell the products under a new label.

Develop a wider product range

Sell a wider range of products under the Hudson label, e.g. trolley-backpacks, document cases, briefcases, name-card holders, shoulder bags for men and women. Sell at lower, competitive prices.

Stretch the Hudson brand

Put the Hudson brand on high-quality watches and jewellery. Make an agreement with the Swiss manufacturers of these top-of-the-range products.

Develop sales using e-commerce

Sell the existing product lines via the Internet at very competitive prices.

Task

1 ***Work in small groups*** as directors of the Hudson Corporation. Hold an informal meeting. Consider the advantages and disadvantages of each option listed above. Choose *two* of the marketing strategies which Hudson should focus on to expand sales in European markets.

2 ***Meet as one group*** and decide which *two* marketing strategies you will use to develop sales in European markets.

Writing

As the CEO of Hudson Corporation, write an e-mail to the head of European Marketing Associates, David Wright, summarising the actions you agreed to take at your meeting, with your reasons. Suggest a time for a meeting with David Wright and his associates.

➡ *Writing file page 127*

Watch the Case study commentary on the **DVD-ROM.**

'Flying? I've been to almost as many places as my luggage.'
Bob Hope (1903–2003), American humourist

STARTING UP

A **Discuss these questions with a partner.**

1 How often do you travel by air, rail, road and sea?

2 Do you enjoy travelling? What don't you enjoy about it?

3 Put the following in order of importance to you when you travel.

comfort	safety	price	reliability	speed

Does the order of priorities change for different types of travel?

B **Choose the correct words from the box to complete the following list of things which irritate people when flying.**

cabin	cancellations	checks	food	jet
luggage	queues	room	seats	trolleys

1 not enough leg............

2 lost or delayed ....

3 long .... at check-in

4 poor quality .... and drink

5 no baggage .... available

6 overbooking of ....

7 flight delays and ....

8 tiredness and .... lag

9 delays for security ....

10 oversized hand luggage in the ....

C 🔊 **CD1.7 Listen to three people talking about their travel experiences. Tick the problems in Exercise B that they mention.**

D **Which of the things in Exercise B irritate you most? Which irritate you least? Discuss your ideas with a different partner.**

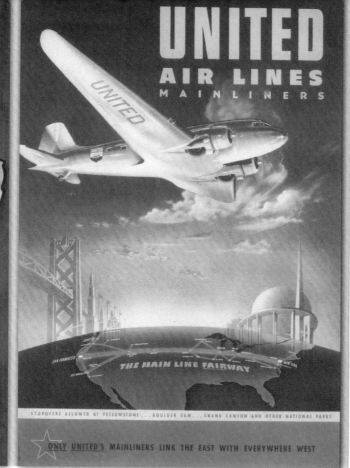

VOCABULARY

British and American English

A **Match the words and phrases which have the same meaning. For each pair, decide which is British English and which is American English.**

1	subway	a)	line
2	city centre	b)	lift
3	carry-on baggage	c)	public toilet
4	one way	d)	schedule
5	return	e)	economy class
6	freeway	f)	single
7	rest room	g)	first floor
8	elevator	h)	bill
9	coach class	i)	booking
10	timetable	j)	round trip
11	car park	k)	downtown
12	queue	l)	motorway
13	check	m)	underground
14	reservation	n)	hand luggage
15	ground floor	o)	parking lot

B **Work in pairs. Use the American English words or phrases from Exercise A to complete this text.**

My last overseas business trip was a nightmare from start to finish. First of all, there was a delay on the way to the airport, as there was an accident on the _freeway_ [1]. When I got there, I found the lower level of the airport .... [2] was flooded. Next, my .... [3] was too big and heavy, so I had to check it in. When we arrived, the .... [4] was closed, and there were no cabs at all. After a long time trying to figure out the .... [5] and waiting in .... [6] for 40 minutes, we finally got a bus .... [7] and found the hotel. Then there was a problem with our room .... [8] and, would you believe it, the .... [9] wasn't working, and our rooms were on the fifth floor.

*See the **DVD-ROM** for the i-Glossary.*

C ◀) CD1.8 **Listen to the recording and check your answers to Exercise B.**

15

LISTENING
Hyatt Hotels

Sholto Smith

A ◀)) CD1.9 **Listen to Sholto Smith, Area Sales Director for Hyatt Hotels, talking about how the company meets the needs of business travellers. Listen to the first part and tick which of the following he mentions.**

Location of hotels	Good links with underground networks	Close to the airport
Totally non-smoking	Good restaurant	Close to client's office
Technology	Internet	Business centre
Swimming pool	Translation services	Free transport to hotel

B ◀)) CD1.10 **Listen to the second part and complete the notes on the ways hotels are adding value to their guests' stay.**

- ....¹ on a daily basis
- Membership to the ....²
- Newspapers
- Transportation to and from the ....³
- A shuttle service to:
  a) the ....⁴
  b) the ....⁵ in which the client works

C ◀)) CD1.11 **Listen to the third part and summarise the future developments in the business travel market that Sholto mentions.**

Watch the interview on the **DVD-ROM**.

D **In groups, discuss what is important for you when staying in a hotel, for either work or pleasure.**

READING
What business travellers want

A **What factors do you consider when choosing an airline?**

B **Work in pairs. Complete the table below for your article. (You may not be able to answer every point.)**

Student A: Read the article on page 17.
Student B: Read the article on page 134.

	Edmond Moutran	John Cox
job	Chairman of Memac Ogilvy & Mather	
nationality		British
travel destinations		
amount of air travel		
choice of class		
choice of airline		
likes		
dislikes		
travel to airport		
hotel requirements		

Article A

FT

Counting the ways to bridge the gulf

by Jill James

As more carriers open up more routes, travelling to and around the Middle East has never been easier.

5 Edmond Moutran, the 63-year-old Chairman and Chief Executive of Memac Ogilvy & Mather, the multinational advertising and communications company, should know. The Lebanese executive 10 reckons he spends 60% of his working week in the air. 'I spend 200 days in Beirut, 40 days in Dubai, 40 days in Bahrain and 25 in the UK. I also spend one week in each 15 of Cairo, Jordan, Jeddah, Riyadh, Kuwait, Tunis and Algeria. I go to South Africa once a year, Barcelona once or twice a year for conferences and I go to Paris four times a year.'

20 He says his choice of airline is dictated by convenience, but his preference is for Middle East Airlines and its 'new aircraft and equipment, and well-trained, fresh and energetic 25 staff'. His second choice is Gulf Air, with Emirates third, followed by British Airways and Air France.

He always travels with his wife, Liliane, who worked with him 30 until very recently, and prefers to travel first class. He also uses business class. He says he will travel economy 'in an emergency'.

He uses airline lounges. 'I want 35 good chairs, plenty of newspapers and television. Airlines that spend millions on décor and have uncomfortable chairs really need to look at themselves.'

40 'MEA gets me a car to the airport and they open a special counter for me as an individual,' he says. 'Staff take your boarding pass, check you in and walk you through to the lounge. 45 The airline saves me about an hour of standing in line. It shows real respect. You don't really get this extra-special treatment on other airlines. With MEA, it's the whole process 50 – that's why I'm so loyal to them.'

So what annoys him most about flying? 'The attitude of crew and

staff sometimes,' he says. 'If they're tired of their jobs, they should 55 give it up. I also dislike the casual attitude of ground staff. Employees should be trained to cope with customers who have problems.'

Mr Moutran says that problems with 60 ground staff are one of the reasons he hates travelling to the US. 'No one ever has time to answer a question there,' he says. He also doesn't like the lack of openness shown by airlines 65 when there are problems and delays.

C In pairs, share information about the two articles. Compare the attitudes of the two travellers. Whose point of view is closest to yours?

D Match the sentence halves to complete the definitions of the words in bold.

1 **Peak travel** happens

2 When you **check in,**

3 **Frequent-flyer points** are

4 An **upgrade** is

5 A **lounge** is

6 A **boarding pass** is

7 **Ground staff** are

a) a change to a better seat or level of service.

b) a room in a hotel/airport where people can sit and relax.

c) a card you must show in order to get on a plane.

d) all the people who work at an airport, but not the pilots or cabin crew.

e) awarded by airlines to reward customer loyalty.

f) at times when the largest number of people are travelling.

g) you go to desk at a hotel/airport to say you have arrived.

E Complete the text with the phrases from Exercise D.

I don't always pay a lot of money and I try to avoid ....[1]. However, I do travel a lot, earn ....[2] and usually get an ....[3] to first class. The airline gets me a car to the airport. I am met by helpful ....[4]. They take my ....[5] and help me ....[6]. Then they take me to the ....[7], where I read the newspapers.

LANGUAGE REVIEW
Talking about the future

We can use different language forms to talk about the future.

- We use *going to* to talk about what we intend to do and have already decided to do.
  *My colleague and I **are going to** attend our Chairman's wedding in Seattle next month.*
  *Some airlines **are going to** increase fuel surcharges this week.*

- We use *will* or *'ll* to talk about something we have decided to do at the time of speaking.
  *The deal's off. **I'll call** the travel agent to cancel the flights.*

- We use the present continuous to talk about a fixed arrangement.
  *I'**m travelling** from Australia to Europe in September.*

- We use the present simple to talk about a timetable or programme.
  *The flight **leaves** Ho Chi Minh City at 11:30 on Tuesday. It **arrives** in Danang at 12:40.*

➡ *Grammar reference* page 146

A **Complete each dialogue with the correct form of *going to* or *will*.**

1 **A** Have you decided where to hold the sales conference?

   B Yes, we .... book the Emory Centre in Atlanta.

2 **A** I can't find my passport.

   B OK, you look in your bag, and I .... check the back seat of the car.

3 **A** What are you planning to do in Tokyo?

   B We .... meet our agent to discuss next year's advertising budget.

4 **A** I'm afraid the flight's been cancelled.

   B I need to get there tonight. I .... take the train. I think it leaves at nine.

5 **A** The Hertz counter is a good place to meet.

   B OK, I .... wait for you there.

B **Choose the correct tense (present continuous or present simple) to complete the sentences.**

1 We *stay / are staying* at the Ritz for next week's conference.

2 According to the timetable, the coach *departs / is departing* from Victoria at 8:00, reaches Lille at 12:30 and arrives in Paris at 13:30.

3 Excuse me, what time *is the conference beginning / does the conference begin*?

4 What *do you do / are you doing* on Tuesday afternoon?

5 What time *is this train getting / does this train get* to Osaka?

6 Next time, I *travel / am travelling* to Madrid by train.

C **In pairs, take turns to complete the sentences below. Use *going to*, *will*, the present continuous or the present simple.**

1 The flight's delayed, so ....

2 OK, I've decided. I ....

3 Let's check the timetable. The flight ....

4 It's OK, I don't need a lift. I ....

5 Friday afternoon? I'll just check my diary. I ....

6 There are two flights to Hong Kong on Friday............ .

7 It's all arranged, we ....

8 Next week, ...

Telephoning: making arrangements

A 🔊 CD1.12, 1.13 **Jennifer North, Sales Director at Madison in New York, makes two telephone calls to Cristina Verdi, a fashion buyer in London. Listen and note a) the purpose of each call and b) the result.**

B 🔊 CD1.12 **Listen to the first call again and complete this extract.**

Jennifer   I'm calling because I'll be in London next week and ....
.... [1] to see you. I want to tell you about our new collection.

Cristina   Great. What .... [2]? I'm fairly free next week, I think.

Jennifer   ....[3]? In the afternoon? Could ....
....................[4] then?

Cristina   Let me look now. Let ....[5]. Yes, that'd be no problem at all. ....[6] two o'clock? Is that OK?

C 🔊 CD1.13 **Listen to the second call again and complete this extract.**

Receptionist   Thank you. I'm putting you through ... Hello, I'm afraid she's engaged at the moment. ....[1] or can I put you through to her voicemail?

Jennifer   Would you be able to take a message for me, please? I'm in a bit of a hurry.

Receptionist   Yes, certainly.

Jennifer   The thing is, I should be meeting Ms Verdi at 2 p.m., ...
....[2]. My plane was delayed, and I've got to reschedule my appointments. If possible, ...[3] tomorrow, ...[4] in the morning. ....
....................[5] here at the hotel, please, to confirm?

Receptionist   Certainly. What's the number?

Jennifer   It's ....[6].

D **Role-play these two telephone situations.**

1   Student A, you are a company employee who has arranged to meet Student B, a colleague from one of your subsidiaries. Explain that you cannot keep the appointment and give a reason. Suggest an alternative day.

2   Student B, you are on a business trip to Singapore and need to stay an extra day. Your hotel is full. Telephone the airline office. Talk to the representative, Student A, to arrange a different flight and a night at another hotel.

USEFUL LANGUAGE

ANSWERING THE PHONE

Hello, Carla Rodríguez speaking.

Good morning, Tiger Ltd.

MAKING CONTACT

I'd like to speak to Martin Krause, please.

Could I have the sales department, please?

IDENTIFYING YOURSELF

This is / My name's Karin Nordby.

Karin Nordby speaking.

STATING YOUR PURPOSE

I'm calling about ...

The reason I'm calling is ...

MAKING ARRANGEMENTS

Could we meet on Monday at 11:00?

How/What about June 12th?

Is 9:30 convenient/ OK?

RESPONDING

That's fine/OK for me.

Sorry, I can't make it then.

No problem.

CLOSING

Good. So, I'll see you on the 8th.

Thank you. Goodbye.

Right. / OK, then.

That's great, I'll see you ...

CHANGING ARRANGEMENTS

I'm afraid I can't come on Friday. I'm very busy that day.

I'm sorry, I can't make it on Tuesday. I've got something on that morning.

We've got an appointment for ten o'clock, but I'm afraid something's come up. Could we fix another time?

BUSINESS TRAVEL SERVICES  BTS

A specialist travel agent has to work hard to retain a key client.

Background

Business Travel Services (BTS) is based in Philadelphia, USA. One of its most important clients is the large multinational corporation NeoTech, whose head office is also in Philadelphia. Recently, NeoTech's senior executives have had problems when they have been on business trips organised by BTS.

| Home | Flights | Hotel bookings | Car rental | Conference | Insurance |

Who we are
BTS provides a full range of corporate travel services. We are highly experienced in handling the requirements of today's business traveller. Among our many clients are multinational companies which are household names.

What we do
Our travel consultants work to produce top-value fares and the best itineraries to suit the needs of your staff. We will minimise your expenses by arranging your staff's travel at the right price, getting additional discounts for you and establishing direct contact with the best service providers. All our overseas partners are selected because of their high standard of service, attention to detail and quality of product.

We offer: Flights, Hotel bookings, Car rental, Conference bookings, Insurance

Stage 1

The Head of Travel at NeoTech phones the Account Manager of BTS to set up a meeting, so that they can discuss the problems that executives have had while on business trips.

In pairs, role-play the telephone conversation to set up the meeting.

Student A:
You are Head of Travel at NeoTech. Turn to page 135 to read the information in your diary and check when you are available for a meeting.

Student B:
You are the Account Manager for BTS. Turn to page 140 to read the information in your diary and check when you are available for a meeting.

Stage 2

NeoTech's Head of Travel phones BTS's Account Manager to change the time of the meeting. Some equipment has been stolen from their office, and the police are investigating. The Head of Travel suggests meeting in two weeks' time on a Wednesday.

BTS's Account Manager cannot meet on the Wednesday – he/she is giving a speech at an international travel conference. He/She suggests an alternative day and time.

Role-play the telephone conversation.

Stage 3

Following a request from BTS's Account Manager, NeoTech's Head of Travel sends summaries of four problems which senior executives at NeoTech had during recent business trips (see page 21).

Hotel Problem

Last Thursday, I checked into the Excelsior Hotel. The receptionist told me I had been upgraded and my room was on the 16th floor. Well, I stayed there for an hour or so, then asked to move to another room. The 'upgraded' room had no safe for my money, and the lighting was very bad. Also, there was a group of noisy people next door.

The new room was no better. I couldn't take a shower because there was no water for four hours. The coffee machine didn't work, the ice machine was out of order and the desk was too small. I called the receptionist to get some action, but she seemed too busy to do anything.

This hotel simply isn't up to standard. What can you do about it for me?

Lost Luggage

Three months ago, I travelled to Atlanta, Georgia. Two pieces of luggage didn't arrive. I reported the loss to the airline. They promised to find the bags and send them to me. Some weeks later, they wrote saying they couldn't find the bags and asked me to fill out a claim form. I didn't hear from them for another month, then they asked me to send receipts for all the missing articles. I didn't have receipts for the lost items.

It's three months later, and still no news from the airline. My e-mails and letters get no response. The airline has recently merged with another company, and I wonder if this is part of the problem. Can you help?

Car Rental Problem

The rental office at the airport couldn't give me the car I had reserved. It was in the medium price range at $250 a week. Instead, they offered me a choice:

- a smaller car, which was uncomfortable and had a small trunk;
- a bigger car for an extra $20 a day.

I was expecting a free upgrade, but the clerk on the desk refused to do that. His attitude was 'take it or leave it'. So I hired the bigger car. When the company billed me, I ended up paying $490 for the car.

Diverted Flight

I was on a flight to Moscow, but the flight was diverted to Helsinki because of bad weather. There was a lot of confusion at Helsinki because the airline sent all the passengers to the same hotel for the night. Some passengers became very aggressive when they tried to get a room. I had to share a room with another passenger. The hotel made all passengers pay for their rooms. The next morning, we had to wait six hours in a cold terminal for the flight to Moscow.

The airline wouldn't pay for our hotel expenses. They said the circumstances were 'beyond their control'. I think we should be compensated for all the inconvenience.

Task

Work in groups of four. One of you is BTS's Account Manager, the other three are travel consultants who work with the Account Manager.

1 Each member of the group (Account Manager/travel consultants) reads one of the problems above and makes notes about it.

2 Each person summarises the problem for his/her colleagues, and answers any questions they may have.

3 After each summary, the groups discuss the following:

- Did the executive in each case deal with the problem effectively? Why? / Why not?

- What can BTS do to help to solve the problem?

- What is the best solution for each executive? What, if anything, should he/she hope to get from the company concerned?

Writing

As the Account Manager for BTS, write an e-mail to NeoTech's Head of Travel, apologising for the inconvenience. Offer some compensation and explain what steps BTS has taken to make sure a similar problem does not happen again.

➡ *Writing file page 127*

Watch the Case study commentary on the DVD-ROM.

UNIT

3 | Change

'If you want things to stay as they are, things will have to change.'
Giuseppe Tomasi di Lampedusa (1896–1957), Italian writer

STARTING UP

A **Which of these situations would you find the most difficult to deal with?**

1 Moving house
2 Losing a pet
3 Moving to another country
4 Changing your job

5 Driving abroad
6 A new boss
7 Getting married (again!)
8 New neighbours

B **What has been the most significant change in your life so far?**

C **Which of these business situations would worry you most? Why?**

1 You find out that your company will be merging with another company.
2 You keep your job after a merger, but you are in a less powerful position.
3 You keep your job after a merger, but you have to take a salary cut.
4 Your company has to relocate to the other side of the city.
5 You are asked to relocate to a foreign country.
6 You are promoted, but are now in charge of a hostile workforce.
7 You have to move from your own office to a large, open-plan office.
8 You have to work with a completely new computer system.
9 You have to decide who to make redundant in your new department after a merger.
10 Your company language becomes English.

VOCABULARY

Describing change

A Write the verbs from the box under the correct prefix to make words connected with change. Use a good dictionary to help you. Some of the words can be used with more than one prefix.

assess	centralise	date	develop	grade	launch
locate	~~organise~~	regulate	size	structure	train

down-	de-	up-	re-
			organise

B Complete these sentences with the correct form of the verbs from the box in Exercise A. Use a good dictionary to help you.

1 Following the merger, the office layout was .*reorganised*. to accommodate the new staff.

2 The most successful change in our company was the decision to .... the company. Now there is more opportunity for promotion.

3 It is now so expensive to rent offices in the city centre that many companies are .... their operations to purpose-built business parks at the city limits.

4 The company has recently .... its workforce. Reducing the number of employees is the best way to stay profitable in the current economic climate.

5 To improve efficiency, the company has introduced new working practices. The HR department will .... all sales staff.

6 One of our products hasn't been selling well recently. The marketing team has decided to take it off the market and .... it next year with new packaging.

7 The IT department report recommended that the company .... the computer system as soon as possible.

8 The CEO thinks that too many decisions are made at Head Office. She wants to .... the decision-making process so that branch managers are more involved at an earlier stage.

9 The company has finalised the plans to .... the disused car-park site. It is going to become a fitness centre for employees.

10 The logo and slogan are very old-fashioned. We need to .... the whole image of the product and bring it into the 21st century.

11 There is a lot of pressure on the government from consumer groups to .... the industry and remove controls, so customers can benefit from increased competition.

12 Following the report by the legal department and changes in the tax laws, the management decided to .... the situation and delay making a decision on the takeover.

C Underline the nouns in Exercise B that make partnerships with the verbs.

example: the office layout was reorganised

See the **DVD-ROM** for the i-Glossary.

D In pairs, describe the changes that have happened in a workplace you know well.

FT

Mercedes star twinkles once more

by Richard Milne

The Mercedes star is gleaming again. In 2002, it suffered as dramatic a fall as any luxury brand could, as it reported its first losses for nearly two decades and saw its quality slip so far that newspapers were full of stories of cars that kept on breaking down.

'Mercedes should not make losses. That is absolutely clear,' says Dieter Zetsche, who became Head of Mercedes in September 2005 and Chief Executive of its parent company, Daimler, three months later. 'But we have great results now and we are starting to change the culture in many ways.'

Indeed, so much has Mercedes changed that in three years it has gone from the worst-performing of the large luxury car makers to the trailblazer. Executives at its bigger-selling rival BMW look enviously at its 9.1-per-cent return on sales last year (and even more so at the 10.4 per cent it made in the fourth quarter – compared with BMW's 5.4 per cent in the third quarter).

Much of that turnaround is due to Mr Zetsche, famous for his walrus moustache. He was not the first automotive executive to take on two jobs, but he has been

one of the most successful with it, using his operational experience at Mercedes to help him at Daimler. Mr Zetsche says that combining roles is essential for his management style. He is also keen to stress that Mercedes has a team approach.

Mr Zetsche was hard from the outset, cutting 14,500 jobs – 8,500 in production and 6,000 administrative staff. That broke the pattern of Mercedes providing a job for life to workers. But it had a dramatic effect on the bottom line. Mr Zetsche says: 'Productivity gains don't get you anything if you don't reduce personnel.' Mercedes' recent success is also linked to a big improvement in its product quality and the launch

of some well-praised models, headed by the new C-Class saloon. 'Mercedes is building cars that people want to buy again and, for once, they even look better than BMWs,' says one London-based analyst.

The debate on reducing carbon-dioxide emissions could hit Mercedes hard. But the company, for now, is choosing to highlight the launch of 20 fuel-efficient models this year.

All of this has put a spring back in the step of a company that, in Mr Zetsche's words, also acts as a 'mirror on German society'. It has also restored lustre to Mr Zetsche's star, which was tarnished by the poor performance of Chrysler, the US car maker that was owned by Daimler.

READING

Mercedes, shining star

A **Read the first two paragraphs quickly and decide if the statements are true (T) or false (F), according to the article.**

1 The fall of the Mercedes luxury brand was not as severe as other brands.

2 In 2002, Mercedes' losses were its first for three decades.

3 In 2002, Mercedes cars were famous for their reliability.

4 Dieter Zetsche is the boss of Mercedes and Daimler.

B **Find words and phrases in the first five paragraphs of the article that mean the same as the following.**

1 sudden and surprising

2 a period of 10 years

3 failing

4 the first company to develop new methods of doing something

5 someone that you compete with

6 jealously

7 a complete change from a bad situation to a good one

8 the financial result of a company's business (i.e. profit or loss)

C Without looking back at the article, try to match the words to form common word partnerships.

1 luxury   a) executive
2 chief   b) models
3 parent   c) effect
4 fourth   d) company
5 management   e) brand
6 fuel-efficient   f) style
7 team   g) approach
8 dramatic   h) quarter

Now check your answers in the article.

D According to the article, which of these factors helped Mercedes improve its performance?

1 Mr Zetsche's walrus moustache
2 Having BMW as a rival
3 Being hard
4 Increasing jobs
5 Giving workers security for life
6 Using Mr Zetsche's operational experience
7 Cutting jobs
8 Building cars the experts want them to build
9 Lowering product quality
10 Improving the looks of new Mercedes cars
11 Producing new models
12 Using a team approach

E Imagine you are Mr Zetsche. What other actions would you have taken at Mercedes?

LISTENING

Helping companies to change

Anne Deering

A ◀) CD1.14 Anne Deering is Head of Transformation Practice at international management consultants AT Kearney. Listen to the first part of the interview and complete the gaps.

1 What are they ....¹, how are they going to ....², and how will they know they've ....³?

2 Make sure people are ....⁴ in the change, that they feel this is something they are doing for............⁵ and not something which is being done ....⁶.

B ◀) CD1.15 Listen to the second part. What are the two main problems that businesses face when going through change?

C ◀) CD1.16 Listen to the final part, where Anne talks about Nokia-Siemens Networks, and answer the questions.

1 What was the main purpose of the merger?

2 What do these numbers refer to?
   a) 8,000   b) 72

Watch the interview on the DVD-ROM.

LANGUAGE REVIEW
Past simple and present perfect

- We use the past simple for actions at a particular point in the past.
  *In 2002, Mercedes **suffered** a dramatic fall.*
  *Dieter Zetsche **became** Head of Mercedes in September 2005.*

- We use the present perfect for actions linking the present to a point in the past.
  *Since 2005, Mercedes **has gone** from the worst-performing of the large luxury car makers to the trailblazer.*

➡ *Grammar reference* page 147

A **Which of the following expressions are used with the past simple and which are used with the present perfect? Which are used with both?**

in 2010	since 2009	yet
this week	yesterday	ever
recently	last year	six months ago

B **Complete this short business brief about Vietnam using the past simple or the present perfect forms of the verbs in brackets.**

Vietnam ....[1] (go) through many changes in its history and ....[2] (experience) many economic changes recently. It is currently experiencing an economic boom. In 1986, the government ....[3] (introduce) economic reforms or *doi moi* (*doi* meaning change and *moi* new). The reforms ....[4] (permit) the setting up of free market enterprises and ....[5] (abolish) the practice of collective farming. However, agriculture remains the most important part of the economy. Vietnam ....[6] (recently/become) the second largest producer of rice in the world after Thailand. The industrial sector ....[7] (show) dramatic improvement and expansion as well. In 1993, the World Bank ....[8] (declare) 58% of the population to be living in poverty. By 2005, this figure was less than 20%. Vietnam ....[9] (also/make) great strides on the international stage in the last decade or so. It ....[10] (become) a full member of ASEAN in 1995, and of the WTO in 2006. The effects of this new-found prosperity can be seen everywhere. Large, glitzy malls ....[11] (appear) in major cities, while streets once filled with bicycles are now overflowing with locally produced Japanese, Korean and Chinese motorbikes and cars. Business visitors wishing to relax in a more traditional Vietnamese town should visit Hoi An. Hoi An ....[12] (be) a major Asian trading port in the 17th and 18th centuries, and its picturesque architecture and relaxed lifestyle ....[13] (change) little over the years.

C **Talk about recent changes that have happened in your town, company or country.**

SKILLS
Managing meetings

A **Think of two meetings you have attended that were a) successful and b) unsuccessful. What were the reasons in each case?**

B 🔊 **CD1.17 Four managers are discussing their company's policy about smoking. Listen to the meeting and answer the questions.**

1 Why are some people not happy with the behaviour of the staff who smoke?

2 What is Eduardo's solution to the problem?

3 Why does Mitsuko object to Eduardo's proposal?

4 What proposal does William make?

5 Do the managers reach a decision about the smoking policy?

C   ◀))) **CD1.17 Listen again and tick the expressions in the Useful language box that you hear.**

USEFUL LANGUAGE

STARTING

OK, let's get down to business.

Right, can we start, please?

SETTING OBJECTIVES

The purpose of this meeting is …

The aims of this meeting are …

ASKING FOR REACTIONS

How do you feel about …?

What do you think?

DEALING WITH INTERRUPTIONS

Could you let him finish, please?

Could you just hang on a moment, please?

KEEPING TO THE POINT

I'm not sure that's relevant.

Perhaps we could get back to the point.

SPEEDING UP

I think we should move on now.

Can we come back to that?

SLOWING DOWN

Hold on, we need to look at this in more detail.

I think we should discuss this a bit more.

SUMMARISING

OK, let's go over what we've agreed.

Right, to sum up then …

D   **You are managers of a retail fashion chain called Young Scene, with stores in most major European cities. You are holding your regular management meeting. Use the CEO's notes below as an agenda for your discussions. A different person should chair each item.**

Briefing notes

1 Performance-related pay

Following changes to the bonus system, sales staff in stores now receive monthly bonuses according to their individual sales. Unfortunately, while the new system is popular with staff, it has led to many complaints from customers about sales staff 'fighting' over customers in order to secure sales and therefore bonuses.
Is the system making staff too competitive?

2 Stock control

Managers at many outlets are reporting problems with the system of organising and finding items for customers in the stock rooms. This is causing delays and causing frustration for both staff and customers.
The main question seems to be how to organise the stock – by size, by style or by colour?

3 Shoplifting

Following a recent increase in shoplifting, Young Scene now employs security guards in all its stores. There has been a number of complaints from customers that they find the guards intimidating. This is starting to affect sales, although shoplifting itself is also down. What can be done about this issue?

4 Carbon footprint

In line with its philosophy as a 'green' company, it has been suggested that Young Scene should be reducing its carbon footprint, meaning that air travel should be kept to a minimum. Buyers and managers would in future travel by train within Europe. Outside Europe, they would use economy class or budget air travel only. Is this practical or indeed desirable?

5 End of clothing allowance

Sales staff in stores currently receive a clothing allowance, which takes the form of a 50% discount on Young Scene clothes, which staff then must wear at work. One suggestion is to cut this to 10%, or stop this completely and introduce a compulsory company uniform.

6 Staff meetings

The current practice is to open all stores two hours later one day a week in order for the store manager to hold a meeting with all staff. It has been suggested that this meeting be held after hours in future to maximise opening hours.

Acquiring Asia Entertainment

How can an international media group integrate the new Hong Kong-based company it has recently merged with?

Background

Last March, readers of an Asia-Pacific business magazine, Investor International, were given information about an Australian company, the Decker Group.

COMPANY **PROFILE**

Company:	Decker Group
Located:	Sydney, Australia
Workforce:	35,000
Turnover:	A$4.6bn

Main activities

Decker is a diversified media group with interests in broadcasting, entertainment and Internet services.

Recent developments

Decker has recently merged with a Hong Kong-based media company, Asia Entertainment. In a press release, the deal was described as a merger, but Decker is the real decision-maker.

Reasons for Decker's acquisition

1 Decker will expand its presence in a dynamic new market, China.
2 It will use Asia Entertainment for further expansion into Asian markets such as Singapore, Malaysia and Vietnam.
3 Asia Entertainment has a growing online presence through its successful DVD viewing service

Comment

Asia Entertainment seems to be a good fit with the Decker Group. However, there may be problems when a different style of management, the 'Australian way of doing things', is introduced into the Asian company.

The new Chairman and Chief Executive will be Scott Henderson. A graduate from the Harvard School of Business, Scott Henderson has a reputation for being a strong leader who is not afraid to take difficult decisions. He is a fluent speaker of Mandarin Chinese.

🔊 **CD1.18** Scott Henderson, the new Chief Executive, gave an interview to a Hong Kong TV business channel. He was asked about the recent acquisition of Asian Entertainment. **Listen and note what he says.**

Problems

It is now a year later. The change of ownership and new management style at Asia Entertainment have caused many problems. The e-mail on the right illustrates some of the difficulties.

To:	Robert Crawford, Vice-President
From:	Cindy Chow, Director, Human Resources
Subject:	Effects of the merger

Staff are very unhappy about the changes. I'm worried about the high staff turnover and low morale. These are some of the reasons for the problems.

1 **Re-applying for positions**
The management has asked all employees to re-apply for their jobs. Staff feel very uneasy and insecure. People do not want to compete against each other for jobs.

2 **Redundancies**
Redundancies are expected. Employees in HR and Sales feel particularly threatened. Many employees from these departments are looking for new jobs, which is affecting productivity.

3 **Compensation**
Staff are already being made redundant. However, the compensation package is poor. They are also receiving no help to find new jobs.

4 **English language skills**
The management has insisted that all staff must improve their English, but no financial help has been offered towards the cost of English courses.

5 **Management style**
These are typical comments made by staff.
- They're trying to do things too fast – there's a new computer system we don't understand; and they're ordering lots of Australian films for our rental service, but we know nothing about the films.
- They want an informal atmosphere, but we don't want to use first names – we're not used to that.
- The food in the staff restaurant is awful. The new manager's Australian, she's changed most of the dishes. We have to eat a lot of food we're not used to. There are too many dairy products and not enough fresh vegetables and fish.
- Most of the management jobs have been given to Australians. There are not many Chinese in senior positions – everyone's complaining about it.
- We don't know what's going on. We don't know where the company is going and what our strategy is. Quite a few of us don't know who our boss is, or what our duties are.
- We feel we're losing our Chinese identity. Our bosses don't understand us, our customs are so different. Our new managers are only interested in results.

Task

A group of senior managers meets to resolve the problems.

1 **Work in two groups.**

Group A: new Australian managers led by Scott Henderson

Group B: senior executives from Asia Entertainment who have kept their jobs following the merger.

Each group prepares separately for the meeting.

2 **Hold the meeting as one group. The agenda is as follows:**

- Background: why are staff resisting the changes?
- What mistakes is the new management making, if any?
- What practical action(s) can be taken to improve the situation?
- What can be learned from this experience? How can the company manage change more effectively in the future?

Writing

Write the action minutes for the above meeting.

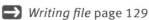 *Writing file page 129*

Watch the Case study commentary on the DVD-ROM.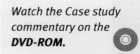

1 Socialising

A In small groups, discuss this question.

If you're listening to spoken English, what do you find most difficult?
- the speaker's accent
- the speed at which he/she is speaking
- the words he/she uses

B Look at these strategies for dealing with accents. Rank them in order of the ones you prefer (1 = best strategy, 6 = worst strategy).

- Ask the speaker to talk more slowly.
- Ask the speaker to repeat what he/she said.
- Check that you understand by saying things like 'Are you saying …?'.
- Interrupt and ask questions to slow the speaker down.
- Listen to English radio on the Internet.
- Watch English-language films.

Are there any other strategies you would use?

C If you were meeting a group of business people for the first time in a social setting, e.g. in the bar of a hotel or the restaurant at a conference, what subjects would you discuss in the first half hour?

D ◀))) CD1.19 Listen to the first part of a conversation between two executives. They are attending a conference in Seattle, USA, on management software systems. They meet at the hotel breakfast table, introduce themselves and have a conversation. Answer the questions.

1 What are the names of the two executives, and where do they come from?

2 Which of these subjects do they mention?
   a) the name of their company
   b) their position in the company
   c) where they are from
   d) the performance of their company
   e) their journey to the conference centre
   f) their reason for coming to the conference
   g) their accommodation

E ◀))) CD1.19 Listen again and answer the questions.

1 What do Antonio Silva and James Whitfield say when they first meet each other?

2 Complete the chart with information from the conversation.

	Antonio	James
Type of company	office equipment	
Job title		Systems Analyst
Company performance		
Flight		
Accommodation		

F ◀))) CD1.20 Listen to the second part of the conversation and answer the questions.

1 Who is:
   a) a senior official?
   b) a director?
   c) a managing director?

2 List the two topics which they discuss in their conversation.

G ◀))) CD1.20 Listen again and fill in the gaps.

James   Let me do the introductions. I'm James Whitfield, I'm from Atlanta, Georgia, and I'm a ………… [1] for New Era. ………… [2] Antonio Silva from Brazil. He's a ………… [3] with an office equipment firm.

Antonio   ………… [4].

Klaus   ………… [5]. I'm Klaus Liebermann, I'm a colleague of James's. I'm the ………… [6] of New Era's ………… [7]. And this is Ludmila Poigina from ………… [8]. She's a director of an engineering company.

H Which of the executives:
   a) has not yet seen the city?
   b) has already seen some of the city's sights?
   c) probably knows the city quite well?

I Two speakers, David Broadus and Jerry Chin, are strongly recommended. What is said about each one?

Task

You are all attending a conference on customer care at a large hotel in New York. You all meet in the hotel restaurant and find yourself on the same table. You must introduce yourself and have a conversation. Find out two things you have in common.

1 **Work in groups. Choose one of the following roles.**

- Manager of a five-star hotel
- Sales Supervisor in a large department store
- Manager of a regional branch of a bank
- Head of Customer Service in a mobile phone company
- Owner of a chain of prestige hairdressing salons
- Manager of a call centre
- Owner of an expensive restaurant
- Sales Representative of a real-estate agency

2 **Prepare for the task by looking at the questions below. Make notes of your answers.**

3 **When you are ready, meet the other members of your group and practise your social English.**

How will you introduce yourself?

What is your name and nationality?

Where are you from?

What is your position and the name of your company or business?

How is the business doing? Is it successful or in difficulties?

How did you travel to the conference? Were there any problems getting there?

Where are you staying? Are you satisfied with your accommodation? If not, why not?

Have you visited the sights of New York yet? If not, do you want to visit them? If so, which ones?

Which speakers interest you? (There are four main speakers from the US, France, Switzerland and Hong Kong.)

1 Brands

VOCABULARY

Complete the text with the correct words.

Topalino is a well-known brand of sweets and chocolates owned by ABG, a company based in Maribor, Slovenia. It focuses mainly on ....[1] products and was the market ....[2] in exclusive confectionery.

In the last two years, however, Topalino's market ....[3] has declined by almost 25%. There are at least two reasons for this decline.

First, supermarkets in the region are now selling sweets of similar quality at much lower prices, so more and more consumers say that Topalino is no longer ....[4] for money. The economic downturn has naturally made people more price conscious, and brand ....[5] is suffering as a result. A possible solution would be to reduce the price of at least a number of products so that they are in the medium ....[6] of prices.

Secondly, a lot of middle-aged people find the logo childish and the packaging old-fashioned and unexciting – in other words, they no longer find the brand ....[7] attractive. In order to appeal to this important market ....[8], Topalino is thinking of ....[9] its main products and expanding its product ....[10].

1 a) inexpensive	b) upmarket	c) influential
2 a) leader	b) launch	c) awareness
3 a) label	b) logo	c) share
4 a) price	b) margins	c) value
5 a) stretching	b) research	c) loyalty
6 a) range	b) order	c) list
7 a) name	b) image	c) label
8 a) segment	b) survey	c) challenge
9 a) endorsing	b) repositioning	c) generating
10 a) numbers	b) range	c) list

PRESENT SIMPLE AND PRESENT CONTINUOUS

Complete the text with the present simple or present continuous form of the verbs in brackets.

Sarika Gupta is a technology programmer, and she ....[1] (love) what she............[2] (do). She............[3] (work) for Datascope, an exciting IT company based in Bangalore, 'the Silicon Valley of India', and she is also a shareholder in the company. Datascope ....[4] (gain) an excellent reputation worldwide for its innovative products and solutions. Not only are its young engineers extremely skilled, they also ....[5] (know) how to market their ideas. As a result, the company's fame ....[6] (spread) rapidly, and currently a number of leading companies............[7] (try) to enter into some form of partnership with it.

That is why this week Sarika and Vijay, her Head of Department, ...[8] (not work) at Datascope. They............[9] (attend) a series of meetings with representatives from global IT companies. Sarika ....[10] (know) that some of these companies............[11] (want) to outsource part of their operations to India, so she............[12] (believe) something good for Datascope will come out of these meetings.

SKILLS

Complete the conversation below with the words in the box.

afraid	how	opinion	perhaps	see	so	views	why

Claire   One proposal is that we bring out a new product under the Topalino brand. So, what are your............¹ on this?

Nikola   In my............², this is the best solution if we want to regain market share.

Ivan   ....³ don't we focus on our pricing policy first? Isn't that the key issue?

Jasmina   I'm............⁴ I can't agree. What we need to do to begin with is reposition our market leader.

Rick   ....⁵ about doing both, Jasmina? We can certainly bring out a new product and reposition another at the same time.

Jasmina   I............⁶ what you mean, but we've got to start somewhere, and thinking about our best-selling product is what's most important at this stage.

Claire   I think............⁷ too. ....⁸ we could agree to bring out a new product later this year.

2 Travel

TALKING ABOUT THE FUTURE

Complete each dialogue with the correct form of *will* or *going to*.

1   A: I'm afraid we haven't received a copy of the booking form yet.

    B: Sorry about that. If I could just have your number, I............ fax it over to you straight away.

2   A: Have you planned the weekend excursion for our visitors from China?

    B: Yes, Tom............ show them round the old town and the harbour.

3   A: I've just heard some bad news.

    B: What is it?

    A: They .... cancel our trip to Brazil.

4   A: What about Tuesday at around nine thirty?

    B: Fine. I............ see you then.

SKILLS

Complete the telephone conversation. Use only one word for each gap.

MG   Marco Gallieri, Travel Section. Good afternoon............¹ can I help you?

KM   Karim Melki speaking, from Marketing. I'd............² to speak to Britta Keller, please.

MG   I'm afraid Britta isn't in today. Would you like to............³ a message?

KM   Yes, please. The............⁴ I'm calling is that Britta is in charge of our travel arrangements for the Dubai conference next month, and there are some changes. First, there are now four of us instead of three. The additional name is Sylvia Lohmar. And then Britta had booked us on flight LH630, leaving Frankfurt at 14.55 on Monday 6th. However, I'm afraid something's come............⁵, and we are now leaving on Tuesday. The flight is at about the same time, I think.

MG   Fine, I've got that, Mr Melki. Was there anything else?

KM   Could you just ask her to call me............⁶ tomorrow morning as soon as she's made the changes?

MG   Right. I'll make............⁷ she gets the message.

KM   ....⁸ for your help. Goodbye.

WRITING

Study the conversation in the Skills section above and write Marco's message to Britta.

3 Change

deregulate
downsize
reassess
redevelop
relocate
restructure
retrain
update
upgrade

Complete each set of sentences with the same verb describing change from the box in the correct form. There are four verbs you will not need.

1   The current economic climate is making people .... all of the purchases they make.

When will the government .... the impact of their economic reforms on the quality of life?

We need to .... the situation before taking any decisions.

2   If your company .... and you are over 50, your working life may be over.

As the car industry .... , many are leaving the country in search of work.

Breaking news: TRN United, the global electronics group, ... its workforce by 20%.

3   Could you perhaps .... us on how the project is progressing?

We continuously .... the files with new information.

We plan to .... our telephone system.

4   The government will soon .... all internal flights, so the industry will probably become more competitive.

They plan to .... the capital markets and privatise most state-owned companies.

Taiwan's government pledged to .... its service sector within four years.

5   We bought new software and had to .... everyone to use the database.

Our agency has seen a huge increase in the number of adults looking to change careers, either as a result of job loss or a desire to .... in a different field.

People are often reluctant to .... until they are convinced that their present skills are not sufficient to enable them to find work.

Complete the two conversations with the words in brackets. Use the past simple or present perfect as appropriate.

A: How long ....[1] (*your offices / be*) in this area?

B: Since April 2007.

A: Where ....[2] (*you / be*) before that?

B: In the city centre. But the rent ....[3] (*be*) outrageously expensive, so we ....[4] (*decide*) to relocate to the suburbs.

A: And ....[5] (*you / ever / regret*) your decision?

B: Frankly, we ....[6] (*be*) slightly worried about all the changes in the first couple of months, but we ....[7] (*soon / realise*) that it was the right move. This part of town is extremely attractive, and in fact, it ....[8] (*develop*) enormously over the last two or three years.

A: So it seems you ....[9] (*have*) a very good year so far.

B: Absolutely! Sales ....[10] (*stand*) at €14m at the end of the last quarter, and they ....[11] (*already / increase*) by 6%.

A: What about your market share?

B: It ....[12] (*remain*) stable since 2008, but we are confident it will increase when we launch our new product.

A: ....[13] (*you / have to*) make anyone redundant?

B: No. At Lortex, we pride ourselves on the fact that there ....[14] (*not be*) any redundancies for over eight years.

Cultures: Socialising

1 Complete the conversation with the words in the box. There are some words that you will not need.

booking	flying	how	I'm	journey	like
nice	please	staying	tired	tiring	where

Laura   Hi, I'm Laura Dumont. Nice to meet you.

Stefan   ....[1] to meet you, too. ....[2] Stefan Kirchner.

Laura   ....[3] are you from, Stefan?

Stefan   I'm from Linz. That's in Austria. ....[4] about you?

Laura   I'm from Ottawa in Canada.

Stefan   You've come a very long way! How was your ....[5] here?

Laura   It was fine, but a bit ....[6]. Nine hours is a long time to be in a plane.

             I managed to get a good rest yesterday, though. By the way, are you ....[7] at the Regency, too?

Stefan   No, they booked me into a small hotel called The Winston.

Laura   What's it ....[8]?

Stefan   Well, it's all right, I suppose. A bit noisy, but the food and service are good. And it's within walking distance of the conference centre, so I can't complain.

2 Write questions for these answers.

1   A   ....?

    B   Not too bad. Sales are up, but we've had some redundancies.

2   A   ....?

    B   I'm a systems analyst.

3   A   ....?

    B   No, but I'll try and see some of the sights before I leave.

4   A   ....?

    B   I flew to Berlin, then I took a taxi.

5   A   ....?

    B   No. The map was very helpful, so we got to the conference centre really quickly.

6   A   ....?

    B   At the Grand Hotel in Friedrichstrasse.

7   A   ....?

    B   It's very spacious and comfortable, with a good view.

8   A   ....?

    B   I'm particularly keen to go to Professor Roger's talk.

Meetings

Objectives

Speaking
Can express opinions and attitudes using a range of basic expressions and sentences.

Listening
Can extract the key details from discussions in meetings conducted in clear, standard speech.

Writing
Can write the agenda for a meeting on a work-related topic.

Lesson deliverable
To plan, prepare and participate in a meeting.

Performance review
To review your own progress and performance against the lesson objectives at the end of the lesson.

A SPEAKING

Discuss these questions with a partner. Then compare your ideas with the rest of the class.

1 How many different types of business meetings can you list, e.g. a board meeting, a client meeting, a project kick-off meeting?

2 How long/short should an agenda be?

3 Is it better to send people the agenda in advance?

4 What language difficulties can there be in international meetings?

B SPEAKING AND LISTENING

1 The CEO of Magnum Hotel Group has called a meeting with her management board. In pairs, look at the two draft agendas and decide which one is better. Why?

①

Annual performance review

1 Key performance figures

2 Customer feedback

3 Turnaround strategies

②

To review the past year's results

• How has the hotel performed?

• What the customers think

• What can we do about it?

2 ◀)) BSA1.1.1 Listen to the CEO opening the meeting. Does she do this well? Why? / Why not? Discuss with a partner.

C LISTENING

1 ◀)) BSA1.1.2 Listen to the next part of the meeting. Which agenda item is being discussed?

2 ◀)) BSA1.1.3 Listen to the last part of the meeting and write the phrases in the box in the correct column.

Global trade is still on the increase, isn't it?
Yes, absolutely.   What's your view?   I agree with Amita.
I don't think changing the customer mix is the right strategy.

Agreeing	Giving an opinion	Asking for an opinion

D LISTENING AND WRITING

◀)) BSA1.1.4 Listen to a hotel manager opening a meeting. In pairs, write the clear agenda he needs for the meeting. Then compare your agendas with the rest of the class.

Task

Pre-task: Context

You are country managers from a worldwide hotel chain. Since its start-up in 1995, the company has been very successful. However, for the last two years, the profits and share price have been falling. Your CEO has given you a simple brief: to refresh the company's brand image by developing a brand-new flagship hotel.

Part 1: Preparation

1 **Work in small groups. Brainstorm a list of essential ideas to consider at a meeting. Think about these points.**

   1 What sort of hotel will it be?
   2 Who will it attract?
   3 What facilities will it offer?
   4 What other points will you need to decide in order to create an architect's brief?

2 **Work in pairs. Write an agenda for the meeting. Make sure it is clear and includes all the essential areas for discussion.**

3 **Compare your agendas with the rest of the class and choose the best one.**

Part 2: Meeting

1 **Turn to page vi, look at the role cards and assign roles. You need one meeting leader and one or two observers. The rest of the class are participants.**

2 **Hold the meeting based on the class agenda. Make sure everyone participates. Use the language you have learnt. (Observer(s): Use the Observer sheet on page vi to make notes.)**

3 **Take one action point from the first meeting and hold a follow-up meeting. Swap roles, with a new meeting leader and (a) new observer(s).**

◎ EXTRA PRACTICE: DVD CLIP AND WORKSHEET 8

E PEER REVIEW

Work in pairs. Use the completed Observer sheets to give each other feedback. Think about these questions.

1 What was good about the agenda you wrote? Be specific.

2 Did you express your opinions clearly in the meeting? Give examples.

3 Did you understand the important information in your meeting? How do you know?

F SELF-ASSESSMENT

Think about your performance and write a 150-word report. Look back at the learning objectives. How successfully have you achieved them? What do you need to improve further? How might you achieve this?

G PROFESSIONAL DEVELOPMENT AND PERFORMANCE GOALS

Identify an opportunity to write an agenda for a meeting in your place of work/study.

Telephoning

Objectives

Speaking
- Can carry out a work-related telephone conversation using polite fixed expressions.
- Can use simple appropriate language to check that information has been understood on the phone.
- Can ask for repetition or clarification on the phone in a simple way.

Listening
Can take messages, communicate enquiries and explain problems.

Lesson deliverable
To plan, prepare and participate in a telephone conversation in a business context and write a short follow-up document.

Performance review
To review your own progress and performance against the lesson objectives at the end of the lesson.

A SPEAKING 1

1 **Work in small groups. Discuss making and receiving a phone call in English. Consider the following in your discussion.**

1 how often you make or receive a call in English

2 challenges with speaking on the phone in English

3 differences between speaking on the phone in your own language and in English

4 differences between speaking on the phone in English to someone you know and to someone you don't know

2 **Use your ideas from Exercise 1 to produce a list of top tips for telephoning in English.**

3 **Share your top tips with the rest of the class and draw up a class list of five top tips for telephoning in English.**

B LISTENING

1 **You are going to hear a telephone call to a company called Global Relocation Consultants. In pairs, think about the name of the company. What kind of business might the company be involved with? Can you predict which of the following they might do? Write Y (Yes), N (No) or M (Maybe) for each point.**

1 Conduct business all over the world.

2 Transport people's furniture and other possessions to another country.

3 Transport other companies' products to another country.

4 Help people find accommodation when they move to another country.

5 Help people learn the language when they move to another country.

6 Provide training to help people get used to living in another country.

2 ◀)) BSA1.2.5 **Listen and check your answers. Were you right?**

3 ◀)) BSA1.2.5 **Listen again and complete these sentences from the call.**

1 I see. .... you?

2 .... an office in Japan at the end of this year.

3 .... with finding accommodation and learning the language?

4 .... about the employees, please?

5 .... you need two apartments – a one-bedded one and one with three bedrooms for the family. .... ?

6 I'm sorry, ... a cultural induction programme?

7 Ah yes, in London, before they go. .... what you'd prefer, ... ?

8 .... the postcode, please?

9 W-H-I-T-E. Is .... ?

10 OK, I .... when the proposal is ready and my secretary .... the information pack in the post this afternoon.

4 Match the sentences in Exercise 3 with the stages of the call in this flow chart.

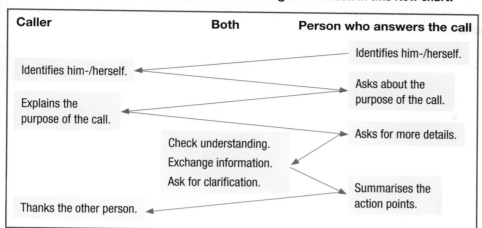

Caller	Both	Person who answers the call

Identifies him-/herself.

Explains the purpose of the call.

Check understanding.
Exchange information.
Ask for clarification.

Thanks the other person.

Identifies him-/herself.

Asks about the purpose of the call.

Asks for more details.

Summarises the action points.

C SPEAKING 2

Work in pairs. Role-play the conversation between Angela Wight and Alex Change. Use the sentences in Exercise B3 and the flow chart in Exercise B4 to help you.

Task

Part 1: Telephoning

Work in pairs to plan and make the following telephone conversations. Student A is the person relocating. Student B's role changes in each call.

Context, conversation 1: Student A is relocating to another country and needs to find a language school in the city where he/she is moving to.

Student A: You are the customer. You are making the call. Introduce yourself, explain the purpose of the call, ask for details about the course you are interested in and check understanding.

Student B: You are the Head of Customer Services at English International language school.

Context, conversation 2: Student A has made all the arrangements for his/her relocation to another country. He/She now needs to organise a car from the hire car company at the airport.

Student A: You are the customer. You are making the call. Ask for availability of a car, make a request for a hire car and ask for details. Think about the size of the car you need, the price and how long you want to hire the car for.

Student B: You work for the hire car company at the airport. Give details about two or three cars that you think would be suitable for your customer. At the end of the call, summarise the details.

Context, conversation 3: The relocation company has organised an apartment for the customer and calls to make arrangements.

Student B: You are making the call. Phone the customer and explain that you are representing the relocation company. Explain the purpose of the call. There is a deposit to be paid and you need to arrange to meet the customer and escort them to the apartment to show them round, sign the documents and hand over the keys.

Student A: You are the customer. Check you understand the information and ask for repetition and clarification where needed. Summarise the arrangement before you end the call.

Part 2: Follow up

Write a summary document of any action points resulting from each of the calls.

D PEER REVIEW

1 Read the follow-up document your partner wrote after the call. Are the details correct? Is all the important information there? Give your partner feedback.

2 Now talk about your telephone conversations with your partner. Look at the lesson objectives and discuss these questions.

  1 What did he/she do well?

  2 Can you suggest some tips to help with the problem areas?

E SELF-ASSESSMENT

Write 80–100 words about your performance. Think about these points.

- the feedback from your partner

- the lesson objectives

- what you did well

- points to work on in the future

F PROFESSIONAL DEVELOPMENT AND PERFORMANCE GOALS

Write two or three sentences about ways you can improve your telephone skills.

Next time I make a call in English, I will … before I make the call.

Next time I receive a call in English, I will …

During calls I make or receive in English, I will …

UNIT

4 Organisation

'Modern organisations have to be built on making conflict constructive.'
Peter Drucker (1909–2005), Austrian-born US management consultant

STARTING UP

A **Discuss these questions.**

1 Would you like to work in the building in the photo above? Why? / Why not?

2 Which people in your organisation have their own office? Do they have their own office because of: a) seniority; b) a need for confidentiality; c) the type of work they do?

B **How important are the following in showing a person's status in an organisation? Give each one a score from 1 (not important) to 5 (very important).**

- a reserved parking space
- an office with a view
- a uniform
- a personal business card
- a company car
- your name on your office door
- the latest company mobile phone

- an assistant
- taking holidays when you like
- the size of your desk
- more than one seat in your office
- flying business class
- a company credit card
- fixed working hours

VOCABULARY

Company structure

A Match the words and phrases (1–8) to their definitions (a–h).

1 subsidiary
2 factory/plant
3 call centre
4 service centre
5 headquarters
6 distribution centre
7 warehouse
8 outlet

a) an office where people answer questions and make sales over the phone
b) a building from which goods or supplies are sent to factories, shops or customers
c) a place through which products are sold
d) a place where faulty products are mended
e) a company which is at least half-owned by another company
f) the main office or building of a company
g) a building for storing goods in large quantities
h) a large building or group of buildings where goods are made (using machinery)

B 🔊 CD1.21 **Listen to the comments from different places in the organisation and write them down. Then match them to the places listed in Exercise A.**

1 Stock levels have been low for two weeks now. *warehouse*

C **What do the following departments do?**

1 *In R&D, people research and develop new products.*

1 R&D
2 Customer Services
3 Human Resources
4 Sales and Marketing

5 Production
6 Finance
7 Administration
8 Legal

9 Logistics
10 Public Relations
11 IT

D **Match these activities (a–k) to the correct department in Exercise C (1-11). Can you add any other activities to any of the departments?**

a) deal with complaints
b) draw up contracts
c) carry out research
d) train staff

e) run advertising campaigns
f) issue press releases
g) operate assembly lines
h) prepare budgets/accounts

i) keep records
j) transport goods and
k) install and maintain systems equipment

E 🔊 CD1.22 **Listen to three people talking about their work. Which department do they work in? Choose from the departments in Exercise C.**

F 🔊 CD1.23 **Look at these words used to describe organisations. Underline the stressed syllable in each word. Then listen and check your answers.**

1 bureau<u>cra</u>tic
2 decentralised
3 impersonal

4 caring
5 democratic
6 market-driven

7 centralised
8 dynamic
9 professional

10 conservative
11 hierarchical
12 progressive

*See the **DVD-ROM** for the i-Glossary.*

G **Which of the words in Exercise F can describe:**

a) good qualities of an organisation?
b) bad qualities of an organisation?

A Read paragraph 1 of the article and choose the best definition for *perks*.

a) happiness and confidence in the workplace

b) something your employer gives you in addition to your pay

c) high-quality food and drink

B Read the article. Look at these key phrases that summarise paragraphs 1–3. Then write similar phrases for paragraphs 4–7.

1 Philosophy behind the perks

2 Competitions and celebratory funds

3 Celebrating special events / friendly place to work

C Decide if the statements are true (T) or false (F). Correct the false ones.

1 Google promotes the idea of staff getting together.

2 Every month, managers get money to build teamwork or reward staff.

3 Ninety per cent of Google Italy workers thought it was a friendly place to work.

4 The furniture in Google offices is different to that in most offices.

5 The work is challenging, and you need a university degree to work there.

6 Employees know what their objectives are and have the freedom to achieve them.

7 Employees have the opportunity to listen to well-known or important authors.

FT

Success can be a game with many players

by Sarah Murray

One of the side effects of the free food for Google staff is what is known as the 'Google 15' – the number of pounds that employees typically gain
5 after joining the Internet company. But whether it is providing snacks and gourmet meals in the canteen, annual skiing trips or games rooms at the office, the philosophy behind such
10 perks is the same – getting staff to meet each other, interact in informal settings and encourage teamwork.

One way the company does this is to hold competitions in everything,
15 from office decorating to dancing and football, with prizes for the winners. Managers also receive a quarterly 'celebratory fund' either to reward accomplishments
20 or to build teamwork by going bowling, go-karting or dining out.

The Best Workplaces survey indicates that such initiatives have a powerful effect. At Google Italy,
25 for example, 90 per cent of the employees agreed that 'people celebrate special events around here'. Also in Italy, 100 per cent agreed that 'this is a friendly place to work'
30 and 96 per cent agreed that 'there is a "family" or "team" feeling here'.

Another part of Google's objective is to make its workplace feel fun. Massage chairs, table-tennis tables,
35 video games, lava lamps, hammocks, beanbags, bicycles, large rubber balls, couches and scooters are all part of the furniture in Google offices.

However, when it comes to the
40 serious business of work, great emphasis is placed on engaging employees. 'What makes Google a great workplace is that the nature of the work itself is very challenging
45 and interesting,' says Nick Creswell, the company's university programmes manager for Europe, the Middle East and Africa. 'And for the type of people who really enjoy
50 an intellectual challenge, that's the biggest appeal of working here.'

Fostering this intellectual activity is a policy giving employees a large degree of independence in deciding
55 how to work – both in terms of the hours they work and how they do their jobs. 'There's a real culture of autonomy and empowerment,' says Mr Creswell. 'Individuals within the
60 business understand what their own goals are within the context of their teams, and they have a lot of freedom to go out and make those happen.'

Even when it comes to learning and
65 development, many programmes are voluntary and informal. Often it may be a case of inviting university faculty in to discuss their latest research. Google also invites prominent writers to give
70 lunchtime talks about their books.

D **Match these nouns from the article (1–5) to their meanings (a–e).**

1 accomplishments (paragraph 2)

2 initiatives (paragraph 3)

3 autonomy (paragraph 6)

4 empowerment (paragraph 6)

5 faculty (paragraph 7)

a) important new plans to achieve an aim

b) success in doing something

c) giving people the power to do something

d) teaching staff

e) independence/freedom to make your own decisions

E **Discuss these questions.**

1 Would you like to work in a company like Google? Why? / Why not?

2 Would Google's philosophy work in your organisation? Why? / Why not?

3 Which of the perks or ideas mentioned in the article appeals to you the most?

LANGUAGE REVIEW

Noun combinations

We can combine two or more nouns in several ways.

1 's possessive: *the company's logo*

2 one noun used as an adjective: ***labour*** *costs*

3 phrases with *of*: *director **of** operations*

4 compound nouns forming one word: ***workforce***

Match these examples from the article on page 38 to the categories above.

a) Internet company

b) culture of autonomy

c) Google's objective

d) teamwork

➡ *Grammar reference* page 147

A **Find noun combinations in the article on page 38 and decide which category they belong to.**

1 's possessive

2 one noun used as an adjective

3 phrases with *of*

4 compound nouns forming one word

B **Underline the most suitable noun combination in each group.**

1 a) the meeting of today   b) today's meeting   c) today meeting

2 a) a letter of credit   b) a credit's letter   c) a letter's credit

3 a) a business card   b) a card of business   c) a businesses' card

4 a) a data's base   b) a base of data   c) a database

C **Compound nouns are sometimes formed with a number to make expressions of measurement. Change these phrases to make compound nouns.**

1 a plan which lasts for 10 years *a 10-year plan*

2 a hotel with five stars

3 a budget worth three million dollars

4 a presentation that lasts 20 minutes

5 a contract worth 200,000 dollars

6 an industrial empire which is 150 years old

D Match each noun (1–10) to two of the following nouns (a–c) to make word partnerships.

1	business	a)	~~virus~~	b)	objectives	c)	plan
2	management	a)	style	b)	technology	c)	consultant
3	sales	a)	team	b)	revenue	c)	trade
4	customer	a)	care	b)	team	c)	loyalty
5	company	a)	house	b)	headquarters	c)	logo
6	product	a)	profit	b)	line	c)	range
7	consumer	a)	goods	b)	logos	c)	awareness
8	research	a)	project	b)	findings	c)	knowledge
9	information	a)	technology	b)	force	c)	desk
10	computer	a)	union	b)	program	c)	virus

E Make sentences with the noun combinations in Exercise D.

example: *We need to agree our business objectives.*

LISTENING

Analysing company organisation

Richard Rawlinson

A ◀)) CD1.24 Listen to Richard Rawlinson, Vice-President of the management consultants Booz & Co. Which four areas does Booz & Co look at when analysing a company's organisation?

B ◀)) CD1.25 Listen to the second part of the interview and answer the questions.

1 What do you need to answer on the website orgdna.com?

2 What are your answers compared to?

3 What can the comparison recognise?

4 How does Booz & Co analyse a company in more depth?

C ◀)) CD1.26 Listen to the third part and answer the questions.

1 How was the American company organised?

2 What did Manufacturing and Marketing do?

3 What was the company not very good at?

4 How did the consultants want to change the organisation?

D ◀)) CD1.26 Listen to the third part again and complete the gaps.

We did a lot of looking at how the business ....[1], where products were ....[2], where they were ....[3], how competitors were ....[4]. And we also had to spend a lot of time thinking about whether we needed ....[5] or whether every single business unit would report back to the ....[6], er, in the US.

Watch the interview on the DVD-ROM.

E Would you prefer to work for a company where the headquarters make the major decisions or for one in which regional offices are given considerable decision-making powers?

SKILLS

Socialising: introductions and networking

A 🔊 CD1.27, 1.28, 1.29 **Listen to the three conversations. Choose the correct description for each one.**

a) Greeting someone and talking about the weather
b) Introducing another person
c) Introducing yourself and giving information about your company
d) Greeting someone and talking about the past / changes

B 🔊 CD1.27 **Listen to the first conversation again and answer the questions.**

1 Which of these expressions do you hear?

a) Nice to see you again.   c) Excellent!   e) I changed my job last year.
b) Fine, thanks.   d) How about you?   f) I'm in banking now.

2 Who is Head of Marketing?   3 Who now works in finance?

C 🔊 CD1.28 **Listen to the second conversation again and complete the chart.**

Name	Company	Activity
Bob Danvers		
Karin Schmidt		

D 🔊 CD1.28 **Listen to the second conversation again and complete this extract.**

Bob   Well, we're basically an ....[1] business. We supply companies and organisations with various services including IT, ...[2], travel and even cleaning services.

Karin   I see. And is it a new company?

Bob   No, we're well established. The company was ....[3] in the mid-1980s, and we've been growing rapidly ever since. It's organised into four ....[4]. We have over 7,000 ....[5]; we've got our ....[6] in London and ....[7] in New York, Cape Town and Sydney – so we're pretty big.

E 🔊 CD1.29 **Listen to the third conversation again and answer the questions.**

1 What expression does Frank use to introduce Nathalie?
2 Why could Nathalie be helpful to Christoph in his work?
3 What interest do they share?

F **Work in groups of four. You are all attending the same conference.**

Student A: } Turn to page 135.
Student B:

Student C: Turn to page 141.
Student D: Turn to page 143.

USEFUL LANGUAGE

GREETINGS
Hello, ... Great to see you again.

Hi, ... How are you?

How's everything going?

RESPONDING
Fine, thanks.

Not too bad, thanks.

Pleased to meet you.

INTRODUCING YOURSELF
I'm from ... / I'm with ... / I work for ... (company)

I'm in sales.

I'm in charge of ...

I'm responsible for ...

I work with ...

INTRODUCING SOMEONE ELSE
Can I introduce you to Miriam?

Robert, have you met Vladimir?

TALKING ABOUT COMMON INTERESTS
You and Tom have something in common.

You both like / enjoy / are interested in ...

TALKING ABOUT YOUR COMPANY
The company was founded in ...

We make/ manufacture/sell/ distribute/supply ...

We have subsidiaries/ factories/branches/ outlets in ...

We have a workforce of 2,000.

NETWORKING
We're very interested in ...

Do you know anyone who could help us?

Could you let me have their contact details?

Could I call him and mention your name?

Let me give you my business card.

InStep's relocation

A US-based shoe manufacturer must decide whether to relocate the head office of its European subsidiary, InStep, from Paris to a small industrial town 120 kilometres away.

Background

Three years ago, InStep moved its factory to Beauchamp, a small, industrial town in northern France. The plant is modern with new equipment. A large warehouse and distribution centre were built near the factory. InStep is now considering moving staff from the Paris office to a purpose-built, six-storey building in the same town. Beauchamp has a population of 25,000, with a high proportion of young people. The relocation, if it goes ahead, will create employment opportunities for local inhabitants.

How do you think staff will react to the proposed relocation? What reasons might some staff have for opposing the relocation?

A 'getting to know you' meeting

The Vice-President of the parent company has come to Paris to discuss the proposed relocation with two senior managers from the Paris subsidiary and an independent relocation consultant. This group will discuss the relocation and make a recommendation to the Board of Directors on whether to go ahead with the relocation or not.

Task

Work in groups of four. Take one of these roles.

Student A: Vice-President, parent company

Student B: Senior Manager, Paris subsidiary

Student C: Senior Manager, Paris subsidiary

Student D: Management Consultant
    (an independent adviser)

As you do not know each other well, you all meet for social reasons in the Paris subsidiary's boardroom. The purpose of the meeting is to get to know each other better. Use your knowledge of social English
to create a warm, friendly atmosphere.

A communication from the Vice-President, parent company

Read the message from the Vice-President. Discuss the questions. How do you think staff will react to this message? Do you think the benefits described by the Vice-President will persuade staff to accept the relocation? Why? / Why not?

MESSAGE FROM THE VICE-PRESIDENT TO ALL STAFF

A decision concerning the proposed relocation to Beauchamp will be made in the near future. The relocation offers our company significant benefits:

- The reduction in costs will boost our profits.

- The town council in Beauchamp has offered us tax incentives to relocate to their town.

- The relocation will result in improved working conditions and better communication.

🔊 **CD1.30** Four members of staff are discussing the proposed relocation. **Listen and note down the worries some staff have about moving away from Paris. Compare your notes with a partner.**

Task

You are members of the Management Committee. Work in groups. Take one of these roles.

Student A: Vice-President, parent company:
    role card page 135

Student B: Manager A: role card page 141

Student C: Manager B: role card page 144

Student D: Independent Management Consultant:
    role card page 144

1 Read your role cards and prepare for the meeting.

2 Hold the meeting. Consider the advantages and disadvantages of relocating to Beauchamp.

3 Argue in favour of or against the relocation.

4 Decide whether or not to recommend relocation to InStep's Board of Directors. If necessary, vote. The Vice-President has the deciding vote if you cannot reach agreement.

Writing

As the Vice-President, write an e-mail to InStep's CEO, informing him of your decision concerning the relocation, with your reasons.

➡ *Writing file page 127*

Watch the Case study commentary on the **DVD-ROM.**

5 Advertising

'Advertising isn't a science. It's persuasion, and persuasion is an art.'
William Bernbach (1911–1982), US advertising executive

STARTING UP

Look at the billboards above. How effective do you think this form of advertising is? Why?

VOCABULARY
Advertising media and methods

A Billboards are one example of an advertising medium. Can you think of others?

B Look at these words. Label each word 1 for 'advertising media', 2 for 'methods of advertising' or 3 for 'verbs to do with advertising'.

advertorials 2
banner ads
billboards (AmE)/
 hoardings (BrE)
cinema
commercials
communicate

endorse
exhibitions
free samples
Internet
leaflets/flyers
outdoor advertising
place

point-of-sale
pop-ups
posters
press/newspapers
product placement
radio
run

sponsor
sponsorship
target
television
viral advertising

Which of the methods do you connect to which media?

C example: *television — commercials*

Which of the verbs you identified in Exercise B combine with these nouns?

D
1 a campaign
2 a product
3 an advertisement
4 an event
5 a consumer
6 a message

E **Choose the most suitable words to complete these sentences.**

1 A lot of cosmetics companies give away *leaflets / commercials / free samples* so that customers can try the product before they buy.

2 Advertising companies spend a lot of money on creating clever *slogans / posters / exhibitions* that are short and memorable, such as the message for Nike: 'Just do it'.

3 Celebrity *exhibition / research / endorsement* is a technique that is very popular in advertising at the moment.

4 If news about a product comes to you by *word of mouth / the press / the Internet*, someone tells you about it rather than you seeing an advert.

5 Many companies use post and electronic *slogans / mailshots / posters* because they can target a particular group of consumers all at the same time.

F **Give examples of:**

1 any viral campaigns you have read about

2 clever slogans that you remember from advertising campaigns

3 sponsorship of any sporting or cultural events.

G **What makes a good TV advertisement? Think about ones you have seen. Use some of these words.**

clever	interesting	funny	inspiring	eye-catching	original
powerful	strange	shocking	informative	sexy	controversial

H **Do you think that these advertising practices are acceptable? Are any other types of advertisement offensive?**

1 Using children in advertisements

2 Using actors who pretend to be 'experts'

3 Using nudity in advertisements

4 Using 'shock tactics' in advertisements

5 Promoting alcohol on TV

6 Comparing your products to your competitors' products

7 An image flashed onto a screen very quickly so that people are influenced without noticing it (subliminal advertising)

8 Exploiting people's fears and worries

I **Which of the following statements do you agree with?**

1 People remember advertisements, not products.

2 Advertising has a bad influence on children.

3 Advertising tells you a lot about the culture of a particular society.

*See the **DVD-ROM** for the i-Glossary.*

READING
A new kind of campaign

A Read the article and choose the best headline.

a) Honda predict record sales as advert breaks new ground

b) Honda skydivers push limits of TV adverts

c) Viewers tune out of normal TV advertising; Honda responds

FT

by Andrew Edgecliffe-Johnson

In a new definition of a publicity stunt, Channel 4 and Honda have turned to a team of skydivers to tackle the problem of viewers tuning out of
5 traditional television advertising.

On Thursday night, the broadcaster was due to devote an entire 3 minute 20 second break in the middle of Come Dine With Me, its dinner
10 party programme, to a live skydiving jump in which 19 stuntmen spelt out the carmaker's brand name. Described as the first live advertisement in modern times, the
15 campaign is the latest attempt by advertisers and broadcasters to find alternatives to the 30-second spot.

The development of digital video recorders such as Sky+ and Tivo,
20 which allow ads to be skipped, has forced advertising agencies and channels' sales teams to collaborate on more innovative attempts to keep the viewer's attention.
25 'We wanted to create something unmissable,' said Andy Barnes, the broadcaster's Sales Director. 'This concept breaks the boundaries of TV advertising,' he added,
30 highlighting a Channel 4 campaign called 'innovating the break'.

The campaign follows initiatives such as LG's 'Scarlet' campaign, in which the television manufacturer
35 ran advertisements appearing to trail a glamorous new television show, which turned out to be a promotion for the design features of its 'hot new series' of screens.
40 Thursday night's live advertisement, while designed to demonstrate the power of television advertising, was backed up by a complex multimedia and public-relations campaign.
45 The campaign's developers – including Channel 4's in-house creative team, Wieden + Kennedy, Starcom, Collective and Hicklin Slade & Partners – spent more
50 than a month pushing the Honda slogan of 'difficult is worth doing' before Thursday night's slot.

A poster campaign, a series of television 'teaser' advertisements and
55 a website have been backed up by digital advertising and press coverage. All are building up to a traditional 30-second advertising campaign, starting on June 1, said Ian Armstrong,
60 Marketing Manager of Honda UK.

'The 30-second ad is alive and well,' Mr Barnes said, pointing to data released this week which showed that commercial television had
65 enjoyed its best April in five years.

For Honda, however, the elements surrounding the core 30-second campaign are designed to generate the intangible buzz of word-of-mouth
70 advertising, Mr Barnes added.

Thursday night's skydive would almost certainly go on YouTube, Mr Armstrong predicted. 'Commercially, that's a fantastic result, as it means our
75 marketing investment becomes more efficient because consumers are doing our marketing for us.'

B Read the article again and answer the questions.

1 Why did Honda need a new publicity stunt with skydivers?

2 Why was the Honda advert unique?

3 Why are Sky+ and Tivo a problem for advertisers?

4 What happened in the Honda advert?

5 What happened in LG's 'Scarlet' campaign?

6 What did the Honda campaign's developers do?

7 What different types of advertising did Honda use?

C Find all the word pairs in the text using the words *advertisement* or *advertising*.

D Match the words in bold in the word pairs (1–5) to their meaning (a–e).

1 publicity **stunt**
2 design **features**
3 Honda **slogan**
4 poster **campaign**
5 **press** coverage

a) newspapers and magazines
b) a short phrase that is easy to remember
c) a series of actions intended to get a particular result
d) an important, interesting or typical part of something
e) something done to get people's attention

E Complete the text with some of the word pairs from Exercises C and D.

PUBLICITY STUNT TIPS

Nothing will get your product noticed faster than a well-thought-out and well-performed ....¹. First, you need to plan an ....². You could start with some ....³ on radio or TV and design some large adverts for a ....⁴. You need to highlight all the key ....⁵. Alert the local media and get good ....⁶. Tip off the local radio or TV station that something is going to happen. When it comes to the actual publicity stunt, ensure that all ....⁷ or logos are visible. And if you have the money, why not try a ....⁸ on TV? Finally, try to get some free ....⁹ and hopefully end up on YouTube.

F In groups, brainstorm some ideas for some live advertisements or publicity stunts.

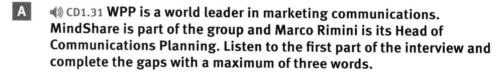

LISTENING
How advertising works

A ◀))) CD1.31 **WPP is a world leader in marketing communications. MindShare is part of the group and Marco Rimini is its Head of Communications Planning. Listen to the first part of the interview and complete the gaps with a maximum of three words.**

I always go back to the beginning and ....¹, what is the person who's paying for the campaign ....²? What is that person's ....³, what is it that that person ....⁴ as a result of ....⁵ on this advertising campaign?

B ◀))) CD1.31 **Listen again. What reasons are there for advertising, apart from selling a product?**

Marco Rimini

C ◀))) CD1.32 **Listen to the second part. What are the four stages of a typical advertising campaign?**

D ◀))) CD1.33 **Listen to the final part and answer the questions.**

1 What are *viral* campaigns?
2 Regarding the Ronaldinho viral, what did people argue about?

Watch the interview on the DVD-ROM.

E **In groups, tell each other about a viral campaign or advertisement that you have discussed with your friends.**

LANGUAGE REVIEW
Articles

a/an
- We use *a* or *an* before singular countable nouns.
  ***a** publicity stunt*
- We use *a* or *an* to introduce new information.
  *They are building up to **a** traditional 30-second advertising campaign*
- We often use *a* or *an* to refer to people's jobs.
  *She's **an** accountant*
- We use *a* before consonants and *an* before vowel sounds
  ***a** commercial, **an** advert*

the
- We use *the* when we think our listener will know what we are talking about. ***the** Internet*
- We use *the* when it is clear from the context what particular person, thing or place is meant because it has been mentioned before.
  ***The** campaign is the latest attempt to ...*

'zero article' We do not use an article before:
- uncountable nouns used in general statements.
  Information is power.
- the names of most countries, companies and people.
  Poland, Honda, Ian Armstrong
- A few countries require *the*:
  ***the** Philippines, **the** United Kingdom, **the** United States*

➡ *Grammar reference* page 148

A **Look back at the article on page 46. In paragraphs 1 and 2, why are *a* or *an* used instead of *the* before these words?**

1 publicity stunt
2 team of skydivers
3 entire 3 minute 20 second break
4 live skydiving jump

B **In the first two paragraphs of the article, which specific examples of the following are referred to?**

1 a problem
2 a broadcaster
3 a brand name
4 a live advertisement
5 a campaign

C **Tick the correct sentences. Add *the* where necessary in the other sentences. You may need to add *the* more than once.**

1 Knowledge of advertising code of practice is vital to those wishing to work in advertising industry.

2 We want to film a TV commercial in Russia.

3 The 'Think small' Volkswagen Beetle advert was one of most successful advertising campaigns of 20th century.

4 Four major brands – AOL, Yahoo!, Freeserve and BT – all achieve awareness of over 40% amongst UK adult population.

5 Next year, I am going to work for an advertising agency in USA.

D **This text is about a television advertisement. Some of the articles are missing. Write in the missing articles – *a*, *an* or *the* – where appropriate.**

Almost as soon as the 'gorilla' television commercial for Dairy Milk chocolate was first shown on 31 August, people started posting it on YouTube. People also started asking questions, like did it feature real gorilla playing drums?

So what role did the extraordinary take-up of gorilla ad on Internet play in Dairy Milk's success?

And was success of the advert a lucky break? For like Unilever and Diageo, Cadbury has benefited from the free 'viral'

distribution of its advertising on Internet as consumers e-mail, post and create spoof versions of gorilla campaign.

Gorilla commercial is most viewed advertisement so far this year on YouTube, the content-sharing website.

SKILLS

Starting and structuring presentations

A What factors do you need to consider when preparing a business presentation?

B 🔊 CD1.34 Listen to two different openings of a presentation. What is the same/different about them? Which do you prefer? Why?

C How many sections is the content of the presentation organised into? Look at the Useful language box below and divide the phrases into two groups, **F** (formal) or **I** (informal). Compare your answers.

D Choose one of these presentation situations. Write and practise the opening of the presentation.

1 Your company is launching a new product. (Audience: a group of potential customers)

2 You are presenting your place of work or study. (Audience: a group of potential customers or students)

3 Your company/organisation is introducing a new way of working. (Audience: a group of colleagues)

E 🔊 CD1.35 An important part of structuring a presentation is letting the audience know what is going to happen next, or signalling. Listen to an extract from later in the presentation in Exercise B and fill in the gaps.

1 ... where this is very important. Just to give you a specific example: .... the next slide, ... the chart that the key age group is 18 to 25, but that this will become less, not more, important as the product matures in the market.

2 As I say, this is reflected across all the markets. Right, ... the target markets. .... the final part, and the media we plan to use. We'll start in ...

3 This will be linked to a coordinated press campaign starting in June. .... , before we go to the storyboard: .... are that firstly ...

F What is the purpose of the missing expressions in each of the three extracts in Exercise E?

a) to introduce a conclusion   b) to change section/topic   c) to refer to visuals

G *Firstly* is an example of a sequencer. What other examples did you hear in the presentation?

H Prepare and deliver a three-minute presentation on your chosen topic from Exercise D. Try and use some signalling language.

USEFUL LANGUAGE

INTRODUCING YOURSELF

On behalf of Alpha Advertising, I'd like to welcome you. My name's Marc Hayward.

Hi, everyone, I'm Marc Hayward. Good to see you all.

INTRODUCING THE TOPIC

I'm going to tell you about the ideas we've come up with for the ad campaign.

This morning, I'd like to outline the campaign concept we've developed for you.

GIVING A PLAN OF YOUR TALK

I've divided my presentation into three parts. Firstly, I'll give you the background. Secondly, I'll discuss the media we plan to use. Finally, I'll talk you through the storyboard.

My talk is in three parts. I'll start with the background to the campaign, move on to the media we plan to use, and finish with the storyboard for the commercial.

INVITING QUESTIONS

If there's anything you're not clear about, feel free to stop me and ask any questions.

I'd be grateful if you could leave any questions to the end.

Alpha Advertising

A large advertising agency with a reputation for creating imaginative and effective campaigns is competing for new business.

Background

Alpha Advertising is based in Turin. It is competing for several new contracts. It has been asked to present ideas for exciting new campaigns to the management of the companies concerned. Concepts are required for the following new goods and services.

Panther Air

- An 'on-demand' jet charter service, based in Hamburg, Germany
- High standards of safety, quality and service
- Expert advice on choice of plane; competitive prices
- Target consumers: top business executives and VIPs

Aim: **To target the world's top business people**

E-Book

- An electronic book recently launched – slim; it can fit into a pocket or handbag
- It has a 200-novel memory and sells at 250 euros.
- When turned on, it takes readers straight to the last page they were reading.
- A 'next read' feature: the E-Book consults a database of related titles which may be of interest to the reader. It then makes recommendations for downloading or purchase.
- The E-Book is pre-loaded with 150 books.

Aim: **An international press and TV campaign**

Safe Haven: a new group of hotels in your country

- Rooms at competitive prices.
- Excellent facilities: a mini-spa on every floor; free aerobic classes three times a week; musical entertainment in the lounge every evening
- Hotels all in downtown areas
- Hotel restaurants offer a wide range of local dishes, prepared by well-known chefs
- A comprehensive advice service for all guests

Aim: **A creative campaign to attract more customers**

Task

You are members of the creative team at Alpha.

1 **Prepare an advertising campaign for one of the products or services. Use the Key questions on the right to help you.**

2 **Present your campaign to the management of the company concerned. When you are not presenting your campaign, play the role of the company's management. Listen and ask questions.**

3 **Use the Assessment sheet below to choose:**

   a) **the best campaign concept**
   b) **the most effective presentation.**

Key questions (advertising team)

• What is the campaign's key message?

• What special features does the product or service have?

• What are its USPs (Unique Selling Points)?

• Who is your target audience?

• What media will you use? Several, or just one or two? If you use:

   – an advertisement, write the text and do rough artwork.

   – a TV commercial, use a storyboard to illustrate your idea.

   – a radio spot, write the script, including sound effects and music.

   – other media, indicate what pictures, text, slogans, etc. will be used.

• What special promotions will you use at the start of the campaign?

Assessment sheet (managers)

Give a score of 1–5 for each category: 5 = outstanding, 1 = needs improvement.

Campaign concept

1 Will it get the target audience's attention? ☐

2 Will it capture their imagination? ☐

3 Does it have a clear, effective message? ☐

4 Will it differentiate the product or service? ☐

5 Will it persuade the target audience to buy the product or service? ☐

6 Will the target audience remember the campaign? ☐
TOTAL: ___ / 30

Presentation

1 Was it interesting? ☐

2 Was it clear? ☐

3 Was it loud and clear enough? Was it varied in pitch or monotonous? ☐

4 Was the pace too quick, too slow or just right? ☐

5 Was the language fluent, accurate and appropriate? ☐

6 Did it impress you? Was there enough eye contact? ☐
TOTAL: ___ / 30

Writing

As the leader of one of Alpha's advertising teams, prepare a summary of your concept for your Managing Director. The summary will be discussed at the next board meeting.

➡ *Writing file page 131*

Watch the Case study commentary on the DVD-ROM. ◎

OVERVIEW

VOCABULARY
Financial terms

LISTENING
Managing
investments

READING
An inspirational
story

LANGUAGE REVIEW
Describing trends

SKILLS
Dealing with
figures

CASE STUDY
Make your pitch

STARTING UP **A** Answer these questions individually. Then compare your answers with a partner.

Money Quiz

1 **How much cash do you have with you at the moment? Do you:**
   a) know exactly?
   b) know approximately?
   c) not know at all?

2 **Do you normally check:**
   a) your change?
   b) your bank statements and credit-card bills?
   c) restaurant bills?
   d) your receipts when shopping?
   e) prices in several shops or online before you buy something?

3 **Do you:**
   a) give money to beggars?
   b) give money to charities?
   c) give away used items such as clothes?
   d) sell things you don't want (for example, on eBay)?

4 **How do you feel about borrowing money? Do you tend to:**
   a) always manage to stay in credit and save regularly?
   b) sometimes go into the red and use an overdraft facility?
   c) usually pay interest on your credit card at the end of the month?

5 **Some people try not to pay the correct amount of tax. Is this:**
   a) a serious crime?
   b) morally wrong, but not a crime?
   c) excellent business practice?

6 **If you lend a colleague a small amount of money and they forget to pay it back, do you:**
   a) say nothing?
   b) remind them that they owe you money?
   c) arrange to go for a drink with them and say you've forgotten your wallet or purse?

B What do your answers to the questions in Exercise A say about your attitude to money? Are your attitudes typical? What do they say about your culture?

VOCABULARY

Financial terms

A **Match the words in the box to the definitions 1 to 6 below.**

equity stake	recession	shares	debt	stock market	forecast

1 equal parts into which the capital or ownership of a company is divided
2 a period of time when business activity decreases because the economy is doing badly
3 money risked when a business owns part of another company
4 a place where company shares are bought and sold
5 a description of what is likely to happen in the future
6 money owed by one person or organisation to another person or organisation

B **Match the sentence halves.**

1 **Profit margin** is   a) a part of a company's profits paid to the owners of shares.

2 **Investment** is   b) the difference between the price of a product or service and the cost of producing it.

3 **Bankruptcy** is   c) money which people or organisations put into a business to make a profit.

4 **A dividend** is   d) the amount of money which a business obtains (in a year) from customers by selling goods or services.

5 **Pre-tax profits** are   e) when a person or organisation is unable to pay their debts.

6 **Annual turnover** is   f) the money a business makes before payment to the government.

C **Complete this news report with the terms from Exercises A and B.**

And now the business news …

There was a further downturn in the economy this month as the …………¹ in the United States and Asia-Pacific region continues. Yesterday was another day of heavy trading on the …………², with big losses in share values. The …………³ for the near future is not good, as market confidence remains low.

Paradise Lane, the struggling luxury hotel group, is seeking new …………⁴ to try and avoid …………⁵, following the announcement of disastrous interim results. It currently has a …………⁶ of nearly $5 billion. There are rumours of rivals GHN taking a large …………⁷ in the troubled hotel group.

Phoenix Media announced a 15% increase in …………⁸ on an …………⁹ of $4.5 million. Added to the strong performance in the last quarter, this is likely to result in an increased …………¹⁰ of over 14 cents per share, well up on last year, which will certainly please shareholders*. Following a rise in sales in the emerging markets of …

* the people who own shares in a business

D ◀)) CD1.36 **Listen and check your answers.**

E **What word partnerships can you identify from the text in Exercise C?**

example: *heavy trading*

F **Discuss with your colleagues.**

- What is the economic situation in your country at the moment?
- Which parts of the economy are doing well or badly?
- What is your forecast?
- Which types of business are making profits or losses?
- What sort of businesses are a good investment?
- Can you think of any businesses which have gone bankrupt recently?
- Which company shares are going up or down at the moment?

*See the **DVD-ROM** for the i-Glossary.*

53

LISTENING
Managing investments

Darrell Mercer

A ◀)) CD1.37 **Darrell Mercer is Investment Director at PSigma Investment Management. Listen to the first part of the interview and complete the gaps.**

The aim of the business is to provide ....[1] for private individuals who have ....[2] that they wish to employ to achieve a certain ....[3]. My role as the Investment Director is to both ....[4] for the client with the intention of meeting that aim, that return, and also then manage that strategy on an ongoing basis.

B ◀)) CD1.38 **Listen twice to the second part and complete the chart. Then go to the audio script on page 157 and check your answers.**

Asset	Example
1 cash	
2 fixed-interest securities	lending to a ....[1] or a ....[2]
3 index-linked securities	linked to the ....[3]
4 equities	a ....[4] or a ....[5]
5 investments not linked to equity returns	.............[6] property ....[7] (e.g. precious metals) ....[8] (an interesting area of development over last 20 years)
6 alternative investments	.............[9] funds ....[10] funds

*Watch the interview on the **DVD-ROM**.*

C ◀)) CD1.39 **Listen to the final part. Which of the following does Darrell not mention?**

1 gold   2 fixed-income securities   3 hedge funds   4 early cycle equities

READING
An inspirational story

A **Find idiomatic expressions in the article heading (page 55) which mean:**

1 someone who does a lot of complicated business transactions

2 a young person who is very skilled or successful at something.

B **Read the article and complete the profile.**

Name	Kieran Prior
Age	
Job	
Duties	
Company	
Work location	
IQ	
Personality/Strengths	
Current area of specialisation	

C **What is your reaction to Kieran's story?**

Kieran Prior: Goldman Sachs's whizz-kid wheeler dealer

Working on the noisy, frenetic **trading** desk at Goldman Sachs's London offices on Fleet Street earlier this decade, Kieran Prior and John Yeatts, two bright and ambitious twentysomethings from very different worlds, became close friends.

Although Prior, then 23, was just a year older than Yeatts when they met, he enjoyed giving practical advice, teasing the American about his Saturday-night dates. Yeatts returned the favour. When **traders** ordered lunch delivered to their desks, Yeatts cut up Prior's food and fed him one small bite at a time. Prior was born with a rare condition that affects his movement and impairs his speech. He cannot get out of his wheelchair unaided, and has never been able to walk.

Yet despite these physical limitations, Prior is thriving on Goldman's trading desk – possibly the most demanding and competitive testing ground in finance – winning the admiration of colleagues while gaining experience, confidence and responsibility.

It's not easy managing investments of any size for the high-powered trading machine that supplies much of the **earnings** of Wall Street's most profitable firm. It is extraordinary that Prior is able to do so with such physical limitations.

Gary Williams, the former head of European equity trading, who hired Prior nearly eight years ago, has enormous respect for his determination. 'He is an exceptionally smart, perceptive guy who has purposefully risen to – and overcome – so many challenges,' said Williams. 'The noise and hurly-burly of the trading floor make trading more difficult for someone in Kieran's position, but the challenge actually appeals to him.'

Intellectually, Prior, now 29, has few limits. Since joining Goldman as a **financial analyst** in the equity division in 2000, Prior – whose IQ score of 238 puts him in the top 1% of the world's population – has risen from performing basic **research analysis** and trading Euro Stoxx futures to running a $50m (£25m) group of European **equities** and **derivatives**.

Prior joined Goldman just four days after he graduated from university. Early on, he caught the attention of John Thornton, Goldman's then-president, as Thornton was walking across the trading floor. Thornton stopped for a brief chat – and was amazed.

'I couldn't help but be impressed,' said Thornton. 'First of all, Kieran's sheer, raw talent is impressive, and when you add to that the determination he shows getting through the day in a place like Goldman Sachs, which is so demanding, it is just breathtaking.'

Prior is free to invest in almost any **business sector**, but recently narrowed his focus to just 20 companies because of the extreme volatility in the markets. 'I joined Goldman in a **bear market**,' he said, 'but these markets are the most difficult I've ever seen, so I'm just using this period of **volatility** to learn as much as I can.'

from the *Sunday Times*

D Find words in bold in the text that mean the following.

1 a financial market in which prices are falling

2 people who deal in shares and bonds

3 someone who carefully examines the financial state of a company

4 sudden and quick change

5 the area of a financial market where a particular company does business

6 the capital that a company has from shares rather than from loans

7 the careful examination of the performance of companies and stocks

8 the part of the economy made up by companies

9 the profit that a company makes in a particular period of time

10 things such as options or futures based on underlying assets such as shares, bonds and currencies

E In groups, discuss which of the following sectors you think are likely to be volatile in an economic recession.

- telecommunications
- advertising
- healthcare
- food
- biotechnology

- cars
- budget supermarkets
- steel
- travel
- construction

LANGUAGE REVIEW
Describing trends

We can describe trends in English in different ways.

1 **Verbs of change**
   Demand for BlackBerries has **soared** *in recent years.*
   Sales are **falling***.*
   Profits **improved** *in July.*

2 **Prepositions**
   Profits rose 5% **to** *$1.4 billion.*
   The sales of Dupont have gone up **from** *$19.6 billion* **to** *$27.4 billion.*
   Sales rose **by** *20% over the holiday period.*
   This represents a decrease **of** *16.4% from the first quarter.*
   The average retail gasoline price stood **at** *$4.11 a gallon yesterday.*

3 **Different verb forms**
   The figures **paint** *a gloomy picture for Japanese growth. (present simple)*
   The unemployment rate **is rising***. (present continuous)*
   Last summer, our market share **fell***. (past simple)*
   This year, orders from Brazil **have levelled off***. (present perfect)*
   If the price of petrol **rises** *further, we'll* **make** *a loss. (first conditional)*

   ➡ *Grammar reference page 148*

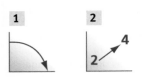

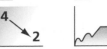

A **What kind of movement do these verbs describe? Match them to the symbols (1–11) on the left. Then compare your answers with your partner. (You will need to use some symbols more than once.)**

decline	increase	double	level off	decrease	peak
gain	rocket	fall	triple	fluctuate	rise
drop	plummet	halve	recover	improve	jump

B **Which of the verbs in Exercise A also have noun forms? What are they?**

example: *to increase — an increase*

C **Look at the graphs below. Complete the sentences about them with appropriate prepositions.**

1 Sales have increased .... €5m .... €7m.

2 Sales have increased .... €2m.

3 There has been an increase .... €2m in our sales.

4 Sales now stand .... €7m.

5 Sales reached a peak .... €7m in July.

6 Sales reached a low point .... €1m in April.

D **Write two more sentences about each of these graphs.**

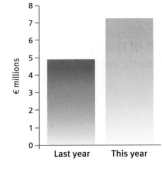
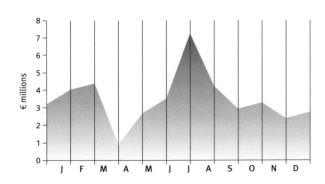

USEFUL LANGUAGE

YEARS

1984 *nineteen eighty-four*
2012 *two thousand and twelve*
or *twenty twelve*

CURRENCIES

£3.15 *three pounds fifteen*
$7.80 *seven dollars eighty*
€250 *two hundred and fifty euros*
¥125 *one hundred and twenty-five yen*

DECIMALS

16.5 *sixteen point five*
17.38% *seventeen point three eight per cent*
0.185 *(nought / zero) point one eight five*

FRACTIONS

$\frac{1}{4}$ *a quarter* $\frac{1}{2}$ *a half*
$\frac{2}{3}$ *two thirds* $\frac{3}{4}$ *three quarters*

BIGGER NUMBERS

3,560   *three thousand five hundred **and** sixty* (BrE)
              three thousand five hundred sixty (AmE)

598,347   *five hundred **and** ninety-eight thousand, three hundred **and** forty-seven* (BrE)
              five hundred ninety-eight thousand, three hundred forty-seven (AmE)

1,300,402 *one million three hundred thousand, four hundred **and** two* (BrE)
              one million three hundred thousand, four hundred two (AmE)
1m   *one / a million (1,000,000)*
3bn   *three billion (3,000,000,000)*
$7.5bn   *seven point five billion dollars*
€478m   *four hundred **and** seventy-eight million euros* (BrE)
           four hundred seventy-eight million euros (AmE)

If you don't specify an exact amount, a plural is used.
*It cost **thousands** of dollars. They spent **millions** of euros.*

A   Work in pairs. Student A, turn to page 136 and read the text aloud to Student B. Student B, listen to Student A while reading this article. Correct any incorrect information.

Business in brief

It was a bad day for the London market. Following disappointing results from FedEx in the US and fears
5 of a credit crunch, the FTSE 100 fell 105 points or 1.8 per cent to 5,756.9, while the FTSE 250 fell 189.1 points or 1.9 per cent to 9,534.8.
10   Only eight blue-chip stocks managed to make gains. The best was Smith & Nephew. Shares in the medical devices group rose 2.9 per cent to 595½p
15 after UBS upgraded the stock to a 'buy' recommendation. S&N was also supported by rumours of a bid approach from a Japanese company.
20   On the other hand, British Airways, down 5.2 per cent to 225¾p, fell even further after Morgan Stanley cut its target to 149p. This was because
25 of worries about increasing fuel prices.
   Tate and Lyle, the sugar and sweeteners group, lost 5.2 per cent to 402¼p after CityGroup
30 lowered its forecasts because of rising corn prices. Following recent floods in the US, the cost of corn has risen 25 per cent.

FT

B   🔊 CD1.40 Listen and check the pronunciation of the figures.

C   Write all the numbers from the correct version of the article in Exercise A in full, according to the way they are pronounced.

example: 105 points   *a hundred and five points*

MAKE YOUR PITCH

Entrepreneurs with new business ideas take part in a TV programme to persuade wealthy people to invest in their project.

Background

BNT is an American TV channel specialising in business news. Currently, it has a weekly programme called *Make your pitch*. In the programme, entrepreneurs of any age can make a pitch (a persuasive sales presentation) to two wealthy business people (tycoons) asking for money to help them develop a business idea, product or service. If the tycoons think the idea will be profitable, they invest some of their own money in the project. However, they usually ask for a large stake in the entrepreneurs' business in return for their investment.

Rules of the competition

Read the rules that the entrepreneurs are given before they make their pitch.

1   Introduce yourself and state the name of your business.

2   Tell the tycoons how much you want them to invest and on what terms.

3   Make a short presentation (2–3 minutes) describing your idea/product/service.

4   Say who the product is aimed at: for example, the type of person and age range.

5   Mention any research you have done or actions you have taken to sell the product/service or develop your idea.

6   Try to convince the tycoons that your idea/product or service will be profitable and make money for them.

🔊 **CD1.41 Listen to an entrepreneur ending a presentation of the product, a storage device, that he and his partner want the tycoons to invest in. Tick the correct statements.**

1 The product can be adapted to any space.

2 It can be used to store different kinds of household objects.

3 It looks impressive.

4 It can only be used once.

5 The entrepreneurs want the tycoons to invest €200,000 in their business.

6 If the tycoons accept the entrepreneurs' offer, they will end up owning 20% of the business.

🔊 **CD1.42 Listen to the questions and answers following the entrepreneurs' pitch. In groups, discuss these questions.**

1 If you were one of the tycoons, what other questions would you ask the entrepreneurs before negotiating a stake in their company?

2 Do you think you would invest in this product? Why? / Why not?

3 If you decided to invest, what stake in the business would you ask for?

4 Apart from investing money, how else could you add value to their business? For example, personal qualities? business experience?

In tonight's programme, there will be four pitches to the tycoons by entrepreneurs.

1 100 sculptures of famous people

2 New Formula XF anti-wrinkle cream

3 Alfresh lunch box with cooler

4 On-the-Spot car cleaning

Task

The tycoons listen to a short pitch (1–2 minutes) from each of the entrepreneurs. Then they ask questions to get additional information. Finally, they decide whether or not they will invest in the project, and on what terms.

1 Work in groups of four. Take turns playing the roles of tycoons and entrepreneurs.

Tycoons: Turn to page 145.

Entrepreneurs: Choose one of the following products and turn to the relevant page.

• Sculptures of famous people (page 136)

• New Formula XF anti-wrinkle cream (page 141)

• Alfresh lunch box with cooler (page 136)

• On-the-Spot car cleaning (page 144)

2 Work as one group. Discuss all four projects. Rank them according to how good an investment they are for the tycoons (1 = excellent investment, 4 = poor investment). If you can't agree, take a vote.

Writing

Write an e-mail to the most successful entrepreneur confirming the investment which the tycoons will make in their project. Give reasons for the tycoons' decision.

➡ *Writing file page 127*

Watch the Case study commentary on the **DVD-ROM.** ◉

2 International meetings

A Think about the last three meetings you attended (not necessarily business meetings, e.g. residents' meetings or sports club meetings) and answer these questions.

1 What was the purpose of each meeting?
2 What size were they?
3 Were they formal or informal?
4 Were they successful or not? Why?

B Do the quiz.

What are the following called?

1 the person in charge of a meeting
a) chief   b) chair   c) boss

2 the people at the meeting
a) audience   b) attenders   c) participants

3 the list of points to be discussed
a) agenda   b) schedule   c) timetable

4 one point on the list
a) theme   b) item   c) topic

5 an official record of what was said or decided
a) protocol   b) notes   c) minutes

6 what you send when you are unable to attend a meeting
a) excuses   b) apologies   c) pardon

7 a method of reaching a decision
a) vote   b) proposal   c) consensus

8 what is decided at the end of the meeting
a) action plan   b) agenda   c) handouts

C Discuss your answers to the quiz with a partner. How important are these things in the meetings you attend?

D International meetings can involve people from very different cultures. Read the experiences of meetings in different cultures on the right and answer these questions.

1 Which would make you feel the most or least comfortable?
2 Which feels the most or least familiar?
3 Do you recognise any of the styles from direct experience?
4 Is there anything in your own business meeting culture which people from other cultures might find unusual?

E ◀)) CD1.43 Listen to an expert talking about international meetings and answer the questions.

1 Which three areas are identified as causing problems in international meetings?
2 What tips does the expert give for successful international meetings?

F ◀)) CD1.43 Listen again. Are the following true (T) or false (F), according to the expert?

1 Punctuality is important in all cultures.
2 In a hierarchical culture, people feel able to express disapproval of the ideas of a superior.
3 Clear meeting aims are a priority in most cultures.
4 The main purpose of meetings is to take decisions.
5 It is easy to misinterpret body language in meetings.

G Complete these expressions used by the expert and discuss the meaning.

1 time is ....
2 stick to the ....
3 loss of ....
4 getting down to ....
5 small ....
6 relationship ....

How important do you think these issues are in your business culture?

A Well, in my experience there's great respect for seniority. Participants will enter a meeting in order of seniority, with the most senior person sitting furthest away. The exchange of business cards is important. They respect silence, as this shows serious work is being done. They do not say 'no' directly, as this is considered impolite.

B The sort of meetings I attended were very goal-focused and efficient. People there like agendas which are clear and they stick to them. They believe in good preparation and they feel that meetings are for clearly defined purposes, with action plans at the end. There seemed to be a general feeling of time being precious and not to be wasted. I think they came up with the idea of business breakfasts.

Task

You work for a large multinational company with over 100 offices worldwide (including in your country). The Communications Director has asked you to discuss the topic of meetings across the company and to report back with your findings. The information you provide will help with the future communications policy of the company.

1   Work in small groups. Hold a meeting using the following as your agenda, and consider the advantages and disadvantages of each recommendation.

   a)   Hold all meetings in English.

   b)   Limit the number of participants in meetings to a maximum of eight.

   c)   Stop holding meetings in the afternoon of the last working day of the week.

   d)   Use more video conferencing or teleconferencing calls for international meetings

   e)   Limit the length of meetings to one hour.

   f)   Conduct meetings standing up, without chairs, tables or refreshments.

   g)   Introduce weekly 'breakfast meetings' across the company.

2   Write some tips for effective meetings based on your discussion.

3   Present your ideas to another group.

C In my experience, meetings follow an established format with a detailed agenda. The use of titles like 'Mr' and 'Mrs' is important. There seems to be a lot of handshaking and sometimes kissing on the cheeks. Discussion is more about process than results, so there may be fewer decisions or action plans. The timetable is changeable, with interruptions and changes likely. The focus is on establishing relationships before moving on to the tasks. A business lunch here can last up to three hours.

D I found that people like to know well in advance about a meeting. They expect an agenda and timetable and dislike alterations. They communicate in a very direct way, follow the agenda precisely and minute all items. My jokes didn't seem to make people laugh, so I guess not being serious is disapproved of. Any proposals were presented in detail with supporting evidence. Generally, the meetings were dominated by the senior person.

E My experience of meetings here was that they are unstructured and often informal, more like a social event. It's normal to have long discussions on other issues, so it's a good idea to prepare and send out an agenda in advance. There was often careful analysis of small details. I found that meetings were more for decision-makers to get input from participants, while key decisions may be made elsewhere.

4 Organisation

VOCABULARY

1 Match the verbs (1–6) to the nouns (a–f) to make common collocations.

1	draw up	a)	press releases
2	install and maintain	b)	contracts
3	keep	c)	research
4	train	d)	systems
5	carry out	e)	records
6	issue	f)	staff

2 Write the name of the activity from Exercise 1 which is typically performed by each of these departments.

1 R&D

2 Public Relations

3 Legal

4 IT

5 Human Resources

6 Administration

NOUN COMBINATIONS

Match a noun from column A with a noun from column B to complete each of the sentences below.

A	B
consumer	style
sales	headquarters
management	range
company	revenue
product	awareness

1 Our ability to attract top people is a reflection of our .... – trying to be close to employees, clients and markets.

2 Arlito's .... has recently been extended and now includes a greater variety of soft drinks.

3 The travel sector is being encouraged to go green by the growing .... of environmental issues.

4 The company's total .... for 2009 was about £1.37bn, compared with £1.8bn the previous year, i.e. a 24-per-cent decline.

5 The new tax regime is an attempt to make our country a more attractive location for ....

Put the sentences (a–g) in the correct order to write an e-mail.

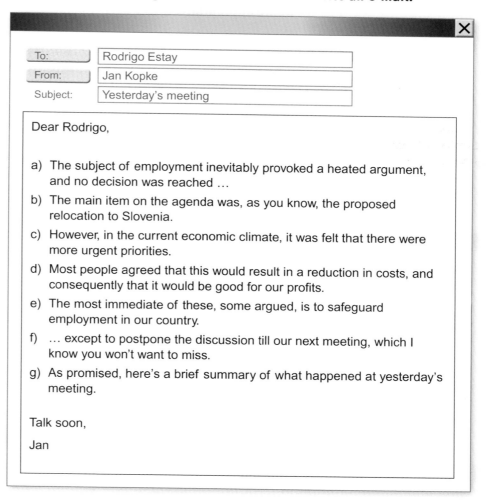

To: Rodrigo Estay

From: Jan Kopke

Subject: Yesterday's meeting

Dear Rodrigo,

a) The subject of employment inevitably provoked a heated argument, and no decision was reached …

b) The main item on the agenda was, as you know, the proposed relocation to Slovenia.

c) However, in the current economic climate, it was felt that there were more urgent priorities.

d) Most people agreed that this would result in a reduction in costs, and consequently that it would be good for our profits.

e) The most immediate of these, some argued, is to safeguard employment in our country.

f) … except to postpone the discussion till our next meeting, which I know you won't want to miss.

g) As promised, here's a brief summary of what happened at yesterday's meeting.

Talk soon,

Jan

5 Advertising

Complete the text with the words in the box. There are some words which you will not need.

| advertorial | commercials | endorsed | flyers | free samples | viral |
| hoardings | placed | point-of-sale | pop-ups | slogans | |

You may disagree that advertising is an art, you may even find it irritating at times, but it has certainly become part of our life. The newspaper article that you started reading turns out to be an ....[1]. The programme you are watching on TV is suddenly interrupted by a series of ....[2] for various consumer goods, including one for Crispin's Crisps, ...[3] by your favourite film star. And no sooner do you start surfing the Internet than ....[4] invade your screen. So you take a break and go for a stroll, only to take in once more how much ....[5] have indeed changed your cityscape. Then, on entering your local supermarket, you notice immediately that ....[6] advertising is alive and well, but do not refuse the ....[7] given away that day. Finally, you just do it – yes, you buy three packets of Crispin's and walk back home with a spring in your step.

ARTICLES

In each sentence of this text, one article is missing. Write *a*, *an* or *the* where appropriate.

Sweden has long history of rules and regulations aimed at guiding citizens on the right path. A majority of Swedes seem content with the prohibitions they believe help keep their country one of safest on Earth. As Sweden is extremely child-focused society, much of the paternalistic protection is directed towards children. For example, all television advertising aimed at children under age of 12 – from junk food to toys to video games – has been banned on terrestrial channels before 9 p.m. since 1991. Although it has many admirers, ban is not entirely successful because the satellite television stations that broadcast from outside Sweden are free to target children as much as they like. Despite this, health professionals say the relatively low incidence of children's advertising has been big factor in the exceptionally low levels of overweight children in Sweden.

SKILLS

Complete this presentation.

Good morning. On b _ _ _ _ _[1] of Lintex International, I'd like to w _ _ _ _ _ _[2] you all. My name's Selim Melki. As you know, I'm here today to t _ _ _[3] about our next global advertising campaign. I have d _ _ _ _ _ _[4] my talk into three p _ _ _ _[5]. F _ _ _ _ _ _[6], I'd l _ _ _[7] to state our objectives. S _ _ _ _ _ _ _[8], I'll explain why this time headquarters has decided to focus on celebrity endorsement, and outline the main ideas so far. And f _ _ _ _ _ _[9], I'll look at our budget.

Please feel free to i _ _ _ _ _ _ _ _[10] at any time if you'd like to ask a q _ _ _ _ _ _ _[11].

6 Money

VOCABULARY

Complete the newspaper article with the words in the box.

bankruptcy	dividend	forecasts	gains	investment
pre-tax profits	recession	share	shareholders	turnover

Stormgard shines when others stumble

While two of its rivals are teetering on the brink of ....[1], Stormgard, one of Europe's largest manufacturers of insulation and roofing products, reports record preliminary results, with sales growth and market share ....[2] made in all three regions of Scandinavia, western Europe and the Mediterranean. ....[3] at Stormgard increased almost 14 per cent last year, with demand for insulation products rising, as companies and individuals looked for ways to cut costs and save energy in the midst of the current ....[4]. ....[5] were €62.4m, up 8 per cent from last year. ....[6] will certainly not be disappointed, as the directors recommended the payment of a final ....[7] of 9.25c per ....[8]. ....[9] are optimistic, and Stormgard even plans to increase its ....[10] in plant and equipment in the near future. Commenting on the results, Lucas Reiner, Chairman of Stormgard, said: 'Against a background of mixed market conditions, our company faces the future with confidence and looks forward to continued progress in the year ahead.'

DESCRIBING TRENDS

1 Complete these verbs, which are all used to describe trends.

Downward movement

1 to p _ _ m _ _ t

2 to d _ _ p

3 to f _ _ _

4 to _ _ c l _ _ _

Upward movement

5 to _ _ c r _ _ _ _

6 to _ i _ _

7 to _ _ c k _ _

8 to j _ _ _

2 Complete the chart.

infinitive	past simple	past participle	noun
to decrease	 1	 2	 3
to fall	 4	 5	 6
to drop	 7	 8	 9
to peak	 10	 11	 12
to rise	 13	 14	 15

3 Complete the sentences below with appropriate prepositions.

Profit figures

2008: €7.5m
2009: €4.5m

1 There was a sharp drop .... profit.

2 Profit decreased .... €7.5m .... €4.5m.

3 Profit decreased .... €3m.

4 Profit now stands .... €4.5m.

5 There was a drop .... €3m .... profit.

SKILLS

Write these numbers in full.

1 14

2 40

3 £8.50

4 €515

5 12.5

6 13.36%

7 0.125

8 $\frac{1}{3}$

9 $\frac{3}{4}$

10 5,678

Cultures: International meetings

Complete the sentences below with the words in the box.

action	agenda	body	building	business	face	key	small	times

1 Different cultural assumptions mean that sometimes .... language can easily be misunderstood.

2 In a hierarchical culture, criticising or disagreeing with a boss or manager can result in a loss of .... for both people involved.

3 In many countries, people like to go away from a meeting with a clear .... plan.

4 Not all cultures have strict approaches to starting and finishing .... or the duration of discussion.

5 The idea of hierarchy in a culture is one of the .... areas to bear in mind.

6 The new manager has a very relaxed attitude towards meetings and sees them as the place for relationship .... and developing trust.

7 The participants made .... talk for a few minutes, then the Chair cleared her throat and said, 'So, let's get down to ....'

8 Their meetings are for clearly defined purposes, and they like to stick to the ....

Small talk

Objectives

Speaking
Can use a basic repertoire of conversation strategies to maintain a discussion.

Listening
Can follow most of an everyday conversation if speakers avoid very idiomatic usage.

Lesson deliverable
To participate in an activity to practise small talk in a business context.

Performance review
To review your own progress and performance against the lesson objectives at the end of the lesson.

A SPEAKING 1

Discuss the questions with a partner.

1 How would you define small talk? Some people think that small talk is a waste of time. What do you think?

2 Think about your small talk skills. What are you good at? What are you not so good at?

3 Make a list of some interesting things you can say about yourselves/your job and company.

4 How important do you think body language is when you meet people?

B READING

Read the text below and discuss the questions.

1 Do you agree with the information in the text?

2 If your country is not mentioned in the text, compare your culture to those mentioned in the text.

Value of small talk

Small talk helps to establish a relationship between people. However, some cultures, for example, Russian and German, often prefer to get down to business with little small talk whereas others, for example Indian, American and Brazilian, expect and enjoy it. Also, the use of titles (Professor, Doctor, etc.) is very important in some cultures (e.g. Mexican, Chinese, German), so it is necessary to listen carefully to how they introduce themselves or are introduced.

Importance of body language

Body language plays a big part as it contributes to the first impression you give. It starts with how and where you stand. Standing too close to someone or touching them is not acceptable in some cultures: it is best to avoid touching Chinese visitors and definitely do not touch the top of the head of an Indian person. Direct eye contact is usually expected in Russia, although too much eye contact may make someone from Japan feel very uncomfortable.

C LISTENING

1 🔊 BSA2.1.6 **Listen to a conversation and answer the questions.**

   1 Which people have met before?

   2 Which people haven't met before?

   3 What mistake does Grant make?

2 🔊 BSA2.1.6 **Listen again and complete the sentences from the conversation.**

   1 Hello, Grant. .... to see you ....

   2 I haven't seen you ....

   3 Are you still .... ?

   4 That's .... , well done! And .... business?

   5 How's .... your company?

   6 Hello, Doctor Sun. .... I .... Grant Corbin?

   7 I believe you .... common.

3 🔊 BSA2.1.7 **Listen to a second conversation and answer the questions.**

   1 How does Dietger feel?   *happy / annoyed / angry / surprised*

   2 How does Grant feel?   *surprised / angry / interested / inspired*

4 🔊 BSA2.1.8 **Listen to a third conversation. Why does Magda say, 'Pleased to meet you, at last'?**

D SPEAKING 2

Work in pairs. Practise asking and answering questions about each other's work and company. Use some of the phrases from Section C in your conversations. Don't forget to introduce yourself and to end the conversation in a suitable way. Turn to page vii for your role cards.

Task

Pre-task: Discussion

When you first meet people from different nationalities, what topics are neutral and could be considered safe to talk about with someone from any cultural background? What can you look for in a person's response to check if the topic is acceptable? In pairs, think about some suitable opening questions for when you meet someone for the first time.

Part 1: Preparation

Context: The international company you work for has just bought another large international company. The regional managers from around the world are visiting the head office for a weekend so that staff can get to know each other.

Work in two groups of four. You are going to prepare for a conversation with regional managers that you are meeting for the first time.

Group A

- You work at the head office and are arranging the event. Discuss how to welcome the other company staff, who are from many different cultural backgrounds.
- How will you deal with any unsuitable conversation topics or body language from your visitors?
- Turn to page vii and choose one Group A role card each.
- Look at your role card, which shows your company role, a characteristic or body language and an unsuitable conversation topic. Try to include these in the conversation along with general small talk.

Group B

- You are the people from the newly-bought company. You come from different cultural backgrounds.
- How will you deal with any unsuitable conversation topics or body language from your hosts?
- Turn to page vii and choose one Group B role card each.
- Look at your role card, which shows your company role, a characteristic or body language and an unsuitable conversation topic. Try to include these in the conversation along with general small talk.

Part 2: Small talk

The two groups meet at the head office. One person from Group A welcomes someone from Group B. Using the small talk phrases you have learnt, have a conversation with the person. After a short while, your teacher will ask you to introduce someone else or move to another person. Talk to as many people as you have time for.

Part 3: Reporting back

Return to your original group and tell each other about the people you met in the other group and what topics you talked about. Were any topics unsuitable for small talk? How did you deal with them? Did you have to deal with any uncomfortable body language?

◎ EXTRA PRACTICE: DVD CLIP AND WORKSHEET 9

E PEER REVIEW

Look back at the lesson objectives and think about the conversations you had. Then answer the questions.

1 Did you manage to start, maintain and end the short conversations?

2 Could you understand the main points discussed and extract the key details?

3 Did you and your partner(s) use suitable body language?

4 What can you and your partner(s) do to improve your skills?

F SELF-ASSESSMENT

Write 80–100 words to assess your performance. Think about these points.

- how well you achieved the lesson objectives

- feedback from your partner(s)

- how body language affected the conversations

- what you can do to improve

G PROFESSIONAL DEVELOPMENT AND PERFORMANCE GOALS

Think of opportunities to practise and improve your skills inside and outside the classroom. Write a few sentences about ways of improving your small talk skills.

Presentations

Objectives

Speaking

- Can summarise the main message from simple diagrams (e.g. graphs, bar charts).
- Can make comments about graphs and charts, using simple language.
- Can use a few basic linking expressions to signal transitions within a presentation.

Listening

Can ask for confirmation of understanding during a live discussion.

Lesson deliverable

To plan, prepare and give a presentation using figures and graphs/charts.

Performance review

To review your own progress and performance against the lesson objectives at the end of the lesson.

Ⓐ SPEAKING 1

1 Work in pairs. Turn to page viii and look at four visuals. Decide which is best for each of these things.

a) showing the market share of a company

b) describing changes in sales figures

c) comparing features of similar products

d) comparing the sales figures of different products

2 In pairs, describe the visuals in Exercise 1 using these sentences. Say more about each visual.

a) Our new model, the X3, is heavier than the X2.

b) Product 1 sold 2.5 million units.

c) Competitor A's market share was 25 per cent.

d) Revenue rose from £40,000 to £50,000.

Ⓑ READING

Read about Life Beverages. What does the company produce? Where and how do they sell their products?

Life Beverages is an American multinational drinks company, manufacturing, retailing and marketing soft drink concentrates and syrups. They work in partnership with bottling companies in over 20 markets in the world, offering canned and bottled drinks in shops, food outlets and through vending machines.

Ⓒ LISTENING

1 Look at the graphs. What has happened at Life Beverages over the last year?

① **Net profit**

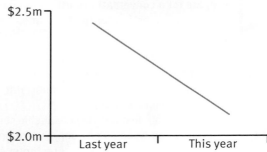

② **Net revenue**

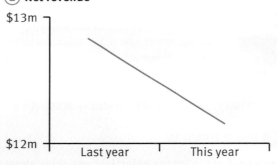

2 🔊 BSA2.2.9 Listen to the CEO of Life Beverages, Carolyn Murphy, and check your answers.

3 🔊 BSA2.2.10 Listen to Carolyn Murphy talking in more detail about the figures and some events which affected the results. Complete the notes.

Reasons:
1 Carbonated drinks sales in .... and .... started .... in April last year.
2 Fruit and sugar prices .... → .... juice prices → lower profits
3 The company .... in restructuring operations in .... and .... last year.

TEAM BUILDING

4 Complete the phrases from Carolyn's presentation with the correct form of *see*, *look* or *show*. When would you use these phrases?

1 So, as we've ...., ...

2 Let's .... in more detail.

3 .... at the next slide, ...

4 Can everyone .... that?

5 This slide ....

6 As you can ...., ...

5 🔊 BSA2.2.11 **Listen to another part of Carolyn's talk. What do these questions refer back to?**

1 Sorry, Carolyn, I thought you said that the volume of carbonated drinks was the same last year and juices are up; so why has revenue fallen?

2 Carolyn, you mentioned other markets. Which ones?

3 Could I just ask, isn't that lower than in previous years?

6 🔊 BSA2.2.11 **Listen again and match Carolyn's explanations (a–c) to the questions in Exercise 5 (1–3).**

a) Products have sold well in India and China.

b) Growth was faster in the past, but markets are healthy.

c) More sales are coming from low-price markets.

D SPEAKING 2

Work in pairs. Practise describing a visual from Carolyn's talk.

Student A: Turn to page ix.
Student B: Turn to page x.

Task

Pre-task: Research

Work in pairs or groups and turn to page x. Read the information and answer these questions.

1 What do you know about the company?
2 What information about the products do you know from the chart/graph?

Part 1: Preparation

Task: Give a five-minute presentation on changes in the company and sales performance year on year.

In your pairs or small groups, read the task and prepare your presentation. Think about the following points.

Structure
- Introducing the presentation: Explain the aim of your presentation and summarise what has happened in the last financial year.
- Presenting: Give reasons for the changes. Focus on parts of the chart/graph in detail.

Techniques and language
- Comment on the information in each graph/chart.
- Signal reasons and refer to slides clearly.
- Be prepared to take questions during the presentation.

Part 2: Presentation

Give your presentation.

Presenters: Use the guidance in Part 1.
Audience: Make notes on the facts and figures while you listen. Ask one question to confirm your understanding. How will you interrupt?

◎ EXTRA PRACTICE: DVD CLIP AND WORKSHEET 10

E PEER REVIEW

Think about another presentation. Give feedback.

1 Did the presentation give clear information?

2 Did the presenter give reasons for changes?

3 What good techniques/language did the presenter use?

4 What could the presenter improve?

F SELF-ASSESSMENT

Look back at the lesson objectives and answer the questions.

1 What techniques did you use:
   a) to refer to graphs and charts?
   b) to signal the stages of your presentation?

2 As audience, how much did you rely on visuals to understand the information? Did you ask for confirmation of any information?

3 What do you think you did well? What would you like to do better next time?

G PROFESSIONAL DEVELOPMENT AND PERFORMANCE GOALS

Think about statistics, numbers and changes related to your job. Write three sentences about how you could use the skills in this lesson to give information about your job.

UNIT

7 Cultures

'When overseas, you learn more about your own country than you do the place you are visiting.' **Clint Borgen, American activist**

STARTING UP

A What do you miss most about your own culture when you go abroad?

B Why is cultural awareness important for businesspeople? Give examples.

C What is culture? Choose the four factors that you think are the most important in creating a culture. Give your reasons.

climate	historical events	language
architecture	behaviour and attitudes	institutions
religion	social customs and traditions	cuisine
geography	ceremonies and festivals	arts

D Do you think cultures are becoming more alike? Is this a good thing or a bad thing? Give reasons for your answers. Think about:

- improved communications
- global business
- cheap foreign travel
- trading groups (such as the EU, ASEAN, USAN)

E How important are these things when doing business in your country? Are they a) important, b) not important or c) best avoided?

- exchanging business cards
- shaking hands
- bowing
- kissing
- being formal or informal
- punctuality
- humour
- eye contact

- socialising with contacts
- small talk before meetings
- accepting interruption
- giving presents
- being direct (saying exactly what you think)
- using first names

LISTENING
Cultural differences

A ◄)) CD1.44 **Jeff Toms is Marketing Director at an international cultural training centre. Listen to the first part of the interview and answer the questions.**

1 What two factors affect the 'Middle East clock'?

2 What can cause problems for Americans when they do business with Latin cultures?

Jeff Toms

B ◄)) CD1.45 **Listen to the second part of the interview and say what qualities companies should look for when sending staff abroad.**

C ◄)) CD1.46 **Listen to the final part of the interview and complete the gaps.**

I think also one of the key features of the successful .... ¹ is to be non-............ ². For instance, if you're coming from an Asian culture to try and do business with a Western culture, for certain the way that people do things will be fundamentally different – the .... ³, the structure, the ....-............ .... ⁴, the seniority and the .... ⁵ of the people you're doing business with – will be fundamentally different.

Watch the interview on the DVD-ROM.

D **If you could be sent anywhere in the world to work, which country would you choose? What aspects of its culture do you particularly like?**

VOCABULARY
Idioms

WELL, LET'S GET DOWN TO BUSINESS, NOW THAT WE'VE BROKEN THE ICE...

A Complete the idioms in the sentences below with the words in the box.

end	eye	eye	fire	foot	~~ice~~	water	water

1 Small talk is one way to *break the* ice when meeting someone for the first time.

2 I was *thrown in at the deep* .... when my company sent me to run the German office. I was only given two days' notice to get everything ready.

3 We *don't see eye to* .... with our US parent company about punctuality. We have very different ideas about what being 'on time' means. It's a question of culture.

4 I *got into hot* .... with my boss for wearing casual clothes to the meeting with the potential Japanese customers.

5 I really *put my* .... *in it* when I met our Spanish partner. Because I was nervous, I said 'Who are you?' rather than 'How are you?'.

6 I *get on like a house on* .... with our Polish agent; we like the same things and have the same sense of humour.

7 When I visited China for the first time, I was *like a fish out of* .... Everything was so different, and I couldn't read any of the signs!

8 My first meeting with our overseas clients was a *real* .... *-opener*. I hadn't seen that style of negotiation before.

B 🔊 CD1.47 **Listen to eight people using the idioms from Exercise A and check your answers.**

C **Consider the context of each idiom in Exercise A and decide which have:**

a) a positive meaning

b) a negative meaning.

D **Match the idioms in Exercise A (1–8) to the correct meanings (a–h).**

a) given a difficult job to do without preparation

b) quickly have a friendly relationship with someone

c) feel uncomfortable in an unfamiliar situation

d) say or do something without thinking carefully, so that you embarrass or upset someone

e) disagree with someone

f) an experience where you learn something surprising or something you did not know before

g) make someone you have just met less nervous and more willing to talk

h) get into trouble

E

Work in pairs or small groups. Discuss the following.

1 What tips do you have for *breaking the ice* at meetings with new clients/people from other cultures?

2 Talk about a place you have visited which was *a real eye-opener*.

3 Describe a situation when you

a) *put your foot in it*

b) *felt like a fish out of water*

c) *got into hot water*

d) *were thrown in at the deep end.*

See the **DVD-ROM** for the i-Glossary.

READING
Culture shock

A Read the article below quickly and decide which of the following (1–5) are:

a) referred to in a positive way in the text
b) referred to in a negative way in the text
c) not referred to at all.

1 understanding the culture of the country you are living in

2 asking British colleagues personal questions when you meet them for the first time

3 hiring staff who are flexible and tolerant

4 providing staff with practical support

5 looking at the role of the spouse (husband or wife) in the selection of candidates for overseas postings.

B Read the article again and answer the questions.

1 What things are people from different countries in an organisation:

a) likely to have in common   b) likely not to have in common?

2 What is 'cultural awareness'?

C Work in pairs. What do you think should be covered in a cultural training course?

D Write a paragraph using information from the article and giving tips to people doing business in the UK.

Standard Bank overcomes culture shock

It is increasingly common for multinational businesses to send employees on international assignments, but without the right cross-cultural 5 skills, staff will often struggle. Wayne Mullen, Head of Learning and Development at Standard Bank, discusses the impact that cultural challenges can have on employees 10 relocating to another country. In order to be successfully transferred, employees must understand the host-country culture, he argues.

Colleagues from different countries 15 might share similar professional knowledge and skills within a single international organisation, but their ways of working, social skills, body language and ways of doing 20 business are likely to be completely different. They may have different patterns of behaviour which need to be understood and appreciated in order for everyone to work together 25 successfully. For example, while it may be acceptable for Chinese office workers in Hong Kong to use the door-close button on a lift no matter how many people are also getting in, doing 30 such a thing in London would make people extremely angry. It is common for South Africans to ask personal questions of their counterparts shortly after being introduced, while a 35 British colleague may perceive this as impolite and inappropriate. Latin Americans' need for personal space is much less than that of their British colleagues.

40 Global companies should never underestimate the effect that culture can have on international assignments. Cultural awareness is much more than simply knowing 45 about a country's history and geography. It is about understanding how and why cultures work differently. It is also important to understand your own cultural make-up in order 50 to work more effectively, maximise teamwork and strengthen global competence.

The Standard Bank group operates in 38 different countries, and 55 its London office alone has 56 nationalities. This wide range of nationalities needs to communicate effectively in order to work as one team. The bank recognised that in 60 order to harmonise working practices within its culturally diverse office, it needed to provide foreign workers with a meaningful understanding of British business culture and communication 65 styles. It also needed to offer practical support which allowed employees to cope with the challenges of living and working in an unfamiliar environment; their reactions to day-to-day issues 70 such as the weather, public transport and social etiquette are often the most visible manifestations of culture shock.

Standard Bank has engaged Communicaid, a European culture and 75 communication skills consultancy, to design a tailored training solution which introduces delegates to some of the key cultural differences that they are likely to face in the UK.

from *Finance Week*

LANGUAGE REVIEW

Advice, obligation and necessity

1 Advice

- We can use *should* and *shouldn't* to give or ask for advice.
  *Global companies **should** never underestimate the effect that culture can have.*
- For strong advice, we can use *must* or *mustn't*.
  *You **mustn't** invade a British colleague's personal space too soon.*

2 Obligation/Necessity

- We often use *must* when the obligation comes from the person speaking or writing.
  *We **must** show more cultural understanding.*
- We use *mustn't* to say something is prohibited or is not allowed.
  *You **mustn't** smoke inside any building.*
- We often use *have to* to show that the obligation comes from another person or institution, not the speaker.
  *You **have to** get a visa to enter the country.* (This is the law.)

3 Lack of obligation / Lack of necessity

- *Don't have to* and *mustn't* are very different.
  don't have to = it is not necessary
  *You **don't have to** hurry. We have plenty of time.*

➡ *Grammar reference* page 149

A **Choose the most appropriate verb. There are some situations where both verbs are possible. Can you say why?**

1 If you are invited to a Brazilian's house for dinner, you *must / should* arrive at least 30 minutes after the time mentioned.

2 You *mustn't / don't have to* give purple flowers as a gift in many countries.

3 All personnel *should / must* read the health and safety notices in the building.

4 Staff *don't have to / mustn't* disclose information on the project unless authorised.

5 I think you *should / must* encourage the team to develop interpersonal skills.

6 Simone *doesn't have to / shouldn't* work so hard – she is looking very tired.

7 When going to a new country to do business, you *should / must* do some research into their culture.

8 You *mustn't / don't have* to pay immediately. We can offer you credit.

B **Read these notes on Chinese business protocol. How does each piece of advice compare with the situation in your country?**

Chinese business protocol and etiquette

Greetings
- You must greet the oldest person first.
- You don't have to be serious all the time. The Chinese have a great sense of humour. You should be ready to laugh at yourself sometimes.
- You mustn't move to a first-name basis until advised to. You should address the person by an honorific title and their surname.

Business cards
- You should exchange cards after the initial introduction.
- You should hold the card in both hands when offering it.
- You mustn't write on someone's card unless asked to.

Gift-giving
- You shouldn't give flowers, as many Chinese associate these with funerals.
- You mustn't give four of anything, as four is an unlucky number.

Entertaining at home
- It is a great honour to be invited to someone's home. If you cannot accept the invitation, you must offer a very good excuse.
- You should arrive on time, remove your shoes, bring a small gift and eat well to show you are enjoying the food.
- You don't have to eat loudly, but if you slurp or belch, it shows that you are enjoying your food.

A ◀)) CD1.48 **Listen to a conversation between two people who have recently met. What is wrong? How can it be improved?**

B **Work in pairs. In what business situations would you use these expressions?**

Congratulations!	I don't mind.	I'm afraid ...	After you.
Cheers!	Excuse me.	Yes, please.	That's no problem.
Make yourself at home.	Sorry.	Could you ... ?	Bad luck.
Help yourself.	It's on me.	That sounds good.	Not at all.

C **What would you say in the following situations?**

1 You don't hear someone's name when you are introduced to them.

2 You have to refuse an invitation to dinner with a supplier.

3 You are offered food you hate.

4 You want to end a conversation in a diplomatic way.

5 You have to greet a visitor.

6 You have to introduce two people to each other.

7 You offer to pay for a meal.

8 You have to propose a toast.

9 Your colleague has been made redundant.

10 You arrive half an hour late for a meeting.

D ◀)) CD2.1 **Listen and compare your answers to Exercise C.**

E ◀)) CD2.2 **What can you say in the first five minutes of meeting someone? Match the questions (1–10) to the answers (a–j). Listen and check your answers.**

1 Is this your first visit to the region? a) At the Metropolitan Hotel.

2 Oh really! What do you do? b) Nearly five years now.

3 How long have you been there? c) No, I come here quite a lot, but usually to Hong Kong.

4 Have you been to Tokyo before? d) I'm an Account Director for a marketing company.

5 Business or pleasure? e) Business, I'm afraid.

6 How long have you been here? f) Until tomorrow evening.

7 How long are you staying? g) No, this is my first trip.

8 Where are you staying? h) Six days.

9 What's the food like? i) I really like it. There's so much to see and do.

10 So, what do you think of Tokyo? j) It's very good, but eating at the Metropolitan can be quite expensive.

F **What are the 'safe' topics of conversation for this sort of situation? Which topics would you avoid?**

G **In your opinion, which of these items of advice for a successful conversation are useful and which are not?**

1 Listen carefully.
2 Give only 'yes' or 'no' answers.
3 Interrupt a lot.
4 Be polite.

5 Ask questions.
6 Stay silent.
7 Keep eye contact.
8 Be friendly.

Case study

Business culture briefing

A group of managers is attending an informal briefing about the business culture of your country.

Background

You work for Better Business Communications, a company which prepares business people who are visiting your country for the first time. A group of top managers will shortly be visiting your country in order to decide on the location of an overseas subsidiary. During their visit, the managers will attend meetings with a number of business people, and be entertained at their homes or in restaurants. They also plan to do some social visits and excursions. You will run an informal business culture briefing for the management group, informing them about aspects of business culture in your country and answering their questions.

Discuss what kind of topics you could include in your briefing about the business culture of your country.

🔊 **CD2.3** Rosana, a Brazilian client, is planning a European trip to Germany, France and Russia. She asks Enrique, who works for Better Business Communications, for advice about the countries she'll be visiting. **Note down the five topics that Rosana mentions. Are they on your list as well? Do you agree with what Enrique says about the three countries? Give your reasons.**

Task

1 **Work individually or in national groups. Prepare an informal talk about the business culture of your country or a country you know well. Use the list of topics and questions below to structure your talk. During each talk, the other members of the class will play the role of the top managers.**

2 **Give your talk to the top managers. Try to answer any questions they may have.**

3 **In one group, discuss the talks. What advice/information surprised you? Which was the most interesting talk? Why?**

Topics

Appearance
- How do men and women dress in business?
- Is casual dress permitted in business meetings?
- How do people dress on social occasions, e.g. at an informal dinner?

Behaviour
- Do people like a lot of personal space?
- Do they usually stand close or far away from another person when talking to colleagues?
- Do staff use first or family names when addressing each other?

Entertainment
- Do businesspeople prefer to entertain guests at home or in a restaurant?
- What advice can you give about gifts?
- What are good/bad topics of conversation?

Meetings
- How important is punctuality in your culture? Is it OK to be late for a meeting?
- Is a person's status important in meetings? Does the most senior person always lead a meeting?
- Is decision-making slow or fast in business?

Business practice
- Do you have to make appointments well in advance?
- What are the usual business hours?
- What is the usual time for a business lunch? How long does it last?

Writing

Write a short report summarising the most interesting information you have learnt about a culture in this unit.

➡ *Writing file page 130*

Watch the Case study commentary on the **DVD-ROM.** ◎

'One machine can do the work of 50 ordinary men. No machine can do the work of one extraordinary man.' **Elbert Hubbard (1856–1915), American writer**

STARTING UP

A **In your opinion, which factors below are important for getting a job? Choose the five most important. Is there anything missing from the list? Which do you think are not important? Why?**

appearance	hobbies/interests	experience	personality
intelligence	marital status	contacts/connections	qualifications
references	age/gender	astrological sign	handwriting
blood group	sickness record	family background	education

B **Think about jobs you've had and interviews you've attended. In pairs, ask each other about your best or worst:**

1 a) job b) boss c) colleague.

2 a) interview experience b) interview question c) interview answer.

C **Discuss the statements.**

1 At work, appearance is more important than performance.

2 You should keep your private life totally separate from your work.

3 People don't change much during their working lives.

4 It is best to work for as few companies as possible.

5 Everybody should retire at 50.

VOCABULARY
Employing the right people

A Complete the text with the words and phrases in the box.

curriculum vitae (CV)/résumé	probationary period	interview
application form	psychometric test	covering letter

These days, many applicants submit their ....¹ speculatively to companies they would like to work for. In other words, they do not apply for an advertised job, but hope the employer will be interested enough to keep their CV on file and contact them when they have a vacancy. When replying to an advertisement, candidates often fill in a(n) ....² and write a(n) ....³. The employer will then invite the best candidates to attend a(n) ....⁴. Sometimes candidates will take a(n) ....⁵ before the interview to assess their mental ability and reasoning skills. These days, it is normal for successful candidates to have to work a(n) ....⁶ in a company. This is usually three or six months; after that, they are offered a permanent post.

B Match the verbs (1–6) to the nouns (a–f) to make word partnerships.

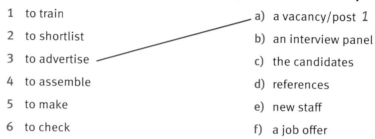

1 to train   a) a vacancy/post 1
2 to shortlist   b) an interview panel
3 to advertise   c) the candidates
4 to assemble   d) references
5 to make   e) new staff
6 to check   f) a job offer

Now decide on a possible order for the events above from the employer's point of view.

C 🔊 CD2.4 **Listen to a consultant talking about the recruitment process to check your answers to Exercise B.**

D **When companies are recruiting, what sort of qualities in employees do they look for?**

E **Look at the different types of people. Which do you think are the most desirable for companies to employ?**

This type of person:
1 is able to come up with ideas
2 is respected and listened to by others
3 is able to see different points of view
4 can see how to put ideas into action
5 is determined to succeed in their career

6 has lots of energy and often gets excited
7 is concerned with details and getting things right even if it takes time
8 likes to assess and evaluate
9 is able to change with new situations
10 is someone you can trust and depend on.

Match the descriptions above (1–10) to the adjectives in the box (a–j).

a) enthusiastic	b) adaptable	c) methodical	d) reliable	e) ambitious
f) objective	g) creative	h) analytical	i) authoritative	j) practical

F 🔊 CD2.5 **Mark the stress on the adjectives in Exercise E. Then listen and check your answers.**

1 Which three qualities listed in Exercise E best describe you?
2 Which of the different types of people have you worked or studied with?
3 Which of the different types of people do you think are easy or difficult to work with?

*See the **DVD-ROM** for the i-Glossary.*

READING

Women at work

A **Work in pairs. Read your article quickly and decide on a heading.**

Student A: Read Article A below.
Student B: Turn to page 137.

Article A

When Nguyen Thu Hang was a child, her mother was a housewife in a small village whose women residents had no
5 say in decision making, either at home or in the community. Now a mother herself, Hang not only shares her husband's burden of earning money for the family and
10 bringing up children, but also has a career and social ambitions.

'Women are much happier than before. They have a good education and careers of their own,'says the
15 39-year-old who lives and works in Hanoi. 'And, of course, they are more respected in the family and society.' Hang, who carries a sleek laptop in her hand, gets
20 out of an elegant black Mercedes and enters a building where she works as the General Director of Viet Hoang Trade and Investment Company, which specialises in
25 construction and real estate.

Like Hang, many other Vietnamese women also pursue careers these days and have stormed the corporate boardroom to affirm
30 their increasingly important roles. Whether in remote farms or in companies, they have become much more self-confident and are discovering their worth and
35 fulfilling their potential.

Women account for nearly 52 per cent of the workforce in the service sector, 50 per cent in the agricultural and fisheries sector and 37 per cent
40 in industry and construction. Almost a quarter of all companies are run by women, many of whom are also the driving forces behind them. As for their status in the family, Hang
45 says that women's position has improved remarkably. 'We jointly decide important issues in our life, such as work or education for our children. My husband always
50 respects my opinions.'

The greater role of women is attributed to the effective policies of promoting them. The state and party are interested in women's
55 advancement. The NA, the national legislature, has approved Law the on Gender Equality and the Anti-Domestic Violence Law. The government has national
60 programmes for vocational training and preventing trafficking of women and children.

Women's own efforts to acquire knowledge and education have,
65 of course, been a major factor in their advancement. They make up over 40.2 per cent of all university graduates, including nearly 9.8 per cent of PhDs and 30.5 per
70 cent of Master's degree recipients.

But women still face a number of difficulties, including poverty, underemployment, domestic violence, prostitution and gender
75 inequality. 'I think the best way to help women overcome these challenges is to help them study and lead an active lifestyle,' says Hang, whose entry into the
80 boardroom began after she obtained a Master's degree in Britain at the age of 27.

from Thanh Nien News

B **Decide if the statements about your article are true (T) or false (F).**

Article A

1 The position of women in Vietnam has improved.

2 Women make up less than half of the workforce in the service, agricultural, fisheries, industry and construction sectors.

3 Nearly 25% of Vietnamese companies are run by women.

4 More than a third of all university graduates and holders of Master's degrees are women.

5 Nguyen Thu Hang lets her husband make important decisions.

6 Nguyen Thu Hang's position with regard to decision-making is different to that of her mother.

Article B

7 Men on their own make a third of car purchases in Japan.

8 Women prefer to buy cars from women.

9 Since 2004, Nissan has more than doubled recruitment of female engineering graduates and saleswomen.

10 The number of female managers at Nissan has increased to 50%.

11 Women make up 5% of managers in the Japanese car industry.

12 Nowadays, men and women are attracted by pictures of families enjoying themselves in a car.

C **In pairs, compare the position of women in Articles A and B.**

D **'The role of women in business is no longer an issue.' Discuss to what extent this is true in your country.**

E **In pairs, find words in both articles that can be grouped under:**

a) people b) business sectors or areas.

Use six of the words in sentences of your own.

LISTENING
Finding a job

A CD2.6 **Carys Owen is a director at Hays, the international recruitment specialist. Listen to the first part of the interview and answer the question.**

In what ways does a Hays consultant work with a candidate?

B CD2.7 **Listen to the second part. What are the three key points that Carys makes about preparing for an interview?**

Carys Owen

C CD2.7 **Listen again and complete the gaps.**

From the point of view of the actual vacancy, we would always ....[1] that you look at the ....[2] within that vacancy and have a think about where in your ....[3] you might be able to ....[4] your ability to do that job.

D CD2.8 **Listen to the final part of the interview and answer the questions.**

1 What two recent changes has Carys noticed in the job market?

2 In what way does one of the changes give candidates and employees a 'unique opportunity'?

*Watch the interview on the **DVD-ROM**.*

E **If you had to change your job, what method would you use to find a new one?**

LANGUAGE REVIEW

-ing forms and infinitives

- We sometimes use one verb after another verb. Often the second verb is in the infinitive.
  *We can't **afford to increase** their pay.*
  *He **intends to sign** the new contract next week.*

- Sometimes the second verb must be in the *-ing* form. This depends on the first verb. (See page 149 for a list of verbs that are usually followed by the *-ing* form.)
  *My job **involves monitoring** sickness levels.*

- Some verbs can be followed by the *-ing* form or the infinitive without a big change in meaning.
  *I **started** working there last month.* / *I **started to** work there last month.*

- With other verbs, however, the meaning changes.
  *We **stopped to have lunch**.* (We stopped what we were doing in order to have lunch.)
  *We **stopped having lunch**.* (We stopped our habit of having lunch.)

➡ *Grammar reference page 149*

A **In each of the sentences, two of the verbs are possible and one is incorrect. Cross out the incorrect verb.**

1 He .... to review our complaints procedures.

   a) promised   b) delayed   c) wanted

2 I .... improving interpersonal skills training.

   a) undertook   b) suggested   c) recommended

3 I .... to meet the HR Director.

   a) decided   b) didn't mind   c) arranged

4 She .... to check the redundancy arrangements.

   a) refused   b) failed   c) put off

5 We .... to review our policy for anti-bullying in the workplace.

   a) consider   b) hope   c) plan

B **Match the sentence halves.**

1 HR **recommends**   a) to raise the minimum wage.

2 The company simply **can't afford**   b) to call me back in a couple of days.

3 This job **involves**   c) smoking after the programme.

4 The manager seemed impressed by my CV and **promised**   d) working weekends sometimes.

5 Three members of staff **stopped**   e) to follow a directive given by his superior.

6 He was fired because he **refused**   f) using the cheapest form of transport.

C **Choose the most appropriate form of the verb to complete the sentences.**

1 HR's new computer programme has stopped *working* / *to work*.

2 She was driving in a hurry, but she stopped *answering* / *to answer* her mobile phone.

3 Did you remember *calling* / *to call* HR yesterday?

4 I can't remember *offering* / *to offer* you a raise.

5 I forgot *telling* / *to tell* you I'd quit my job.

6 I'll never forget *making* / *to make* my first sale.

D **Make sentences of your own with the verbs in bold in Exercise B, using either the *-ing* form or the infinitive.**

SKILLS

Getting information on the telephone

A 🔊 CD2.9 **Cindy Tan calls the Guangdong Trading Company (GTC) to get information about an advertisement in the *China Post* for the position of Marketing Assistant. Listen to her talking to Li Ping, a member of the Human Resources department. Tick the points about which she needs further information.**

a) the closing date

b) what the duties would be

c) if there's an application form

d) when she would be expected to join the company

e) how many days' holiday she would get

f) what the starting salary would be

B 🔊 CD2.9 **Listen to the call again and complete the extracts.**

Cindy   .... [1] if you could give me a little more information.

Li Ping   Certainly, what do you need to know?

Cindy   Well, first of all, am I .... [2]?

Cindy   Just one or two more questions. .... [3] when the successful candidate has to start work with you. I mean, if I get the job, will I be able to give my present employer sufficient notice?

Li Ping   OK, that's a good question. How much .... [4]?

Cindy   OK, so, ... [5], I probably wouldn't have to start working until February, and maybe even later?

Li Ping   .... [6].

Cindy   One last question. Could I ask you .... [7]? It wasn't given in the advert.

Li Ping   You're right. It would depend on a lot of things: qualifications, experience, personal qualities, that sort of thing.

Cindy   .... [8] you can't give me a figure?

Li Ping   That's right. The salary's .... [9].

C **Role-play this telephone situation in pairs. A department store will be hiring a number of temporary workers from Omnia Employment Agency. The Human Resources Manager calls the agency to discuss some of the terms and conditions of the contract. Read your role cards, then role-play the call.**

Human Resources Manager: Turn to page 137.
Employment agency consultant: Turn to page 142.

USEFUL LANGUAGE

SAYING WHO YOU ARE

Good morning, my name's Lisa Mann.

Hello, Ben speaking.

STATING YOUR PURPOSE

I'm calling about ...

The reason I'm calling is ...

ASKING FOR INFORMATION

I was wondering if you could give me ...?

Could you tell me ...?

I'd also like to know ...

Could I ask you ...?

CHECKING INFORMATION

Just to get this clear ...

There's just one other thing, I'd like to check ...

Are you saying ...?

SHOWING INTEREST

Certainly, what do you need to know?

No, don't worry.

I look forward to getting it.

That's correct.

Good luck.

ENDING A CALL

OK, I think that's everything.

Right, I think that's all I need to know.

FastFitness

A chain of health clubs needs to find a new manager in Brazil. Appointing the right person is essential for the success of the business.

Background

Fast Fitness owns and operates a chain of health and leisure clubs in the United States. Two years ago, the company decided to enter the South American market. It began by opening six clubs in São Paulo, Brazil. The clubs appeal mainly to people aged 20–40. All the clubs have a gymnasium, with the latest equipment, an aerobics studio, a swimming pool, sun decks, a café, bar and clubroom. Four of the clubs are located in areas where large numbers of Japanese, Spanish, Chinese and Italian immigrants live.

The performance of the clubs has been disappointing, and none of them has reached their turnover and profit targets. Many members have not renewed their membership, and the clubs have not attracted enough new members. Fast Fitness recently advertised for a General Manager. His/Her main task will be to boost sales at the clubs and increase profits.

FastFitness

General Manager

Required for our chain of Health and Leisure Clubs

- Salary negotiable
- Excellent benefits package

The job
- Leading, co-ordinating, and motivating staff.
- Increasing the revenue and profits of the six clubs in São Paulo
- Exploiting new business opportunities
- Liaising with and motivating our team of managers and their staff
- Contributing to marketing plans and strategies

The person
- Dynamic, enthusiastic, flexible
- A strong interest in health and fitness
- A good track record in previous jobs
- The ability to work with people from different cultural backgrounds
- Outstanding communication and interpersonal skills
- A flair for new ideas and organizational skills

Fast Fitness, 80 Front St,
New York NY 10003–1324

Task

You are directors of Fast Fitness.

1 **Study the file cards on the four shortlisted candidates on the opposite page. Hold a meeting to discuss the strengths and weaknesses of each person. Try to rank the four candidates in terms of their suitability for the job.**

2 **Listen to the interview extracts with each of the candidates and come to a final decision on who should get the job.**

🔊 **CD2.10** Sean Wilder 🔊 **CD2.12** Martha Gómez

🔊 **CD2.11** Paulo Goncalves 🔊 **CD2.13** Silvia Cominelli

Name: Martha Gómez
Age: 34
Nationality: Brazilian
Marital Status: Divorced, two children

Education: Finished secondary school; two years' training at a School of Dance and Theater.

Experience: Several years as professional dancer in theaters and on television. Joined a small fitness center as instructor.

Outstanding achievement: Introduced fitness programs in the center for people suffering from Parkinson's Disease and multiple sclerosis. Received an award for this work.

Skills: Qualified in first aid. Fluent Spanish and Portuguese.

Personality/appearance: Warm, friendly, dynamic. Appearance: rather a "hippy" look.

Comments: *"I hope to build new schemes and initiatives to help people in the community to achieve a healthier lifestyle. If we promote that idea, people will flock to Fast Fitness clubs."*

Believes her main asset is her creativity.

Interests: pop music, running a weekly aerobics class.

Name: Silvia Cominelli
Age: 38
Nationality: American
Marital status: Married, no children

Education: Trained as a dietician (Berkeley University, U.S.); Masters in Sports Psychology.

Experience: Worked for several years as adviser to the national football team.

Currently sports organizer in a women's college.

Outstanding achievement: "Helping the national football team to win the World Cup."

Skills: Fluent English, Portuguese, and Spanish.

Personality/appearance: Ambitious, assertive, outspoken. *"Nothing will stop me from achieving my goals in life."* Wore casual clothes to the interview.

Comments: *"I love being able to motivate people to exercise and then seeing their faces."* Believes Fast Fitness must spend a lot of money on multimedia advertising to improve profits, and offer big discounts to new members. Is taking an evening course in Business Studies to upgrade her academic qualifications."

Interests: hiking, photography.

Name: Sean Wilder
Age: 52
Nationality: American
Marital status: Married to Brazilian, four children

Education: B.Sc. Physics, Yale University; M.A. Sports Management, University of Southern California.

Experience: Taught English and Spanish at high schools for 10 years. Ran sports programs for the schools.

Currently teaches English in a private language school in São Paulo.

Outstanding achievement: *"Achieving happiness by marrying the right person."*

Skills: Fluent English, Portuguese, and Spanish.

Personality/appearance: Very good-looking, relaxed, self-confident. Dressed very casually for the interview.

Comments: He believes that his greatest quality is to be calm under pressure. *"The secret of being a good manager is to delegate tasks and not get too friendly with staff,"* he said.

Did not have many ideas for improving the clubs' profits. Thinks Fast Fitness is spending too much on advertising. It should focus on existing members and persuade them to sign up new members.

Interests: jogging, cinema, his wife and family.

Name: Paulo Goncalves
Age: 36
Nationality: Brazilian
Marital Status: Single

Education: Left school at 16. Three years' training at RADA (Royal Academy of Dramatic Arts), London.

Experience: Did two trips around the world in his early twenties. Taught English in Japan for two years. Played a variety of roles in Brazilian movies, then specialized in action movies. Has spent the last two years in Florida, U.S., working as a gym instructor.

Outstanding achievement: "Playing a role in a successful Hong Kong movie with Jackie Chan."

Skills: Has a black belt in karate; extensive knowledge of martial arts; fluent Portuguese, Spanish, and Japanese.

Personality/appearance: Looked very fit and muscular. Dressed formally in an Armani suit. Strong personality, confident, articulate.

Comments: Some interesting ideas for improving First Fitness profits. Thinks many people will join the clubs when they know he is the manager. Wants to use his name and photograph in all publicity for the clubs.

Interests: Politics, cooking, socializing.

Watch the Case study commentary on the DVD-ROM.

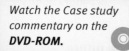

Writing

Write a letter offering employment to the successful candidate.

→ *Writing file page 126*

STARTING UP

companies
competition
environment
gap
opportunities
poverty
prices
standards
unemployment
workers

A **The sentences below represent a variety of views on international markets. Complete the sentences with the words in the box.**

'International markets for labour, capital, goods and services ...

1 provide *opportunities* for people to work/study abroad and improve their lives.'

2 increase .... and improve the choice of goods and services.'

3 create .... and lead to job losses in richer countries.'

4 reduce .... and increase wealth everywhere.'

5 exploit .... in poorer countries.'

6 widen the .... between rich and poor nations.'

7 mean lower costs and cheaper retail ...., which benefit consumers.'

8 give large multinational .... and trading blocs too much power.'

9 lead to damage to the natural ...., local cultures and industries.'

10 promote higher .... of living, working conditions, technology, education, etc.'

B **Work in pairs. Which of the statements in Exercise A do you agree with?**

C **Work in pairs. How has the development of international markets affected:**

a) you as a consumer?   b) your company/institution?   c) your country?

D **How do you think international markets will develop in the future?**

VOCABULARY
Free trade

A In pairs, discuss the question.

What is free trade?

B ◀))) CD2.14 Listen to the first part of a radio interview with Ian McPherson, an expert on international trade. Complete the definition of free trade he gives.

It's a situation in which goods come into and out of a country without any _controls_ [1] or ....[2]. Countries which truly believe in free trade try to ....[3] their trade, that's to say, they take away ....[4] to trade. [...] They have open ....[5] and few controls of goods at ....[6].

C ◀))) CD2.15 Listen to the second part of the interview. Note down five things which stop people trading freely. Explain briefly the meaning of each one.

example: *1 Tariffs: These are taxes on imported goods.*

D ◀))) CD2.16 Listen to the third part of the interview and do these exercises.

1 **Choose the best answer.**

When there is a policy of deregulation, ...

a) companies compete freely.

b) there are a lot of government controls.

c) companies must follow regulations.

2 **Which benefits of free trade does Ian McPherson mention? Tick the ones you hear.**

a) greater choice of goods

b) better-made products

c) lower taxes

d) better pay

e) a wider choice of jobs

3 **Complete the gaps.**

Some countries do not practise free trade because they wish to:

• fight against ....[a] competition, for example, dumping;

• protect their ....[b] industries, which are important to their economy;

• be less reliant on ....[c], because their own economies need developing.

4 **Answer the questions.**

a) What trend in international trade does Ian McPherson mention?

b) Why does he think the trend is a good one?

E Use the words and phrases in the box to complete the table below. Use a good dictionary to help you.

barriers	open borders	free port	developing industries	dumping
tariffs	strategic industries	restrictions	quotas	laissez-faire
liberalise	customs	deregulation	subsidise	regulations

Open markets	Protected markets
(Trade without restrictions on the movement of goods)	(Trade with restrictions on the movement of goods, for example, import taxes)
open borders	*barriers*

F **Match the sentence halves.**

1 We're trying to break into

2 You should carry out

3 If you would like to place

4 If you can't meet

5 They've quoted

6 Let us know if you want us to arrange

7 It's essential to comply with

a) all regulations if you want the delivery to go through without problems.

b) the delivery date, let us know as soon as possible.

c) insurance cover for the shipment.

d) a market survey before you make a major investment.

e) the Japanese market.

f) an order, press one now.

g) us a very good price for the consignment.

G **Find verb + noun partnerships in the sentences in Exercise F.**

example: *1 to break into a market*

Which of them is normally done by:

a) the supplier?   b) the buyer?   c) both the supplier and the buyer?

H **Discuss the questions.**

1 To what extent do you have free trade in your country?

2 Should certain industries in your country be protected? If so, which ones?

3 Is free trade always a good thing, in your opinion?

*See the **DVD-ROM** for the i-Glossary.*

READING

Trade between China and the US

A **Work in pairs. Read the two articles quickly and choose the best title for each one.**

a) US–China trade has cost 2.3 million American jobs

b) US protectionism is not the way forward

c) Stop blaming China for US trade deficit

d) Yuan needs to rise against the US dollar

Article 1

by Xin Zhiming

'The US should focus on improving its overall economic competitiveness instead of seeking protectionism to combat its economic slowdown,' said the latest 2008 White Paper: American Business in China.

'And it should not argue for a stronger currency to reduce its trade deficit with China, since the value of the yuan is not the fundamental cause of the deficit,' said the White Paper, which was released by the American Chamber of Commerce (AmCham) China, AmCham Shanghai and AmCham South China Tuesday.

The US economy is currently slowing, while its trade deficit with China remains high, standing at $163.3 billion last year. The deficit has led to protectionism against Chinese goods and investment in the US.

The two countries should make 'defending and preserving the openness of the trade relationship a core commitment', the White Paper said. 'Instances of co-operation between China and US far exceed instances of dispute.

'An open US and an open China will lead to sustained benefits for both US companies and citizens back home,' said Harley Seyedin, Chairman of AmCham South China.'

from China Daily

Article 2

BY ANDREA HOPKINS

The US trade deficit with China cost 2.3 million American jobs over six years, the Economic Policy Institute said on Wednesday.

5   Even when they found new jobs, workers who had lost jobs to Chinese competition saw their earnings decrease by an average of $8,146 each year because the new jobs paid less, according to the

10 report, funded in part by labor unions.

   "(We hope) it will help to focus the debate on trade to where it needs to be right now with respect to China," said Scott Paul, Executive Director of the

15 Alliance for American Manufacturing.

   US manufacturers, labor unions, and many lawmakers have long accused China of manipulating its currency to give Chinese companies an unfair advantage

20 in international trade, and are pressing China to continue to allow the yuan to rise against the US dollar.

   China has said the United States should recognize how much its yuan

25 currency has already risen against the dollar—it is about 20 per cent higher since China revalued its currency in July 2005.

   China has also said the fact that Americans save much less of their incomes

30 than the Chinese do has increased the trade deficit. Chinese-made goods have been extremely popular in recent years with US consumers looking for low prices.

from *Reuters*

B **Look at the articles again. Decide if the statements are true (T) or false (F).**

Article 1

1 The US should concentrate on being more competitive economically.

2 The US should be protectionist.

3 The US should argue for a stronger Chinese currency in order to reduce the US's trade deficit with China.

4 The US and China should focus on the openness of their trading relationship.

Article 2

5 The US should recognise how much the Chinese currency has already risen against the dollar.

6 US labour unions say China has manipulated its currency to give Chinese companies an unfair advantage in international trade.

7 The Chinese save less of their income than Americans.

8 Americans have recently bought Chinese-made goods at low prices.

C **Find the opposites of these words in the articles.**

1 free trade   2 upturn   3 surplus   4 dispute   5 decreased   6 spend

D **Complete the sentences with the words you found in Exercise C.**

1 Economists know that .... and import taxes promote inefficiency.

2 The study was done in .... with local businesses.

3 There has been a .... in the tourist trade.

4 The figures show a trade .... of $4 billion.

E **What do you think will happen to the trade situation between China and the US?**

LANGUAGE REVIEW
Conditions

- We use the first conditional when we think the expected outcome of a situation is very likely.
  *If you **give** us a 10% discount, we'**ll place** a firm order of 2,000 units.*
  (This is a promise.)
  *If you **don't deliver** on time, we **won't order** from you again.* (This is a threat.)
  *Will you give us a discount **if** we **double** our order?*

- We use the second conditional when the outcome is less certain or is imaginary. We also use it in negotiations to make the offer or proposal less direct.
  *If you **gave** us a 5% discount, we **would place** a much bigger order.*
  *If they **didn't have** a guaranteed market, their business **wouldn't** survive.*
  *What discount **would** you **offer** us **if** we **decided** to go to another supplier?*

➡ *Grammar reference page 150*

A ### Choose the correct verbs to complete the sentences.

1 If you *give us* / *'ll give us* a discount of 5%, we *'ll place* / *place* a firm order.

2 *Will you deliver* / *Do you deliver* by November if we *pay* / *'ll pay* the transport costs?

3 If you *will lower* / *lower* your price by 5%, we *buy* / *'ll buy* at least 4,000 units.

4 *Would* / *Does* it help you if we *sent* / *are sending* the goods by air?

5 If you *aren't improving* / *don't improve* your delivery times, we *'ll have* / *had* to find a new supplier.

6 If we *will join* / *joined* an association of producers, we *would get* / *will get* a better price for our coffee.

B 🔊 CD2.17 **Naoko Nakamura, a buyer for a large Japanese department store, is negotiating with Li Bai, Sales Director for a clothing company in Hong Kong. Listen and complete the conversation.**

Naoko   If I .... [1] 30,000 silk scarves, what discount will you offer us?

Li   On 30,000, nothing. But if you buy 50,000 scarves, then .... [2] offer you 10%.

Naoko   OK, I'll think about that. And tell me, if we placed a very large order, say 80,000 units, ... [3] to despatch immediately?

Li   We can normally guarantee to despatch a large order within three weeks. But if you .... [4] at a peak time, like just before Chinese New Year, it will be impossible to deliver that quickly.

Naoko   I take it your price includes insurance?

Li   Actually, no. Usually, you'd be responsible for that. But if the order .... [5] really large, that would be negotiable, I'm sure.

Naoko   What about payment?

Li   To be honest, we'd prefer cash on delivery, as this is our first contact with you. If you .... [6] a regular customer, ... [7] you 30 days' credit, maybe even a little more.

Naoko   That's all right. I quite understand.

Li   Look, how about having some lunch now, and continuing later this afternoon? Then we could meet for an evening meal. I know an excellent restaurant in Wanchai.

Naoko   Yes, let's continue after lunch. If I had more time, ... [8] to have dinner with you, but unfortunately my flight for Tokyo leaves at eight tonight, and I need to be at the airport by six.

C ### Make a list of the conditional sentences in the dialogue in Exercise B. For each sentence, decide if the events are:

a) very likely

b) less certain or imaginary.

LISTENING
Training for negotiating

Andy Simmons

Watch the interview on the DVD-ROM.

A 🔊 CD2.18 **Andy Simmons is a partner at The Gap Partnership and is an expert on negotiating. Listen to the first part of the interview. What three things does Andy say are important in negotiating?**

B 🔊 CD2.19 **Listen to the second part and complete the gaps.**

In fact, this concept of .... [1] – that's what we teach – says that there is no one way, there are many .... [2] ways, ranging from the very .... [3], very high-............ [4] negotiations that are generally win–lose, all the way through to the very, very .... [5] negotiations, which are deemed as .... [6]. And there's no right or .... [7], or there's no good or bad, it's just what's appropriate to the .... [8].

C 🔊 CD2.20 **Listen to the final part and answer the questions.**

1 What behaviours are appropriate for being a good negotiator?

2 How do you tell if there is more scope for negotiation?

D **Discuss the questions.**

1 What do you think makes a really good negotiator?

2 Do you prefer high-conflict win–lose negotiations or cooperative win–win negotiations?

3 How common is negotiating in your country?

SKILLS
Negotiating

A **Work in pairs. Try to sell something you have on you (a watch, bracelet, etc.) or a household object to your partner.**

B **Discuss the questions.**

1 Were you pleased with the outcome of the negotiation in Exercise A?

2 What strategy or tactics did your partner use to achieve his/her objective?

C **In his book *The Art of Winning*, Harry Mills says that most negotiations have seven stages. These are listed below, but in the wrong order. Put the stages in order. What word do the initial letters of the stages spell?**

- **Tie up loose ends**
  Confirm what has been agreed. Summarise the details on paper.

- **Explore each other's needs**
  Build rapport. State your opening position. Learn the other side's position.

- **Ready yourself**
  Prepare your objectives, concessions and strategy. Gather information about the other side.

- **Probe with proposals**
  Make suggestions and find areas of agreement.

- **Close the deal**
  Bring the negotiation to a clear and satisfactory end.

- **Signal for movement**
  Signal that you are prepared to move from your original position. Respond to signals from the other side.

- **Exchange concessions**
  Give the other side something in return for something you need or want.

D 🔊 CD2.21 **Listen to seven extracts from a negotiation between two buyers from an exclusive department store in Moscow and Pierlucci, an Italian supplier of leather goods. Match each extract (1–7) to one of the stages of Harry Mills's list (a–g).**

Extract 1

Extract 2

Extract 3

Extract 4

Extract 5

Extract 6

Extract 7

a) Tie up loose ends

b) Probe with proposals

c) Ready yourself

d) Close the deal

e) Explore needs

f) Signal for movement

g) Exchange concessions

E **Study the Useful language box below, then role-play these negotiations. Try to get a good outcome in each situation.**

Student A: Look at this page.
Student B: Look at page 138.

Student A

1 **You are a handbag supplier.**

Because there is strong demand for your new range of handbags, you want to:

- increase your list prices by 20%
- increase your delivery time to three weeks
- only offer the buyer a one-year contract.

2 **You are an agent for an overseas kitchen equipment company.**

You exceeded your sales target by 25% last year. You want the company to:

- increase your commission on sales from 5% to 10%
- invite you for a visit to their head office and pay all the expenses of the trip
- make you an exclusive agent for their goods
- offer you a five-year contract.

USEFUL LANGUAGE

STARTING POSITIONS

We'd like to reach a deal with you today.

Right, let's try to get 10% off their list prices.

EXPLORING POSITIONS

Can you tell me a little about ...?

What do you have in mind?

MAKING OFFERS AND CONCESSIONS

If you order now, we'll give you a discount.

We'd be prepared to offer you a better price if you increased your order.

CHECKING UNDERSTANDING

What do you mean?

Have I got this right?

If I understand you correctly, ...

You mean, if we ordered ... , would ...?

Are you saying ...?

REFUSING AN OFFER

I'm not sure about that.

That's more than we usually offer.

That would be difficult for us.

ACCEPTING AN OFFER

Sounds a good idea to me. As long as we ...

Good, we agree on price, quantity, discounts ...

PLAYING FOR TIME

I'd like to think about it.

I'll have to consult my colleagues about that.

CLOSING THE DEAL

I think we've covered everything.

Great! We've got a deal.

FOLLOWING UP THE DEAL

Let me know if there are any problems.

If there are any other points, I'll e-mail you.

Pampas Leather Company

An Argentinian exporter is negotiating to sell into the US market.
It must reach a deal on the best possible terms while seeking to build
a long-term relationship with its distributor.

Background

The Pampas Leather Company is based in Buenos
Aires, Argentina. This well-established business
exports leather and fur jackets, as well as
accessories such as handbags, belts and wallets,
to world markets. It uses the best quality leather,
introduces creative designs in its collections,
has excellent quality control and a reliable
delivery service.

A major US distributor in Seattle, West Coast
Apparel (WCA), has contacted Pampas Leather
about marketing a range of Pampas's men's
leather jackets under the WCA brand name. WCA
has a chain of stores in all the large cities on
the West Coast of the US. WCA's President, Brad
Schulz, wants to put three models of the jackets

on the market: the Clubman (the most expensive
model), the Nightrider and the Look.

It is now May. Pampas Leather has agreed to make
the jackets and have them ready for shipment to
Seattle early in November. This will not be easy,
as Pampas has to fulfil several large orders before
dealing with the WCA order.

Several points of the contract need to be
negotiated. Roberto González of Pampas has flown
to Seattle to meet Brad Schulz. The Marketing
Director of each company will also be present at
the meeting. The purpose of the meeting is to
make a deal acceptable to both sides, which could
be the basis for a long-term relationship.

Task

You are negotiating as either:

- the Pampas Leather team (Roberto González
  and his Marketing Director): Turn to page
  138.

- the WCA team (Brad Schulz and his
  Marketing Director): Turn to page 142.

**Read your information files, identify your
priorities and work out your strategy and tactics.
Then negotiate so that you get the best deal
for your company.**

Writing

**As the owner of either the Pampas
Leather Company or West Coast Apparel,
write an e-mail summarising the points
agreed during the negotiation. Indicate
any terms of the contract requiring
further discussion or clarification.**

➡ *Writing file page 127*

*Watch the Case study
commentary on the **DVD-ROM**.*

3 Doing business internationally

A Tim Collins goes to Saudi Arabia

Tim Collins, Sales Manager, travelled to Riyadh to present his company's TV sets to Karim Al-Jabri, president of a retail group.

The meeting, arranged for Monday, was postponed two days later. When Collins finally met Al-Jabri, he was surprised that several other Saudi visitors attended the meeting. He turned down Al-Jabri's offer of coffee, and when asked about his impressions of Riyadh, said that he had been too busy dealing with paperwork to see the sights.

During the meeting, Al-Jabri often interrupted the conversation to take telephone calls. Collins wanted to get down to business, but Al-Jabri seemed to prefer to talk about English football teams. When Collins admired a painting on the office wall, Al-Jabri insisted on giving it to him as a gift. Collins was very embarrassed.

Two days later, Collins presented his company's new products. A large number of staff attended and asked technical questions which Collins couldn't answer. The following day, Collins asked Al-Jabri if he wanted to place an order for the TV sets. 'If God pleases,' was the answer. Collins thought that meant 'Yes'.

Collins did not secure the contract. When he e-mailed Al-Jabri a month later, he was informed that Mr Al-Jabri was away on business.

> **Task**
>
> 1 **Tim Collins made several mistakes because he lacked knowledge of the local business culture. In pairs, discuss his mistakes and note them down.**
>
> 2 **Turn to page 138 and check your answers.**
>
> 3 **Draw up a list of advice you would give a visitor like Tim Collins.**

B Carson Martin visits Japan

Carson Martin, Managing Director of a Canadian golf equipment company, travelled to Osaka to meet Yasuo Matsumoto, General Manager of a sports goods business.

Martin arrived punctually for his meeting with Matsumoto. He hoped it would be with Matsumoto alone, but some of Matsumoto's colleagues were also present. After introductions, they exchanged business cards. When Martin received Matsumoto's card, he put it away in his wallet. However, Matsumoto examined Martin's card closely for some time.

After a short discussion, Martin said, 'Well, are you willing to be an exclusive agent for us or not?' Matsumoto looked embarrassed, then he said, 'It will be under consideration.' Martin was not clear what Matsumoto meant. Matsumoto went on to say that he had to consult many colleagues in other departments before they could make a decision.

After the meeting, Matsumoto invited Martin to join him for dinner. Matsumoto complimented Martin on his ability to use chopsticks. Later, Martin gave Matsumoto two gifts: a guide book for Ontario, Canada, wrapped in red paper, and a bunch of beautiful white water lilies for his wife. 'I hope they appreciate my gifts,' he thought.

He did not hear from Matsumoto for some while. However, six months later, he received an e-mail from Matsumoto: 'Please return to Osaka as soon as possible. We would like to meet you to discuss the agency agreement.'

Read the case, then discuss the questions in pairs.

1 Why was Martin disappointed when:
   a) he first entered Matsumoto's office?
   b) Matsumoto said, 'It will be under consideration'?
2 What mistakes did Martin make when he:
   a) exchanged business cards?
   b) asked the question about an exclusive contract?
   c) gave Matsumoto's wife white water lilies?

> **Task**
>
> CD2.22 **Listen to an expert on Japanese culture analysing the case. Make notes and discuss her comments.**

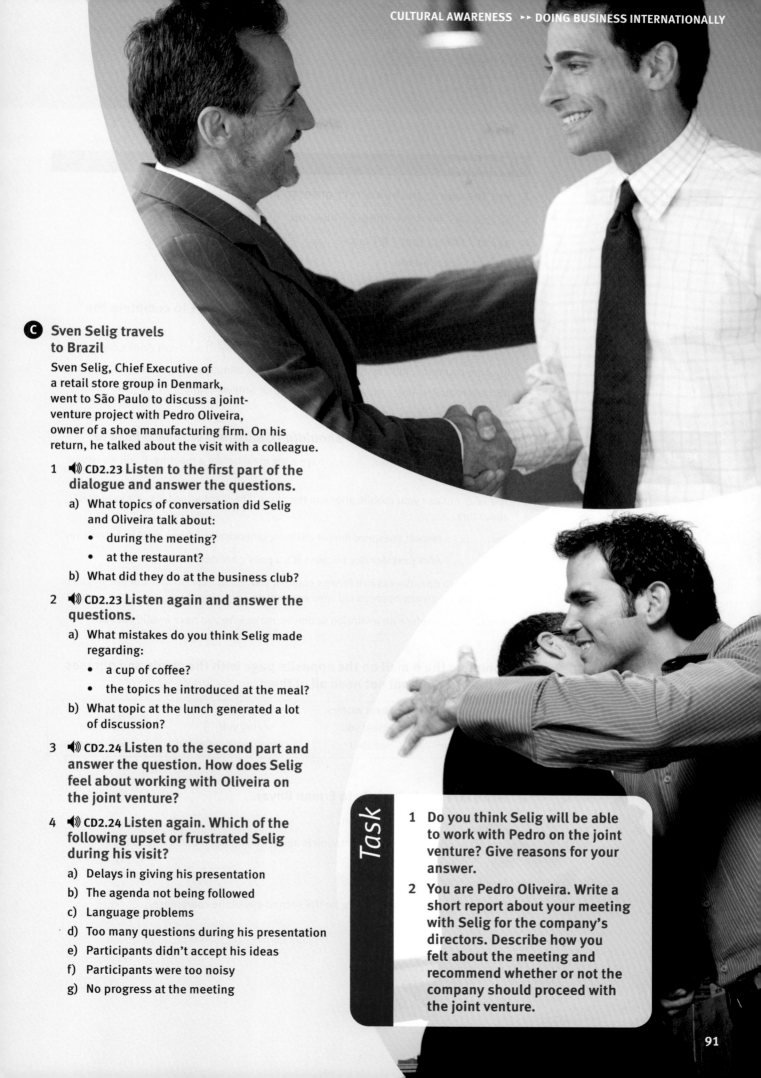

C Sven Selig travels to Brazil

Sven Selig, Chief Executive of a retail store group in Denmark, went to São Paulo to discuss a joint-venture project with Pedro Oliveira, owner of a shoe manufacturing firm. On his return, he talked about the visit with a colleague.

1 ◀◀ CD2.23 **Listen to the first part of the dialogue and answer the questions.**

   a) What topics of conversation did Selig and Oliveira talk about:
- during the meeting?
- at the restaurant?

   b) What did they do at the business club?

2 ◀◀ CD2.23 **Listen again and answer the questions.**

   a) What mistakes do you think Selig made regarding:
- a cup of coffee?
- the topics he introduced at the meal?

   b) What topic at the lunch generated a lot of discussion?

3 ◀◀ CD2.24 **Listen to the second part and answer the question. How does Selig feel about working with Oliveira on the joint venture?**

4 ◀◀ CD2.24 **Listen again. Which of the following upset or frustrated Selig during his visit?**

   a) Delays in giving his presentation

   b) The agenda not being followed

   c) Language problems

   d) Too many questions during his presentation

   e) Participants didn't accept his ideas

   f) Participants were too noisy

   g) No progress at the meeting

Task

1 Do you think Selig will be able to work with Pedro on the joint venture? Give reasons for your answer.

2 You are Pedro Oliveira. Write a short report about your meeting with Selig for the company's directors. Describe how you felt about the meeting and recommend whether or not the company should proceed with the joint venture.

7 Cultures

1 Put the words in the correct order to make idioms.

1 to / on / a / fire / get / house / like / on

2 to / in / one's / foot / it / put

3 to / ice / the / break

2 Use the correct form of the idioms from Exercise 1 to complete the sentences.

1 I .... at the party when I asked for a glass of wine. It was soft drinks only!

2 In some countries, talking about the weather for a minute or two is a way to ....

3 My new manager has a great sense of humour, and we really ....

Complete the sentences with *should(n't)*, *must(n't)* or *(don't) have to*.

1 If you want my advice, you .... have a big meal before a meeting. It will make you feel sleepy.

2 You .... use your mobile phone in the plane. The flight attendants are very strict about this.

3 You .... respect the speed limit at all times, otherwise your licence will be taken away.

4 We .... work next Monday because it's a public holiday.

5 If you plan to do business in a foreign country, you .... learn some of the language. That's always greatly appreciated wherever you go.

6 If you .... refuse an invitation to dinner, make sure you have a valid excuse.

1 Complete the e-mail on the opposite page with the words and phrases in the box. You will not need all of them.

are willing	best wishes	faithfully	invited
inviting	meet you	seeing you	sincerely
very much hope	wanted	would be delighted	would like to

2 Write Mr Ferreira's reply to Erman Bayar.

• Thank Mr Bayar for the invitation.

• Explain briefly what your presentation is about and mention that the abstract is attached.

• Mention your fee.

• Explain why you cannot be there for the second day of the conference.

To:	J. Ferreira
From:	Erman Bayar
Subject:	Forthcoming IRTA Sales Conference

Dear Mr Ferreira,

We .... [1] invite you to attend our international sales conference, which is being held in Izmir this autumn. Your latest book on cross-cultural communication, *Bridges to Success*, has become a best-seller throughout the region. Therefore, we .... [2] if you could deliver a 30-minute keynote address at this event.

The conference will be on Wednesday and Thursday, November 4–5, from 9.00 till 15.00.

If you .... [3] to accept this invitation, could you please send us the abstract of your speech at your earliest convenience and also let us know what your fee is.

You are also cordially .... [4] to the dinner which will be given in honour of the presenters and of our prominent guests on Thursday evening.

We .... [5] that you can accept this invitation and look forward to .... [6].

Yours .... [7],

Erman Bayar

8 Human resources

VOCABULARY

1 Match the verbs (1–7) to the nouns (a–g).

1 to apply   a) a candidate
2 to fill in   b) a probationary period
3 to attend   c) a psychometric test
4 to work   d) a vacancy
5 to shortlist   e) an application form
6 to advertise   f) an interview
7 to take   g) for a job

2 Choose the correct verb–noun combinations from Exercise 1 to complete the sentences.

1 A potential employer will often ask job seekers to .... in order to form a better idea of their personality.

2 If the selection panel members consider that your application has sufficient merit, you will be contacted and invited to ....

3 Many companies would never .... whose contact e-mail address is anything like 'cool_dude1987@bluedreams.net'.

4 The successful applicants will be required to .... of six months, during which time their suitability for the post will be assessed.

5 Before you .... , it is useful to know what kind of company or institution is offering the position, so do your homework!

3 Look at the Case study on pages 80–81. You have decided to appoint Martha Gómez to the job. Complete the letter with the correct words.

Dear Ms Gómez

It was a ....¹ meeting you here at our Fast Fitness headquarters last Tuesday. As you certainly realised, the panel was extremely interested in your innovative fitness programs and how you would introduce those in our clubs.

Since then, we have ....² your ....³, and all three were very positive.

Therefore, we are ....⁴ to offer you the ....⁵ of General Manager for our chain of health and fitness clubs.

We can offer a starting salary of $75,000 a year, plus an excellent ....⁶ package, including free accommodation and insurance.

We expect you to commence work on September 1. However, we would like you to ....⁷ a two-day induction meeting at our headquarters on 3–4 August, which will help you to get to know the company and some of your future ....⁸.

Please could you ....⁹ that you wish to take up this post and also let us know whether you are able to come to New York for the induction course?

We look forward to ....¹⁰ from you.

Sincerely

1	a) welcome	b) pleasure	c) good	d) enjoy
2	a) found	b) checked	c) controlled	d) written
3	a) employers	b) managers	c) sponsors	d) references
4	a) please	b) informing	c) delighted	d) deciding
5	a) position	b) work	c) skill	d) employment
6	a) benefits	b) assets	c) bonus	d) profits
7	a) attend	b) assist	c) participate	d) take part
8	a) colleges	b) workmen	c) colleagues	d) workers
9	a) inform	b) confirm	c) prefer	d) refer
10	a) hear	b) heard	c) have heard	d) hearing

WRITING

Write a letter to one of the applicants who failed to get the job. Include the following points:

- thank the applicant for coming to the interview
- explain why you are not able to offer him/her the job, despite his/her skills and experience
- say you will keep his/her name on file and let him/her know about any future job openings.

9 International markets

Match the verbs (1–6) to the nouns (a–f).

1	to comply with	a)	a market
2	to carry out	b)	a price
3	to break into	c)	an order
4	to place	d)	a market survey, an enquiry, an investigation, tests
5	to quote	e)	the delivery date, a deadline
6	to meet	f)	the regulations, a rule, an order

1 Match the sentence halves.

1	If they didn't offer such good terms,	a)	we'll have to cancel it.
2	If you ordered a larger quantity,	b)	the consignment will reach us in time.
3	If we offer them a 10% discount,	c)	we can start production as scheduled.
4	If you don't confirm your order soon,	d)	we wouldn't do business with them.
5	As long as we get the parts in May,	e)	we could negotiate a better price.
6	Provided that it is sent by air,	f)	they say they'll place an order today.

2 Complete the sentences with 'll, 'd, won't or wouldn't.

1 We .... have to look for another supplier if you can't deliver this month.

2 You .... get such a good commission if you didn't win so many deals.

3 We .... cut the price by 10% if you gave us a firm order in advance.

4 If we don't retrain our staff, they .... be able to use the new software.

5 Unless we hear from you within five days, we .... assume that the deal is off.

6 If you met your sales targets, we .... consider offering you a three-year contract.

Match the expressions (1–5) to the functions (a–e).

1	If you order more, we'll give you a discount.	a)	Refusing an offer
2	What exactly do you mean?	b)	Playing for time
3	I'd like to think about it.	c)	Making offers and concessions
4	I'm not sure about that.	d)	Closing the deal
5	Right, I think we've covered everything.	e)	Checking understanding

Cultures: Doing business internationally

Decide whether these sentences are typically about doing business in Brazil (B), Japan (J) or Saudi Arabia (SA). One applies to more than one country.

1 People tend to stand close together when talking and are not afraid to touch each other.

2 Don't be afraid of silence.

3 On receiving a business card, examine it carefully, then place it on the table in front of you.

4 Initial meetings are generally not private.

5 If you are offered coffee, accept, even if you do not normally drink coffee.

6 During a presentation, you can expect to be interrupted and asked a lot of questions.

7 Don't give white flowers as a gift, because they remind people of death.

8 Avoid direct questions, especially questions which may require a 'no' answer.

9 A meeting may be postponed by one or two days once you arrive.

10 Don't bring up topics of conversation such as crime, the government or deforestation.

Negotiations

Objectives

Speaking

- Can negotiate a change in price in a simple transaction using basic language.

- Can negotiate simple terms and conditions of a basic sale or contract.

- Can use simple language to convey the basic facts about a negotiating position.

Lesson deliverable

To participate in a business negotiation, negotiating price and simple terms and conditions, and practising language for possible present or future outcomes.

Performance review

To review your own progress and performance against the lesson objectives at the end of the lesson.

A SPEAKING

Work in pairs or groups. Discuss the questions.

1 How often and with whom do you negotiate in your daily life:
   a) in your own language?
   b) in English?

2 What strategies help when you have to negotiate price, terms and conditions?

3 What are some of the difficulties of negotiating with people from other cultures?

B LISTENING

1 ◀)) **BSA3.1.12 Listen to the first part of a negotiation between Luca Tessaro, an Italian buyer for an international clothing retailer, and Rahul Darzi, an Indian fabric supplier. Answer the questions.**

   1 Complete the saying Luca uses at the start of the meeting: When in ....

   2 What two things is Luca worried about?

   3 What does Rahul suggest regarding the zips on the bags?

   4 What else does Rahul offer Luca?

2 ◀)) **BSA3.1.13 Listen to the second part of the negotiation and choose the options you hear.**

   1 If you order more than *400 / 500* metres, I'll give you a *20 / 12* per cent discount.

   2 We'd be prepared to offer you a good price on *silk / man-made fabrics* if you *increased / decreased* your order.

   3 I'll buy your *zips / silk* as long as you can guarantee the *shipment / quality*.

   4 Sure, provided they're ready by *6 / 7* p.m. *this* evening / *tomorrow*!

3 ◀)) **BSA3.1.14 Listen to the final part of the negotiation. Complete Luca's e-mail based on the summary at the end of the recording.**

✕

Dear Rahul,

Many thanks for your hospitality during my visit. I'm sending you a brief summary of our last meeting.

As agreed, Darzi & Sons Fabrics will supply us with stronger zips for our ....[1], but if we receive any more ....[2], I'm afraid we'll have to ....[3] the terms of our order. In addition, if we have problems with the new zips, you say we can ....[4] them free of charge.

I understand you will charge us the new price of ....[5] per metre if we order over ....[6] of quality silk.

Regarding fabrics, we will order the same quantities as before, but ....[7] will be man-made fabric and ....[8] will be quality silk for our luxury sleepwear collection.

Finally, as I explained, we need the quality silk to be sent by ....[9], to ensure it arrives in excellent condition and in time for our campaign. You agreed to send the silk consignments by air as long as we offer you ....[10] credit terms.

Please confirm and I'll send a detailed document of our new agreement.

Regards,

Luca Tessaro
Head Buyer
DifrenT Fashions

C VOCABULARY

Complete the flow chart sho____ e stages of a typical negotiation with the words in the box.

agenda body concluding points purpose started

Stages of a negotiation

Getting ....¹ ➤ Stating the ....² ➤ ....³ ➤ ....⁴ of the negotiation ➤ Action ....⁵ ➤ ....⁶ the meeting

Task

Pre-task: Context

You have decided to buy new staff T-shirts for each person in your organisation. You are going to negotiate the price, terms and conditions with a supplier. Think about: product, price, discounts for large quantities and terms and conditions for delivery dates and payment.

Part 1: Preparation

Work in pairs or groups of three. Your teacher will assign your role: Group A or Group B. Discuss the information on your role cards and establish what you want to achieve by the end of the negotiation. Prepare a possible agenda for the negotiation.

Group A: You are buyers. Turn to page xi.

Group B: You are suppliers. Turn to page xii.

Part 2: Negotiation 1

Work in a groups of four or six. The suppliers and buyers meet at the client's office. Hold the first part of the negotiation, including stages 1, 2 and 3.

- Choose one person to lead the negotiation.
- Confirm the agenda.
- Ask questions and state your negotiation positions.
- Make sure at least one person in each party takes notes.

Part 3: Rethinking positions

Regroup as buyers or suppliers and compare notes. Check your negotiating positions and plan the next part of the negotiation.

Part 4: Negotiation 2

Hold the next part of the negotiation (stage 4).

- Choose one person in each group to lead the negotiation.
- This is when you need to discuss prices, discounts, terms and conditions, bargain and make any concessions. Try to reach a 'win–win' situation.
- When you have finished, regroup as buyers or suppliers.
- Check your notes and consult each other before the final part.

Part 5: Final negotiation

Hold the final part of the negotiation (stages 5 and 6).

- Choose one person in each group to summarise the action points.
- Clarify any points that are not clear and end your negotiation in a professional way.

○ **EXTRA PRACTICE: DVD CLIP AND WORKSHEET 11**

D PEER REVIEW

Find a partner from another group and give him/her feedback at the end of the task. Think about these points.

1 Did you achieve a win–win situation? Why? / Why not?

2 Did everyone understand the same prices, terms and conditions? Which action points need to be clarified?

3 What worked well? How could you improve if you were going to negotiate the deal again?

E SELF-ASSESSMENT

Look back at the lesson objectives and think about the feedback from your teacher and colleagues. Write answers to these questions.

1 Which learning objectives did you achieve?

2 What useful language did you use from Section B?

3 What do you need to improve when negotiating?

F PROFESSIONAL DEVELOPMENT AND PERFORMANCE GOALS

Think of opportunities to practise and improve your negotiation skills in your place of work/study. What kinds of things can you negotiate in class? Write a short dialogue and then practise and record it with a colleague. If you record your dialogue, listen to it before your next class. Write a short summary of the agreement. Use the e-mail in Exercise B3 to help you.

E-mails

wing th...

Objectives

Writing

- Can write a simple e-mail requesting information, emphasising the most important points.

- Can write an e-mail giving some detail of work-related news and events.

Reading

- Can understand standard e-mails on work-related topics.

- Can understand factual details in work-related e-mails.

Lesson deliverable

To write two e-mails requesting/delivering key information.

Performance review

To review your own progress and performance against the lesson objectives at the end of the lesson.

A SPEAKING

1 **How often do you write e-mails in English? Is it difficult? Why? / Why not?**

2 **Read the e-mail below. In pairs or small groups, discuss these points.**

   1 the *accuracy* of the English

   2 the *clarity* of the message

   3 its *effectiveness* – will Tomasz respond in time?

☒

Subject: Request for sales numbers again

Tomasz,

As I requested in my e-mail three days ago, I need Poland's half-year sales figures from you to create the mid-year report. You need to send it today – latest 4 p.m. – or I have to deliver the international report to the board without the Polish numbers, which is not a good idea!

Olivia

B LISTENING

1 🔊 **BSA3.2.15 Listen to Richard, Head of International Sales, talking to Olivia about getting sales data from international colleagues. Answer the questions.**

   1 Which sales forecasts are needed? Why?

   2 When is the data needed?

   3 What will be a problem for people delivering the data?

   4 What advice does Richard give Olivia?

2 **In your opinion, is Richard's advice good or bad? Why?**

C READING

Richard recommends an article on e-mail strategies. In pairs, read the list and choose the three most important tips.

Key e-mail strategies	
1	Give more than enough information to ensure full clarity.
2	End on a clearly positive note.
3	Use paragraphs to make it easy to read.
4	Make clearly positive social opening.
5	Suggest a specific time to call.
6	Confirm status of information.
7	State purpose of e-mail.
8	Highlight information to read.
9	Refer to a previous request.
10	Offer to call.

D WRITING

1 Complete the e-mail Olivia writes after her conversation with Richard using the phrases in the box.

feel free to call   I apologise for   I wouldn't spend   it is essential that   ~~it urgently needs~~   it would be great
let me have   thanks in advance   there's no need to worry   you may need to   you must send

---

Dear Colleagues,

Our management board plans to discuss next year's sales forecasts next week and *it urgently needs*[a] some information from you. Could you ....[b] your expected next year's sales for your top five products and top five corporate customers? ....[c] too much time working on this, but please make sure numbers are realistic, as ....[d] justify them at a later date. Don't use gross numbers. ....[e] if you could give figures which are net of any discounts. Can you also give an overview of any special sales activities you already have planned/completed?

In terms of deadline, ...[f] your data by close of day on Friday. I realise that the schedule is very tight and ....[g] putting you under any pressure, but ....[h] we have the numbers as the board needs to make some investment decisions.

If you have any questions or need any support, ...[i] so we can discuss. I am available most of this afternoon and tomorrow morning. As I said, ...[j] too much about formatting the data. Richard will do all that here.

Many ....[k],

Olivia

---

2 Turn to page xiii and read Jean Paul's reply. In his e-mail, he uses the key e-mail strategies from Exercise C. Match the strategies to the parts of the e-mail.

Task

E-mail 1

Context: You have to prepare a short business report for your management board and need some information from your international colleagues.

1 Work in two groups. Decide:
- the name of your company and its main activity
- the name of your international colleague and their role in the company
- what information you need for your report
- when you need this information.

2 Now form pairs within your group and write an e-mail. Think about:
- how to start the e-mail and explain its objective
- how to communicate that this information is needed urgently and is a priority
- what to say at the end to offer support.

3 Give your e-mail to a pair from the other group.

E-mail 2

1 Read the e-mail you received and write a reply. Decide:
- how to start the e-mail, referring back to the original request for information
- how to make clear what information you are sending, how accurate/correct it is, etc.
- how/if you are going to offer to discuss the information by phone
- how to express appreciation for the offer of support
- how to end the e-mail.

2 When you have finished, pass your e-mail back to the pair who sent it.

E PEER REVIEW

In small groups, evaluate the e-mails you received. Is the information you got the right information? Is it clearly stated and presented? Is the tone polite and professional?

F SELF-ASSESSMENT

Look back at the lesson objectives and the e-mails you wrote in this lesson. Which parts were effective in requesting and giving information clearly? Why? To what extent have you achieved the lesson objectives?

G PROFESSIONAL DEVELOPMENT AND PERFORMANCE GOALS

Find two examples of recent e-mails in which you requested information. Look at the replies you received. Were there any gaps between the information you asked for and the information you received? Complete the sentences to create an action plan.

1 One thing I will do to improve further is to …

2 Another thing I can do is …

3 Finally, I will try to …

'Morality is largely a matter of geography.'
Elbert Hubbard (1856–1915), American writer

STARTING UP **A** **Discuss this list of unethical activities. In your opinion, which are the worst? Are any common in your country?**

1   Finding ways of paying as little tax as possible

2   Using your work computer or phone for private purposes (e.g. online shopping)

3   Accepting praise for someone else's ideas or work

4   Selling something as genuine when you know it is not

5   Using your influence to get jobs for friends or relatives (nepotism)

6   Phoning in sick at work when you are not ill

7   Not telling the truth about your age or experience on an application form

8   Not saying anything when you are charged too little for something by mistake

9   Paying people in cash for jobs done around the home in order to reduce the cost

10 Claiming extra expenses (e.g. getting a taxi receipt for more than the actual fare)

B **Are some jobs/professions more ethical than others? How ethical do you think these professions are? Which are seen as more/less ethical in your country?**

accountant   civil servant   lawyer   police officer   politician   banker   estate agent
nurse   university lecturer   soldier   car sales executive   journalist   doctor   taxi driver

C **Discuss the questions.**

1   What is the purpose of a business, in your opinion? Is it just to make money?

2   What do you understand by the term 'an ethical business'?

VOCABULARY
Right or wrong

A **Look at the situations. Which do you think are the most serious?**

1 A new contact suggests that a payment into his private bank account will enable a company to win a valuable supply contract.

2 An employee informs some friends about a company takeover before it is generally known so they can buy shares and make a profit.

3 A company is making copies of luxury branded products and selling them in street markets.

4 An upmarket private airline only employs attractive women under 25 years old as cabin crew and ground staff.

5 An industrial company is disposing of waste chemicals in the sea.

6 A car manufacturer is secretly taking photos of a rival's new model at a test track.

7 A cosmetics and pharmaceutical company tries out all its products on rats and mice.

8 Some criminals buy property and expensive cars with money they got from illegal activities. The goods are then sold and the now 'clean' money is used in other businesses and new bank accounts.

9 A group of rival mobile phone companies get together and agree to charge approximately the same amount for a range of services and packages.

10 A company tells the authorities that it is making a lot less profit than it actually is.

B **Match words from Box A and Box B to make word partnerships which describe the activities in Exercise A.**

example: *1 bribery and corruption*

A
| ~~bribery~~ | price | environmental | sex | insider |
| tax | counterfeit | money | animal | industrial |

B
| ~~and corruption~~ | testing | discrimination | fraud | trading |
| fixing | laundering | goods | pollution | espionage |

C ◀)) CD2.25 **Mark the stress in each word partnership from Exercise B. Then listen to the correct answers.**

D **Discuss the questions.**

1 Which of the activities described in Exercise A are illegal in your country?

2 Are there any which you think should not be illegal because this damages business?

3 In your opinion, which are the easiest or most difficult to control?

E **Work in groups. What should you do in each of these situations?**

1 Your boss has asked you to make one member of your department redundant. The choice is between the most popular team member, who is the worst at his job, or the best worker, who is the least popular with the other team members. Who do you choose?

2 The best-qualified person for the post of Sales Manager is female. However, you know most of your customers would prefer a man. If you appoint a woman, you will probably lose some sales.

3 You work for a travel company which is in serious financial difficulties and will go bankrupt in the near future. Your boss has ordered you to continue to accept deposits and payments from customers until the company officially stops trading. You fear that these people may lose their money or may be left abroad when the company collapses.

4 Your company has a new advertising campaign which stresses its honesty, fairness and ethical business behaviour. It has factories in several countries where wages are very low. At present, it is paying workers the local market rate.

See the **DVD-ROM**
for the i-Glossary.

READING

The ethics of résumé writing

A **In groups, discuss the question.**

Is there ever a time when it is OK to lie on a résumé?

B **Read the headline and subheading of the article. In pairs, predict five words that will appear in the article. Include some words connected to dishonesty. Check the article to see if you were correct. Underline all the words in the article connected with dishonesty.**

The ethics of résumé writing

It's never OK to lie on a résumé. But what about stretching the truth?
by Clinton D. Korver

How much can you "dress up" your résumé to make yourself as strong a candidate as possible without crossing the ethical line of deception? Consider a few conflicting thoughts:

- Over 50% of people lie on their résumé.
- A Monster.com blog about the dangers of lying on your résumé elicited 60 comments from job seekers recommending lying and only 46 discouraging it. Recommenders justified lying by claiming: everyone else is doing it, companies lie about job requirements, and it's hard to get a good job.
- Executives caught lying on their résumés often lose their jobs.

If you are reading this blog, you probably are not tempted by dishonesty. But what about the following:

- Claiming a degree that was not earned because you did most of the work and were only a few credits short.
- Creating a more impressive job title because you were already doing all of the work of that position.
- Claiming a team's contributions as your own, because other members did not carry their weight.
- Inflating the number of people or range of functions for which you had direct responsibility because you really did have a great deal of influence over them.

These are called rationalizations—constructing a justification for a decision you suspect is really wrong. You create a story that sounds believable but doesn't pass close examination. You begin to fool yourself. You develop habits of distorted thinking.

So where is the line? You need to decide that for yourself. Here are some tests to keep your thinking clear:

- Other-shoe test: How would you feel if the shoe were on the other foot and you were the hiring manager looking at this résumé? What assumptions would you draw and would they be accurate?
- Front-page test: Would you think the same way if the accomplishment in question were reported on the front page of the Wall Street Journal? Or your prior employer's internal newsletter?

But wait, you say. My résumé doesn't quite pass these tests, but there is something real underneath my claims, and I do not want to sell myself short.

When in doubt, ask an old boss. While asking an old boss may be difficult, it has many benefits. Precisely because it is difficult, it forces you to think clearly and sometimes creatively. Asking also checks the accuracy of your claims, trains your old boss in how to represent you during reference checks, and sometimes your old boss may give you better ways to represent yourself.

from Business Week

C **Read the article again and answer the questions.**

1 What reasons are given for not being totally honest on your CV?

2 What can happen to senior managers who lie on their CVs?

3 Which of the four rationalisations do you think is the most serious? Why?

4 What happens to you when you start using rationalisations?

5 What are the advantages of asking an old boss?

D **Discuss the two situations and decide what you would do in each case.**

1 You discover that one of your top employees, who has done an excellent job for the last 15 years, lied about their qualifications when she joined the company.

2 One of your employees, who is not a good worker, has asked you to give him a good reference. You would be happy if this employee left the company.

LISTENING

Helping environmental research

A ◀)) CD2.26 **David Hillyard, Director of Programmes at EarthWatch, is describing his organisation. Listen to the first part of the interview and complete the gaps.**

EarthWatch is an .... ¹ research and .... ² and .... ³ organisation, and we have over .... ⁴ field research projects around the .... ⁵. That involves, er, ... ⁶ looking at how animals and .... ⁷ are coping in their natural .... ⁸.

David Hillyard

B ◀)) CD2.26 **Listen again and answer the questions.**

1 Where does EarthWatch have offices?

2 How are EarthWatch's field research projects designed?

C ◀)) CD2.27 **Listen to the second part of the interview and answer the questions.**

1 Why do businesses need to change the way they operate?

2 What opportunity do companies have with respect to the environment?

D ◀)) CD2.28 **Listen to the final part and write three sentences about the collaboration with HSBC. Compare your sentences with a partner's.**

Watch the interview on the DVD-ROM.

E **In what other ways could businesses involve their employees in environmental issues?**

LANGUAGE REVIEW

Narrative tenses

A ◀)) CD2.29 **Listen to a conversation about a woman who was fired from her job and put these events in the order that they happened.**

a) She lost her job.

b) She felt desperate.

c) She lied on her CV.

d) There was an HR initiative.

e) The company found out she did not have a Master's degree.

f) She got a really good job.

g) She got strong performance reviews.

We can use different tenses to narrate a story.

Past simple	*The company **fired** her.*
Past continuous	*Everything **was going** really well.*
Past perfect	*She **had lied** on her CV.*
Present perfect	*Since then, **I've advised** everyone to be honest.*

Which tense is normally used for:

1 setting the scene and providing background information?

2 events which happen before the story begins?

3 events in the story?

4 saying what the present results of the story are?

➡ *Grammar reference* page 150

B ◀)) CD2.29 **Listen to the conversation again. Follow the audio script on page 163 and note down examples of each of these tenses.**

a) past simple

b) past continuous

c) past perfect

d) present perfect

C **Complete this text about a pharmaceutical company with the correct tenses of the verbs in brackets.**

We like to think we are an ethical company, but we .... [1] (have) a problem last year when we .... [2] (launch) our new product.

Let me give you the background to the problem. The new product .... [3] (sell) very well, we .... [4] (get) good feedback, and sales .... [5] (increase) month by month. Everyone was happy.

Then it all .... [6] (go) wrong. In August, we .... [7] (start) to get complaints from some doctors about one of our salesmen. They .... [8] (complain) about the methods that the salesman .... [9] (use) to persuade them to endorse the product. He .... [10] (offer) them expensive gifts and .... [11] (take) them to expensive restaurants. The doctors .... [12] (feel) under pressure to promote the product.

By the end of the year, we .... [13] (receive) over 30 complaints about that particular salesman. In December, articles .... [14] (start) to appear in the press about our unethical sales methods. In the end, we .... [15] (fire) the salesman. As a result of this, we .... [16] (recently issue) guidelines to all sales staff about appropriate gifts.

D **Tell a story about any of these ideas.**

1 A significant news event you remember well

2 An ethical problem you know about

3 A memorable event in your life (good or bad)

4 An unusual or memorable experience while you were travelling abroad

5 Your first or last day in a job or organisation

SKILLS
Considering options

A 🔊 CD2.30 **Listen to two directors talking about a top salesman, Tom Pattison, who is not doing his job properly. Then answer the questions.**

1 In what ways is Tom behaving unprofessionally?

2 What two options does one of the directors mention?

3 What do the directors finally decide to do?

B **Which of the headings (a–g) in the Useful language box should these comments go under? Some may go under the same heading.**

1 I'd say there are two ways we could deal with this.

2 We could have a chat with him about his sales reports.

3 If we take a firm approach, there's a risk he may get upset and look for another job.

4 OK, let's look at it from another angle …

5 It might be the best way to deal with the problem.

6 Yeah, the problem is, he's a really good salesman, but I agree he needs tighter control.

7 If we just have a friendly chat with him, he may not take it seriously.

C 🔊 CD2.30 **Listen again. Tick the expressions from the Useful language box that you hear.**

USEFUL LANGUAGE

a) STATING THE PROBLEM

The problem is, he's a really good salesman.

The way I see it is he doesn't like rules.

b) LOOKING AT OPTIONS

So, what are our options?

There are (two/several) ways we could deal with this.

c) DISCUSSING POSSIBLE EFFECTS

If we do that, he may come to his senses.

One consequence could be that he gives in his resignation.

d) CHANGING YOUR APPROACH

Let's look at it from another angle.

Let's consider another approach.

Why don't we deal with it in a different way?

e) EXPRESSING QUALIFIED AGREEMENT

I'm with you up to a point, but it may not work.

You could be right, but it's a risky strategy.

f) MAKING A DECISION

The best way to deal with the problem is to talk to him.

Let's see if we can sort this out.

g) STATING FUTURE ACTION

I'll arrange for Tom to meet us.

The next thing to do is fix up a meeting.

D **Role-play this situation.**

You are senior managers of a department store. Your business is losing market share. You strongly suspect your main rival is using unfair methods to compete against you. For example, you are almost sure that your rival has been:

a) trying to obtain information about your marketing strategy from an employee who has just left your company;

b) offering members of your award-winning window-display team exceptionally high salaries and bonuses to leave your organisation.

Hold a meeting to consider how to solve the problems.

Principles *or* profit?

An international drugs company is struggling with a number of ethical dilemmas. Its future success depends on making the right choices now.

Background

Universal Pharmaceuticals (UP) is based in Atlanta, Georgia. During the 1990s, it was highly successful thanks to the effective treatments it developed for people suffering from diabetes and Parkinson's Disease. However, the company has been less successful in recent years because its drug for the treatment of asthma turned out to have harmful side effects and was withdrawn from the market. The company's image was also damaged when a newspaper ran a series of articles criticising some unfair methods used by UP's sales representatives to sell the company's products. The writer of the articles questioned whether UP was living up to its mission statement that it was an 'ethical company which will always put principle before profit'.

Ethical dilemmas

At present, the management of UP are faced with three ethical dilemmas which they must discuss and resolve in the best interests of the company. The first concerns a new drug which could benefit poor people in Africa.

◀)) **CD2.31** Two directors of the company, Ernesto and Ingrid, are talking about the problem. **Listen and make notes on the problem. Then, working with a partner, summarise the ethical dilemma which the company must deal with.**

Discussion topics for the management meeting

The first item on the agenda is the new drug to treat river blindness. Then there are two other problems relating to drugs that the company is developing. They are summarised below in a discussion document which has been circulated to all participants attending the meeting.

Read about the problems relating to two other drugs and note the key points.

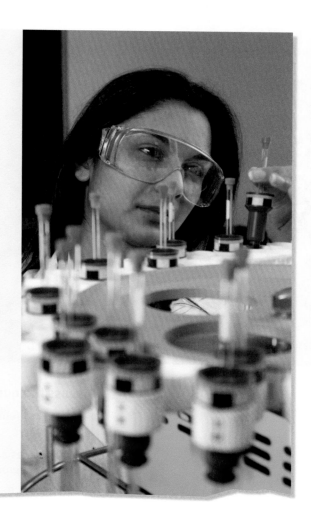

›› Test results on PX200, our new drug for treating heart disease

There is great interest in PX200, which is in the final stages of development. Up until now, the test results have been impressive. However, the recent series of tests has produced disappointing results. It seems that some patients have experienced severe breathing difficulties and other unpleasant side effects after taking the drug, while most patients have received significant benefits from it in terms of lower blood pressure and less pain.

Should we make public the results of this test, as we have done with previous test results, or should we withhold the information at this stage?

New dieting product

Our R&D department has been developing a new diet drink which will help people lose weight. The drink has been tested on animals, but some became sick in the early trials. Up until now, we have been reluctant to test new products on animals since we claim to be an ethical company. However, the new drink could be extremely profitable when it is launched. Should we continue to test this product on animals or try to develop it without using them for our research?

Task

You are members of UP's board of directors. Hold a meeting to discuss the three ethical dilemmas. One of you should lead the discussion.

1 **Use the agenda on the right to guide your discussion. The chairperson starts by briefly summarising each problem.**

2 **In each case, start by discussing the options which are available to UP to deal with the problem. Then decide how to deal with the situation. If you can't agree, take a vote.**

Agenda

1 The new drug for River Blindness
2 Test results for the PX200 (heart problems)
3 Animal testing for a dieting product

Writing

Write a short report from the chairperson, summarising the decisions reached at the UP board meeting and giving reasons for them.

 Writing file page 130

Watch the Case study commentary on the **DVD-ROM.**

'*The key to successful leadership today is influence, not authority.*'
Kenneth Blanchard, American author and management expert

STARTING UP

A **Discuss the questions.**

1 Which modern or historical leaders do you most admire? Which do you admire the least? Why?

2 What makes a great leader? Write down a list of characteristics. Compare your list with other groups.

3 Are there differences between men and women as leaders? Why have most great leaders been men?

4 Do you think great leaders are born or made?

5 Do you think first-born children make the best leaders?

6 What is the difference between a manager and a leader?

B **In groups, think of someone you know who is in a powerful position.
List three positive qualities and three negative qualities about this person.
Then compare your ideas.**

VOCABULARY
**Character
adjectives**

A **Match the adjectives in the box to make pairs of contrasting ideas.**

example: *assertive/diffident*

cautious	casual	idealistic	~~assertive~~	encouraging
~~diffident~~	formal	critical	decisive	realistic

B **Do the same with the adjectives in this box.**

dynamic radical ruthless distant conservative approachable principled laid-back

C Complete the sentences with suitable adjectives from Exercises A and B. (For sentences 1–4, use Exercise A; for sentences 5–8, use Exercise B.)

1 She doesn't like to rush into things. She's careful and ....

2 He's very good at pointing out problems with people and systems in the company. He's often .... , but this helps make improvements.

3 He's a serious, ... person, both in the way he dresses and in his dealings with people. Everyone knows he's the boss.

4 She has a very clear vision for the long-term future of the company, but many people think she is too ....

5 He is a very .... man. He sacked anyone who got in his way.

6 Our boss is friendly and .... She's very easy to talk to.

7 He's very .... He doesn't like to try anything new now he's running the company.

8 She's very .... She would never approve any policies that were remotely unethical.

D Match the phrasal verbs (1–6) to the nouns (a–f).

1	to take on	a)	a proposal/suggestion
2	to be up to	b)	the job
3	to put forward	c)	criticism
4	to deal with	d)	your resignation
5	to hand in	e)	responsibility for something
6	to come in for	f)	a problem

E Which of the phrasal verbs in Exercise D mean the following:

a) to manage c) to receive e) to be good enough

b) to give d) to accept f) to propose

F Discuss the questions.

1 Can you think of any leaders who were not up to the job?

2 When was the last time you took on responsibility for something?

3 What sort of problems do business leaders have to deal with? Give two examples.

4 Why do leaders hand in their resignations? Can you give any examples?

5 Has any leader (business, political or other) come in for criticism recently in your country? Why? What was your opinion?

See the **DVD-ROM** for the i-Glossary.

listening
Qualities of leadership

A ◀)) CD2.32 **Listen to Elizabeth Jackson, Managing Director of DirectorBank, an executive recruitment company. Which five areas does Elizabeth think are important for a good business leader?**

B ◀)) CD2.33 **Listen to the second part and answer the questions.**

1 What qualities do natural born leaders possess?

2 Can people who have acquired leadership skills beat natural born leaders?

Elizabeth Jackson

Watch the interview on the **DVD-ROM.**

C ◀)) CD2.34 **Listen to the final part and decide if these statements about Elizabeth Jackson's husband are true (T) or false (F).**

1 He is younger than her. 3 He is a natural leader. 5 He is a strategic thinker.

2 He used to be a boxer. 4 He is a creative thinker.

A In groups, write down four things that you know about L'Oréal.

B Read the article quickly to check if any of your points were mentioned.

FT

Father of the feel-good factory

by Jenny Wiggins

Sir Lindsay Owen-Jones does not like being photographed. 'Do I have to smile?' he says gruffly. He exudes the air of a man who has done this many, many times before.

Such expertise derives from the fact that Sir Lindsay is frequently photographed with models, girls far taller than he is, who wear lipstick, eyeshadow and nail polish made by L'Oréal, the company he has worked for since 1969. For nearly 20 years, he was Chief Executive of L'Oréal, the world's biggest beauty company and owner of brands such as Maybelline, Redken, Lancôme and Vichy.

Although he stepped back from the day-to-day running of the company two years ago, handing over the job to Jean-Paul Agon, he remains Chairman.

Sir Lindsay, who turns 62 this month, has spent the better part of his life trying to convince women and men that buying L'Oréal's lotions and shampoos will make them feel good.

L'Oréal is a curious destination for a man who had 'no intention' of taking a job in the consumer goods industry. Yet he was drawn to the beauty company. 'It was still quite a small company, but was thought to

be going places and was considered a great example of creative marketing and original advertising campaigns. Cosmetics is a business of intuition. Consumers don't tell you what they need; you've got to guess.'

He credits his predecessor, François Dalle, with teaching him basic business sense while he was working his way up the ranks of L'Oréal.

'He single-handedly ran this company and did every marketing job for every brand, all at the same time. But he was a genius. I think one of the reasons I got responsibility so young was that I could interpret the things he said, which often were the opposite of what he actually said literally. So when I got the job as Chief Executive, it came totally naturally to me that my priority was going to be to write L'Oréal in the sky of every country in the world.'

Under Sir Lindsay's leadership, L'Oréal did just that. Annual sales rose from a few million euros to more than €17bn as the company acquired foreign cosmetic groups such as Shu Uemura in Japan, Kiehl's in the US and the Body Shop in Britain.

Sir Lindsay harboured international ambitions even as a child. 'My mother dreamed of parties at Monte Carlo and the bright lights. She transmitted to me the idea that excitement and fun was being international and travelling and speaking languages. It was easy as a teenager in a slightly grim 1950s Britain to see the cars going into Monte Carlo and to say, "Wow, one day I'm going to be there."'

C Read the article again and match the descriptions below (1–10) to these four people. Two of the descriptions are not mentioned in the article.

a) Lindsay Owen-Jones	c) François Dalle
b) Jean-Paul Agon	d) Lindsay's mother

1 had international ambitions from a very young age.

2 runs L'Oréal.

3 is Chairman of L'Oréal.

4 was attracted to L'Oréal before it became very successful.

5 relaxes by sailing and skiing.

6 was attracted by the lifestyle of the rich and famous.

7 ran the company on his own.

8 likes going to concerts and reading.

9 climbed the career ladder at L'Oréal.

10 dreamed of parties at Monte Carlo.

D Take three minutes to make some notes about L'Oréal. Use your notes to give a one-minute presentation to your partner. Your partner will then ask you a question about it.

E   Without looking back at the article, complete the gaps with prepositions.

1   Such expertise derives .... the fact that Sir Lindsay is frequently photographed.

2   Although he stepped .... the day-to-day running of the company two years ago, handing .... the job .... Jean-Paul Agon, he remains Chairman.

3   He credits his predecessor, François Dalle , ... teaching him basic business sense.

4   ... while he was working his way .... the ranks of L'Oréal.

5   My mother dreamed .... parties at Monte Carlo.

F   Discuss the questions.

1   Would you like to work for Sir Lindsay? Why? / Why not?

2   What kind of leader would you like to work for?

3   Who is the worst leader you have come across?

LANGUAGE REVIEW
Relative clauses

Defining clauses provide essential information about the subject or object of a sentence. Without this information, the sentence often does not make sense or has a different meaning.

- *Who* or *that* are used for people.
  *He exudes the air of a man **who** has done this many, many times before.*

- *Which* or *that* are used for things.
  *Boldness and vision are qualities **that/which** all leaders should have.*

Non-defining clauses provide extra information about the subject or object of a sentence. The sentence still makes sense without this information. The extra information is separated by commas.

- *Who* (not *that*) is used for people.
  *Sir Lindsay, **who** turns 62 this month, is now the chairman.*

- *Which* (not *that*) is used for things.
  *I could interpret the things he said, **which** often were the opposite of what he actually said literally.*

➡ *Grammar reference* page 151

A   Complete the sentences in the job advertisement with *who* or *which*.

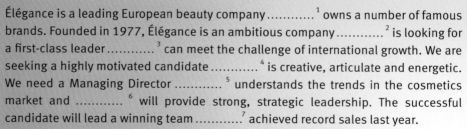

Élégance

Managing Director
Paris-based, competitive salary

Élégance is a leading European beauty company .... [1] owns a number of famous brands. Founded in 1977, Élégance is an ambitious company .... [2] is looking for a first-class leader .... [3] can meet the challenge of international growth. We are seeking a highly motivated candidate .... [4] is creative, articulate and energetic. We need a Managing Director .... [5] understands the trends in the cosmetics market and .... [6] will provide strong, strategic leadership. The successful candidate will lead a winning team .... [7] achieved record sales last year.

In the first instance and in complete confidence, please write with CV to Yvonne Roland at: Agence Richaud, 19 boulevard Gobelins, Paris 75005, France.

B Complete the quotations below with the relative pronouns in the box.

who	which	that	where

1 'The job for big companies, the challenge .... we all face as bureaucrats, is to create an environment .... people can reach their dreams.' *Jack Welch (US business leader)*

2 'He .... has never learned to obey cannot be a good commander.' *Aristotle (Greek philosopher)*

3 'A leader shapes and shares a vision, ... gives point to the work of others.' *Charles Handy (British writer)*

4 'A leader should be humble. A leader should be able to communicate with his people. A leader is someone .... walks out in front of his people, but he doesn't get too far out in front, to where he can't hear their footsteps.' *Tommy Lasorda (US sports personality)*

5 'A leader is someone .... knows what they want to achieve and can communicate that.' *Margaret Thatcher (British politician)*

C In this article, the relative pronouns are missing. Add the pronouns where appropriate.

FT

America will find opportunity in scarcity

by Eric Schmidt

We now need to encourage investment in new high-technology industries such as clean energy and environmental technology. These are sectors we have lacked political leadership not just recently, but for decades.

The Internet, enables the open and free exchange of information, is critical to our future economic growth. It has already proved to be vital to entrepreneurs and America's small businesses, generate up to 80 per cent of new jobs in the US. But continuing this record will require a strong federal commitment to keeping the Internet open.

Technologies such as the Internet can also help make our government more open and responsive to citizens. But even those of us are technology's biggest enthusiasts must recognise its limitations. In the end, it is people have to make the decisions.

More than ever, we need a leader will look beyond the old thinking and orthodoxies and understands the importance of investment in ideas and technology for our future.

This article expresses the personal opinion of Eric Schmidt, is the Chief Executive of Google.

SKILLS
Presenting

A Comment on the following statements. In your opinion are they:

a) essential?   b) helpful?   c) unhelpful for a successful presentation?

1 Tell a joke at the beginning to relax the atmosphere.

2 Speak more slowly than you normally do.

3 Smile a lot.

4 Involve the audience.

5 Invite questions during the presentation.

6 Always keep to your plan.

7 Move around during your presentation.

8 Use gestures to emphasise important points.

9 Read out your presentation from a script.

10 Stand up when giving your presentation.

B What other useful techniques do you know for giving a presentation?

C ◄)) CD2.35 Listen to a presentation addressed to a company's sales team about the launch of a new range of tennis rackets, under the Excel brand. Tick the expressions in the Useful language box that you hear.

USEFUL LANGUAGE

WELCOMING

Good morning, everyone.

Hello, everyone, welcome to …

STRUCTURING THE PRESENTATION

I'm going to divide my talk into four parts.

First, I'll give you … . After that, … . Next, … . Finally, … .

INVITING QUESTIONS

If you have any questions, don't hesitate to ask.

I'll be glad to answer any questions (at the end of my talk).

GIVING BACKGROUND INFORMATION

I'll give you some background.

Let's start with the background.

REFERRING TO THE AUDIENCE'S KNOWLEDGE

As you know, …

As you are aware, …

REFERRING TO VISUALS

If you look at the graph …

Could I draw your attention to the chart?

CONCLUDING

To sum up, …

To summarise, …

ENDING

Thanks very much. Any questions?

Well, that's all I have to say. Thank you for listening.

D Prepare a short presentation of three to five minutes. Choose one of these topics.

Topic	Audience	Suggestions
A country you have visited on holiday or done business in	A group of people who will shortly be working there	• way of life • transport • accommodation • food and drink • standard of living • customs and traditions • weather • language • people • entertainment
Your company's main competitors	The Board of Directors of your company	• identifying the competition • their strengths and weaknesses • how powerful they are in the market
Your job	A group of high-school students at a careers evening	• responsibilities and tasks • the future • perks and special advantages, e.g. foreign travel • qualifications • career structure

E In groups, make your presentations. After each presentation, rate the following aspects of the presentation from 1 to 5 (1 = unacceptable, 2 = fair, 3 = average, 4 = good, 5 = excellent).

	1	2	3	4	5
The presentation was interesting.					
The presentation was clear.					
The presentation's beginning made an impact.					
The presentation had a logical structure.					
The presentation had a summary or conclusion.					
TOTAL: ____ / 25					

Case study

LINA SPORTS

A sportswear manufacturer
is in need of new leadership.
Which of the three candidates
has the right style and strategy to
lead the company back to success?

Background

Lina Sports S.p.A is an Italian sportswear manufacturer. It was founded by Franco Rossi in 1978 and has since become a world-famous company. Originally, it specialised in tennis shoes, but later it diversified into football, athletics, tennis and volleyball clothing. The directors of the company are of different nationalities, and the working language of Lina Sports is English.

During the last three years, Lina Sports's annual results have been disappointing. Profits have fallen steadily while costs have risen, and competition in its main markets has been fierce. At present, it is reviewing its strategy in order to improve its performance. It also faces the possibility of being taken over. A giant French retailing group has announced that it would like to acquire the company, but only in the event of a 'friendly takeover', with full agreement from the present management.

Franco Rossi is now 58 years old. He would like to become Chairman of the company in the near future and to appoint one of the present directors as CEO to run Lina Sports. There are three possible candidates for this position. Each candidate will present his/her ideas for the company's future strategy to the board of directors. The director who makes the most persuasive presentation will replace Franco Rossi as CEO of the company.

Problems faced by Lina Sports

A report by JPS Consultants identified four reasons for Lina Sports's poor results in recent years. The company had:

- launched too many product lines in a wide range of sports
- invested in too many expensive endorsements with top sports people
- suffered from fierce competition from stronger rivals
- lost its reputation for being innovative.

Strategies for turning round the company

The leadership candidates will present three alternative strategies for the Board to consider. Consider which, in your opinion, appears to be the best one for the company. Do not discuss your choice at this stage.

Strategy 1

Lina Sports must give up its independence and merge with, or be taken over by, a larger, financially stronger company.

Strategy 2

Lina Sports should acquire a number of smaller companies and focus more on making sports accessories.

Strategy 3

Lina Sports should grow organically by revising its organisation, product ranges and marketing strategy.

Task

1 **Divide into two groups:**

   Group A: The three directors, each presenting a different strategy to the board

   Group B: Members of the board.

2 **Look at your role card and prepare for the meeting.**

   Director 1: Turn to page 139.   Director 3: Turn to page 139.

   Director 2: Turn to page 143.   Group B: Turn to page 145.

3 **Each director presents his/her ideas for the company's future strategy and answers any questions the other board members wish to ask.**

4 **The other board members discuss the three presentations and decide which director has given the most convincing presentation.**

5 **All board directors discuss the future strategy of Lina Sports and add any comments they wish.**

Writing

As Chairman of Lina Sports, write an e-mail to the Head of JPS Consultants summarising the three business strategies and indicating which one has been chosen, giving reasons for your choice. Ask the Head of JPS to comment on your decision.

Watch the Case study commentary on the DVD-ROM.

 Writing file page 127

12 Competition

'Business is Darwinism: only the fittest survive.'
Robert Holmes à Court (1937–1990), Chairman of Bell Group

A   **Before doing the quiz below, say whether you are:**

a)   very competitive   b)   fairly competitive   c)   not at all competitive.

B   **Answer the questions in the quiz. Then turn to page 140 to find out your score. Compare your score with a partner.**

How competitive are you?

1 Which of the following statements do you agree with?
a) Winning is everything.
b) It's not the winning that counts, it's the taking part.
c) We are in this world to help each other.

2 Which of the following would satisfy you?
a) Earning more than anyone else you know.
b) Earning more than most of your friends.
c) Earning enough to have a comfortable life.

3 You have just won €50,000 and need to buy a new car. Do you:
a) spend €12,000 on a reliable car that will get you from A to B?
b) spend €26,000 on a middle-range car?
c) spend the entire €50,000 on a flashy, top-of-the-range car that will impress all your friends?

4 If a colleague did something very successful, would you feel:
a) pleased for them?
b) pleased for them, but a bit jealous?
c) very jealous and unhappy?

5 If you lose at something, do you:
a) forget about it immediately?
b) think about it for a while?
c) never forget?

6 How do you feel when you win? Do you:
a) boast about it and tell everyone?
b) feel good, but keep it to yourself?
c) feel sorry for the person who lost?

7 What do you want for your children? Do you want them:
a) to be happy?
b) to achieve more than you did?
c) to be the best at everything?

8 You are at the traffic lights next to another car. The lights change to 'go'. Do you:
a) let the other car go first?
b) move away slowly, without being aware of the other car?
c) try to be the first away?

9 You are waiting to check in at a crowded airline counter. There does not seem to be a system of queuing. Would you:
a) push your way to the front?
b) insist loudly that a fair system is adopted?
c) keep quiet and wait?

10 How do you feel about doing this quiz? Do you want to:
a) show you are the most competitive person in the group?
b) show you are the least competitive person in the group?
c) find out something about yourself?

VOCABULARY

Competition idioms

A There are many idioms from sport used in business, particularly when talking about competition. Complete the idioms below with the nouns in the box. Which sports do you think they come from?

| player | ropes | game | ~~field~~ | ball | seat | horse | goalposts | race | neck |

1 a level playing field
2 in the driving............
3 to be neck and............
4 flogging a dead............
5 a major............

6 move the............
7 keep your eye on the............
8 ahead of the............
9 a one-horse............
10 on the............

B Which of the idioms in Exercise A refer to:

a) a situation of fair competition?
b) being in front of the competition?
c) being at the same level as the competition?
d) being the only competitor?
e) wasting your time on a hopeless situation?

f) staying focused?
g) a change in the rules?
h) being in control?
i) being in a very bad situation?
j) an important company or person with a lot of power or influence?

C Complete the extracts with the most suitable idioms from Exercise A. Remember to change the verb form where necessary.

1 It's not a level playing field any more. As a small, family-owned company, it's very difficult for us to compete with the big multinationals in terms of price.

2 They are so far ahead of their competitors in terms of new products that it has become .... It will be years before their rivals catch up with them.

3 There's no point continuing with the project. It'll never work. We're............ .... We need to look elsewhere if we're to fight off the competition.

4 With our market dominance in Asia, we're in an extremely powerful position. We are really............ ....

5 We have exactly the same market share as our nearest rival. According to independent research, we're also............ .... in terms of sales so far this year as well.

6 Although the market has expanded, there are still really only two............ .... They will fight it out for market dominance.

D Discuss the questions.

1 Have you ever felt you were *flogging a dead horse*

a) at work? b) in your private life?

2 Which companies are *ahead of the game* in your industry or the industry you would like to work in?

3 Can you give an example of a situation when

a) someone *moved the goalposts*? b) you were *in the driving seat*?

How did you feel?

4 Name some *major players* in the following industries:

automotive, telecoms, computing, electronics, an industry you know well

*See the **DVD-ROM** for the i-Glossary.*

113

A   In groups, discuss what you know about Starbucks and McDonald's.

B   Read the first two paragraphs of the article. Which company is focusing more on the international market?

C   Read the whole article, then look at these company plans. Write 'M' (McDonald's) or 'S' (Starbucks) for each one.

1   start competing in the coffee-bar market

2   replace their Chief Executive

3   slow expansion in the US

4   introduce coffee bars with 'baristas'

5   close under-performing stores

6   focus on international plans

7   allow customers to see drinks being made

8   use simple sizes for coffees

9   probably offer coffee at a lower price than their major competitors

McDonald's stirs up battle with Starbucks

by James Quinn

Starbucks' Chief Executive Jim Donald – who has presided over a 50 per cent decline in the retailer's share price in the last 12 months – is to be replaced by founder and Chairman Howard Schultz.

His appointment comes after a dark 12 months for Starbucks, which has seen it lose out to rivals such as Dunkin' Donuts and McDonald's, who have begun to replicate its success. Schultz is now set to slow the expansion of the retailer's growth in the US, closing under-performing stores in direct response to the slowing North American economy. Instead, he will focus on the company's international plans, using money originally earmarked for US store openings for its global expansion plans.

Fast-food giant McDonald's is set to take on Starbucks in the competitive coffee market, with plans to open coffee bars across the United States. McDonald's, until now better known for Big Mac burgers than its beverages, yesterday detailed plans to roll out coffee bars complete with their own 'baristas' in its near-14,000 North American stores.

Although there is no fixed timescale for the roll-out, trials are already under way, and it is believed the push could add $1bn a year to McDonald's $21.6bn of annual sales. The aim is to compete head-to-head with Starbucks in the ever-increasing brewed coffee market.

The trial involves recruiting 'baristas' – a term made famous by Starbucks – to stores, where espresso machines are displayed at the counter, so allowing customers to actually see the drinks being made. This is in direct contrast to McDonald's traditional approach, where products tend to be made out of sight from the consumer.

McDonald's is also trying to demystify the at times confusing Starbucks approach to coffee, replacing sizes such as 'venti' and 'grande' with a simplistic small, medium and large.

In a direct side-swipe at its coffee-focused rival, it is even going so far as to use the difficulties customers often have in pronouncing words like 'latte' in consumer advertising in Kansas City, where one of the trials is taking place.

A McDonald's spokesman told the Daily Telegraph that the push is part of the company's global focus on offering 'great products at great value', suggesting the price point will be somewhat lower than that of Starbucks. The move follows on from a previous roll-out of its coffee products, and is part of a wider re-imaging of many of its stores.

from the Daily Telegraph

D   Reread the article's headline and first three paragraphs and find the prepositions that go with these verbs.

1 stir   2 replace   3 lose   4 focus   5 take

E Match the verbs and prepositions in Exercise D (1–5) with the meanings (a–e).

a) to not get something because someone else gets it instead

b) to compete or fight against someone

c) to give all your attention to a particular thing

d) to take something else's place

e) to deliberately cause problems

F Match the phrasal verbs with *take* (1–5) with the meanings (a–e).

1   be taken aback
2   take off
3   take on
4   take out
5   take over

a) grow rapidly
b) give employment to
c) be surprised
d) gain control of a company
e) arrange (of money)

G Complete the sentences with an appropriate form of *take* and a preposition.

1   We were going to .... five new staff next month, but then the economy crashed.

2   They pretended it was a merger, but it feels like we were ....

3   We were .... when the president announced his resignation.

4   It is very difficult to .... a loan these days.

5   After the new product launch, sales are expected to ....

H Answer the questions.

1   Do you think that McDonald's strategy will be successful?

2   How do you think Starbucks will respond?

LISTENING

The Competition Commission

Rory Taylor

Watch the interview on the **DVD-ROM.**

A ◀)) CD2.36 **Rory Taylor is Media Relations Manager for the UK's Competition Commission. Listen to the first part of the interview and answer the questions.**

1   What does the Competition Commission do?

2   Why are they investigating the ownership of UK airports?

B ◀)) CD2.37 **Listen to the second part and decide whether the statements are true (T) or false (F).**

1   For the Competition Commission, the most important thing is the number of providers in a market.

2   In static markets, there is not much competition.

3   The UK grocery market is dominated by a few companies.

4   The grocery market is not competitive.

C ◀)) CD2.38 **Listen to the third part and complete the extract.**

We found a far more ....[1] market. Er, we found that customers were not ....[2] between the companies, the companies were not ....[3] with each other, erm, and consequently we were finding higher ....[4], less ....[5] and less ....[6].

Passives

- We make passive verb forms with the verb *to be* + the past participle.
  *Starbucks **was started** by Howard Schultz.*

- We often choose a passive structure when we are not interested in who performs an action or it is not necessary to know.
  *Howard Schultz **was awarded** an athletic scholarship to Northern Michigan University.*

- If we want to mention who performs the action, we can use *by*.
  *Howard Schultz **was named** Chief Executive **by** the company's Board.*

- We often use a passive structure to be impersonal or formal (for example, in notices, announcements or reports).
  *It has **been agreed** that the prototype **will be tested** next month.*

- Some verbs can only be used in the active, e.g. *occur, rise, happen, arise, fall, exist, consist (of), depend (on), result (from).*

- Some verbs which often appear in the passive are: *(be) born, situate, design, estimate, base, test, accuse, jail, shoot, bother.*

➡ *Grammar reference page 151*

A **Look at the sentences. Correct the incorrect ones.**

1 The result of the leadership contest was based on the boardroom vote.

2 The leadership contest was depended on the boardroom vote.

3 Where were you when the president was be shot?

4 The CEO has been accused of stealing funds from the pension fund.

5 They are depend on the CEO to show strong leadership.

6 He was jailed for six months.

7 I can't be bothered to finish this report.

8 All the candidates need to be tested.

9 Problems may be occurred after the leadership vote.

10 The CEO's strategy is based on her second book.

11 The President of the company was born in 1962.

12 The audience is consist largely of senior executives.

B **Look at the minutes of a company meeting. Complete the gaps with the appropriate passive form of the verbs in brackets.**

Minutes of the planning meeting

The monthly meeting .... [1] (hold) at 14.00 hrs on Wednesday 15th February. The meeting .... [2] (attend) by the Chief Executive Officer, LP Williams, J Morrison (Sales), SP Thompson (Marketing), LK Tin (Property Management) and SH Ho (Human Resources).

Item 1: Agenda

The CEO stated that although the agenda for the meeting .... [3] (circulate) earlier and that it .... [4] (intend) to deal with routine matters, a slump in sales and a lowering of profits as a result of strong competition meant that the company .... [5] (force) to deal with the crisis now.

Item 2: Reports

The CEO asked for reports from those present. The Sales Manager reported that prices .... [6] (cut). The Marketing Manager confirmed that the advertising budget .... [7] (increase) substantially and that new customer surveys .... [8] (commission) to see how strong competition had affected the company's products. The meeting .... [9] (inform) by the Property Manager that agreement .... [10] (reach) about the sale of 40 of the company's high-street shops and that 20 better-located sites .... [11] (investigate) with a view to creating new outlets. The Head of Human Resources reported that the new redundancy scheme .... [12] (implement) and that so far, 50 long-serving employees .... [13] (consider) for voluntary redundancy.

Negotiating

A 🔊 CD2.39 **An Italian bicycle manufacturer wants to enter the Swedish market, using an agent. The manufacturer and the agent disagree about some terms of their proposed contract. Listen to the discussion between them and answer the questions.**

1 Which of these points did the two sides agree on during the negotiation?

   a) the type of relationship they want   c) payment of commission

   b) who sets prices   d) who pays for promotion

2 Why does the agent want the contract to be longer than two years?

B **Match the direct phrases (1–5) to the more diplomatic versions (a–e).**

1	We must talk about price first.	a) Your price seems rather high.
2	There's no way we can give you any credit.	b) Unfortunately, I can't lower my price.
3	I want a discount.	c) Could you possibly give me a discount?
4	I won't lower my price.	d) I'm afraid we can't give you any credit.
5	Your price is far too high.	e) I think we should talk about price first.

C 🔊 CD2.40 **Listen to and complete the extracts from the negotiation in Exercise A. Then decide whether the speakers are being diplomatic (D) or not diplomatic (ND).**

1 A non-exclusive contract .... for us, too.

2 No, that's .... for us.

3 We know the market conditions .... than you.

4 I .... a rate of 15% on all the revenue you obtain.

5 Fifteen per cent is too low. We .... 20%.

6 We .... with this.

7 How much .... ?

8 We'll .... the commission later.

9 .... , with a new distributor, we prefer a shorter period.

10 It .... at least three years.

D **Role-play the negotiation between a store owner and the manufacturer of Sheen, a hair shampoo for women. Be diplomatic.**

Store owner

- You want to order 50 bottles of Sheen at the quoted price.
- You want a 10% discount.
- You want 60 days' credit.
- You want delivery in two weeks.

Shampoo manufacturer

- You get a bonus if the order is over 100 bottles.
- You don't give a discount for orders of less than 100 bottles.
- You want payment on delivery.
- You can deliver in three weeks.

USEFUL LANGUAGE

DIPLOMATICALLY GIVING BAD NEWS

I'm sorry, we can't agree to that.

I'm afraid your price is rather high.

Unfortunately, we can't deliver any earlier.

To be honest, we'd need credit terms.

USING SPECULATIVE LANGUAGE

It would probably arrive late.

It could be a problem.

It may be difficult to deliver.

We might not be able to do that.

USING A PAST FORM TO EXPRESS DISAPPOINTMENT

We were hoping for ...

We were expecting ...

We were looking for ...

We had in mind ...

fashionhouse

A jewellery retailer wants to expand its range of suppliers. It is keen to negotiate new contracts with exciting producers who will give it excellent value and reliable service.

Background

Fashion House Inc., based in Miami, Florida, owns a chain of stores selling high-class jewellery products. Its best-selling lines are top-of-the-range necklaces, bracelets and earrings, made by overseas manufacturers who have outstanding design capability. Its profit margin on most of these products is at least 80 per cent.

Today is 1 October. The buying department of Fashion House wishes to purchase 5,000 necklaces and bracelets and 3,000 earrings. Delivery of the items, if possible, should be by 15 November, in time for the Christmas buying season. The company is confident of selling 3,000 necklaces and bracelets and 2,000 earrings and the remaining items should sell if prices are competitive and the demand is high. Fashion House has a temporary cashflow problem, so it wishes to pay for the goods as late as possible.

Members of the buying department are now visiting companies in India, Peru and Chile. They are looking for a reliable supplier with whom they can build a long-term relationship. They have contacted three companies who have shown interest in doing business with them.

Supplier 1: Rashid Singh Enterprises (Mumbai, India)

Quantity	Necklaces/bracelets: 2,000 of each item in stock Additional 3,000 necklaces and bracelets should be available by 15 November Earrings: 3,000 available by 30 November
Product features	Original designs by a young Indian selected as 'Designer of the Year' by well-known fashion magazine. Stones available: jade, amber, crystal and marcasite. All chains are silver.
Unit cost (US$)	Necklaces $100–$120; bracelets $80–$100; earrings $40–60
Delivery	No information
Payment	50% deposit when order placed; remainder payable when goods are shipped
Discount	No information
Returned goods	No information
Guarantee	No information

Supplier 2: Pacific Traders (Lima, Peru)

Quantity	All quantities of the products are in stock, but several large orders for important customers must take priority
Product features	Handmade jewellery with semi-precious stones in a variety of colours and designs, reflecting local culture.
Unit cost (US$)	Necklaces $20–$40; bracelets $20–$30; earrings $25–$50.
Delivery	No information
Payment	Pay the full amount as soon as the goods are shipped; no initial payment required.
Discount	No information
Returned goods	No information
Guarantee	No information

Supplier 3: The Artisans Co-operative (Santiago, Chile)

Quantity	Necklaces and earrings: all quantities are in stock and will be available by 15 November. Bracelets: only 1,000 available by 15 November as orders from important customers must be serviced first.
Product features	Beautiful, elegant jewellery made from precious stones Vibrant colours, high standard of craftsmanship
Unit cost (US$)	Necklaces $60–$70; bracelets $40–$60; earrings $60–$90
Delivery	No information
Payment	40% deposit when order placed; remainder to be paid after 30 days on receipt of the company's invoice
Discount	No information
Returned goods	No information
Guarantee	No information

Task

1 Read the information about each supplier. Some information is missing. Which supplier looks the most attractive at this stage? What problems, if any, could there be with each supplier?

2 Work in groups of three buyers and three suppliers.

Buyers 1–3: Turn to page 139.
Supplier 1: Turn to page 143.
Supplier 2: Turn to page 145.
Supplier 3: Turn to page 145.

3 Each buyer meets *one* of the suppliers. Find out the missing information concerning delivery, discount, returned goods and guarantees. Negotiate to get the best terms for your company.

4 Buyers: meet and discuss how the negotiation went. Decide which supplier to use.

Suppliers: meet and discuss how the negotiation went. What are you happy and unhappy about? What would you do differently next time?

5 Buyers: announce your decision and, diplomatically, explain why you rejected the suppliers who were not chosen.

Suppliers: say how you would negotiate differently next time.

Writing

Write an e-mail to the person you were negotiating with confirming the details of your negotiation and any outstanding points to be agreed.

➡ *Writing file* page 127

Watch the Case study commentary on the DVD-ROM.

4 Communication styles

A In groups, answer the questions.

1 How close do you like to be when speaking with a business colleague?
2 How much eye contact are you comfortable with?
3 Are you comfortable with long periods of silence?
4 How do you feel about interruptions?

B ◀)) CD2.41 Listen to a short talk at the beginning of a workshop on communication styles and cultural awareness. Complete the table with the appropriate cultures.

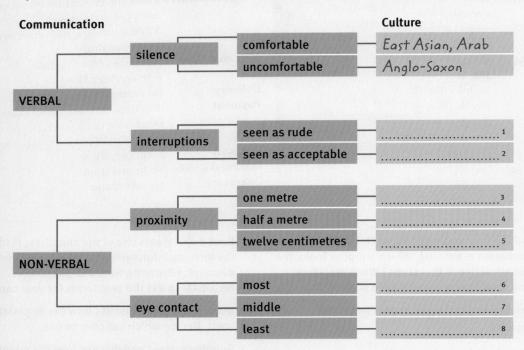

Communication

Culture

VERBAL
- silence
  - comfortable — *East Asian, Arab*
  - uncomfortable — *Anglo-Saxon*
- interruptions
  - seen as rude — 1
  - seen as acceptable — 2

NON-VERBAL
- proximity
  - one metre — 3
  - half a metre — 4
  - twelve centimetres — 5
- eye contact
  - most — 6
  - middle — 7
  - least — 8

Do you agree with the information presented?

C Look at the audio script on page 165 and list the sentence(s) which:

1 use rhetorical questions to get the audience's attention
2 give the topic of the talk
3 describe the speaker's expertise
4 outline what the audience will gain from the talk
5 emphasise that something is important
6 outline the structure of the talk
7 ask the audience a question.

D In groups, discuss some of the things that would be seen as rude in your culture and also any things that you know would be rude in other cultures.

Task

Prepare a short presentation to a group of businesspeople who wish to do business in your country, but who do not know much about your culture, customs and etiquette. Choose four topics from the list below to talk about in your presentation.

- Proximity
- Interruptions
- Eye contact
- Greetings
- Saying goodbye

- Gift giving
- Dining etiquette
- Punctuality
- Dress etiquette
- Business cards

Use the following structure for your talk:

- gain the audience's attention at the beginning
- state the topic of the short talk
- describe your expertise
- state what the audience will gain from the talk
- outline the structure of the talk
- give the main body of the talk
- ask a question at some point to keep the audience involved.

Look at the audio script on page 165 for help with the language of how to organise your presentation. Give your presentation to other members of the group. Discuss which was the most interesting presentation and why.

10 Ethics

1 Match the words from column A to those from column B to make word partnerships.

A	B
money	testing
sex	laundering
animal	goods
counterfeit	fixing
price	discrimination

2 Choose the correct word partnership from Exercise 1 to complete the sentences.

1 A few years ago, British Airways and Korean Air were each fined $300m by the US Justice Department for their roles in separate .... conspiracies in both their cargo and passenger operations.

2 According to a survey, 91% of doctors believe .... is important to medical progress.

3 An anti-............ directive was passed to prevent the proceeds of organised crime circulating through the financial system.

4 In 2008, it was estimated that $135bn of .... were sold online.

5 Banks were recently accused of ...., as apparently female staff are often paid 40% less than their male counterparts.

Choose the correct tenses to complete the text.

Two years ago, we had a lot of trouble with one of our new shampoos. It was selling really well, but then one day dozens of customers ....[1] (*started / had started*) phoning and complaining that the shampoo was burning their scalp. The newspapers ....[2] (*heard / were hearing*) that one of our products ....[3] (*caused / was causing*) allergies nationwide, and of course they started calling us too to ask what we ....[4] (*did / were doing*) about this problem.

Honestly, we didn't understand what ....[5] (*happened / was happening*). We are a responsible company and, as you would expect, we ....[6] (*were testing / had tested*) the shampoo for months before launching it, and there had been no bad reaction to it whatsoever. We had invested a lot of money in the testing and marketing and now we ....[7] (*were losing / had lost*) money because of bad publicity. We ....[8] (*realised / had realised*) that the growing number of complaints was harming our image, so we ....[9] (*decided / had decided*) to recall the shampoo.

Read the e-mail on the opposite page. In each line (1–6), there is one wrong word. Find them and correct them.

Dear Mr Pattison,

1 Please find attached the expenses claim form that you send to our Accounts Department last
2 week. I was afraid we cannot process it as it is, because it is incomplete.

3 Firstly, we need to know the names of the customers that you taken for lunch on May 12, as
4 well as the name of the restaurant which you took them. We also need to know the reason for
5 the £60 that you entering under 'sundry expenses'. Finally, we would like to remind you that all
6 expenses had to be authorised by your manager.

Best wishes,

Lisa Ristic
Accounts

11 Leadership

VOCABULARY

1 Complete the keyword in the statements about leadership qualities.

1 Someone who is **a p p** _ _ _ _ _ _ _ _ _ is friendly and easy to talk to.

2 An _ **n c** _ _ _ _ _ _ **i n g** person gives you confidence or hope.

3 Someone who is _ _ _ _ **l i s** _ _ _ believes firmly in something which is good but probably impossible to achieve.

4 If you describe people as _ _ **f f** _ _ _ **n t,** you mean that they do not have much confidence in themselves.

5 _ _ **t h** _ _ _ **s** people are determined to get what they want and do not care if they hurt other people.

6 Someone who is _ _ _ _ **e r v** _ _ _ _ _ is unwilling to accept changes and new ideas.

2 Write the phrasal verb which can form word partnerships with all the nouns and noun phrases in each line.

1 to .... the job / the standards / someone's expectations

2 to .... your homework / your keys when you leave the hotel / your resignation

3 to .... extra work / responsibility for something

4 to .... a hard time / heavy criticism

5 to .... issues / enquiries / complaints / problems

6 to .... an argument / a plan / a suggestion / a proposal

RELATIVE CLAUSES

Complete the sentences with a relative clause using the information in the box.

He came from Brazil.

It organised business travel for top executives.

It was on my desk this morning.

~~Li had recommended a workshop to us.~~

She is fluent in four languages.

We had invited some speakers.

We had put forward some proposals.

You are going to attend a talk.

1   We went to the workshop *that Li had recommended to us*.

2   Most of the proposals .... were eventually accepted.

3   The firm, ..., went bankrupt last month.

4   What's the title of the talk .... ?

5   Mrs Martens, ..., heads our translation service.

6   Two of the speakers .... were unable to come.

7   My favourite manager was a young man ....

8   Where is the report .... ?

12 Competition

Complete the idioms in the sentences with the words in the box.

ball	field	game	goalposts	horse	neck	seat

1   Dave's views on management may have seemed practical and attractive 20 years ago, but now he's just flogging a dead .... None of his ideas could possibly be put into practice.

2   Given our country's industrial policy and the new global economic environment, we should clear unreasonable hurdles and provide a level playing .... to all businesses, regardless of their size and nationality.

3   Smaller countries became frustrated, believing that the big powers kept moving the .... and failed to outline fixed rules that all should play by.

4   The creativity of our R&D people has enabled our company to stay ahead of the .... in this highly competitive market.

5   The two rival companies were running neck and .... in the push to achieve national leadership through local dominance.

6   Unprecedented state involvement in the car industry has put governments in America, Germany and elsewhere in the driving .... in deciding their carmakers' fate.

7   We are a French company, but our goal is to go international. However, we don't want to go global too early. It's extremely important for us to keep our eye on the .... in France.

1   **Complete the second sentence in each pair with a passive form so that it means the same as the first.**

1   Someone tests all our new products in our laboratory.

    All our new products *are tested* in our laboratory.

2   Every member of staff reads our weekly newsletter.

    Our weekly newsletter .... by every member of staff.

3   A company driver will meet the conference delegates at the airport.

    The conference delegates .... at the airport by a company driver.

4   We must review our health and safety regulations as soon as possible.

    Our health and safety regulations .... as soon as possible.

5   They have closed three of their subsidiaries over the last year.

    Three of their subsidiaries .... over the last year.

6   We are currently developing a new sugar-free soft drink.

    A new sugar-free soft drink .... currently ....

2 Complete the sentences with the appropriate passive form of the verbs in the box.

accuse	discuss	estimate	found	know	own	supply	sell

1 A number of multinational enterprises taking advantage of lower wages and labour standards abroad .... recently .... of practising unfair competition.

2 Arnontov's last painting, Crescendo, ... at auction tomorrow. Its value .... at $1m–$1.5m.

3 Currently seven of the UK's airports .... by a company called the British Airports Authority.

4 Google .... by Larry Page and Sergey Brin in 1998.

5 Liquid petroleum gas, which .... also .... as propane, is essentially for domestic users who .... not .... with energy through pipes, for example because they live in remote areas.

6 There are rumours of a takeover. Apparently, the matter .... currently .... at the highest levels.

WRITING

1 Match the sentence halves.

1 Whether we send you replacements or credit the amount to your account

2 This is just to confirm the main points

3 The goods will be shipped to you

4 Secondly, we agreed that you would receive

5 However, the deluxe items will not be sent until mid-May,

6 Finally, it was also agreed that faulty or damaged goods

a) a trade discount of 5% off list prices.

b) may be returned within one month.

c) as they are not available from stock at present.

d) by sea immediately on receipt of order.

e) that we agreed on during our negotiation last Monday.

f) will then be negotiated on a case-by-case basis.

2 Put the sentences in Exercise 1 in the correct order to form a paragraph.

Cultures: Communication styles

1 Put the words in the correct order to make questions about communication styles.

1 How / like to be / a business colleague / you / speaking with / when / close / do / ?

2 How / eye contact / with / comfortable / much / are you / ?

3 How / prolonged periods / comfortable / are / of silence / you with / ?

4 How / do / interrupted / you / being / feel about / ?

2 Plan a short presentation in which you explain how people in your culture feel about the four aspects of verbal and non-verbal communication mentioned in Exercise 1.

Objectives

Speaking

- Can respond to follow-up questions at a presentation using fixed expressions.
- Can ask for confirmation of understanding during a live discussion or presentation.

Listening

- Can extract the key details from a presentation if delivered slowly and clearly.
- Can follow most of a clearly structured presentation within their own field.

Lesson deliverable

To plan, prepare and give a presentation about a range of company issues and deal with audience questions.

Performance review

To review your own progress and performance against the lesson objectives at the end of the lesson.

Ⓐ SPEAKING 1

1 **What, in your experience, makes an effective presentation and why?**

2 **Work in pairs. Discuss and complete the sentences.**

  1 The end of a presentation is important because ...

  2 At the end of a presentation, the presenter should ...

Ⓑ LISTENING 1

1 ◀)) **BSA4.1.16 Listen to the end of a presentation by a production manager. What is the topic of the presentation?**

2 ◀)) **BSA4.1.16 Listen again and number the stages in the order you hear them (1–5).**

  a) Thank the audience. ☐

  b) Signal the end. ☐

  c) Invite questions. ☐

  d) Summarise the main points. ☐

  e) Give a conclusion. ☐

3 **Complete the descriptions with *summary* or *conclusion*. Are both a summary and a conclusion necessary in a presentation?**

1 A .... briefly repeats the key points of a presentation as a reminder to the audience. Depending on how long the presentation is, it can be a useful reminder, but may not always be necessary.

2 A strong .... is always good practice. This includes a 'call to action' or 'final remarks' which indicate clearly what you want the audience to know or do.

Ⓒ SPEAKING 2

In your opinion are the comments below true (T) or false (F)? Discuss your opinions in pairs.

1 The question and answer section is the most stressful part of any presentation.

2 You should never admit you don't know the answer to a question.

3 It's polite to answer all the questions people ask, including irrelevant ones.

4 It's much better to leave questions until the end.

Ⓓ LISTENING 2

1 ◀)) **BSA4.1.17 Listen to the question and answer session. Tick what happens.**

  1 The presenter doesn't know the answer. ☐

  2 He doesn't want to answer a question. ☐

  3 He answered a similar question earlier. ☐

  4 He doesn't hear a question. ☐

  5 He thinks the question is not relevant. ☐

  6 He thinks the answer would be too long. ☐

2 ◀)) **BSA4.1.18 Look at six strategies for answering questions. Then listen and complete the phrases. Have you ever used any of these strategies?**

1 Listen carefully to the question and paraphrase it if necessary to check understanding.
- ᵃSo, your .... how many ... Is .... ?

2 Ask the speaker to repeat the question if you didn't hear or understand it.
- *Do you mean ...?*
- ᵇ............, I didn't .... Could............ ?

3 Show you value the question.
- *I'm glad you asked me that question.*
- ᶜ............ question.

4 Show sympathy with the speaker if appropriate.
- ᵈ............ concerns.
- ᵉI know ....
- ᶠ............ point.

5 Check you answered the question fully and clearly.
- ᵍHave I .... ?
- ʰDoes .... ?

6 Politely avoid answering a question.
- ⁱ............ to answer that.

3 Why do you think the speaker repeats his conclusion after the question and answer session?

E SPEAKING 3

1 Work in pairs. Student A: complete the sentences in box A. Student B: complete the sentences in Box B.

A	B
The best thing about remote working is …	The best location for a company's offices is … because …
… is the worst day for meetings because …	The ideal working hours are …
If I had to entertain visitors at work, I would …	In five years' time I would like to …

2 Take turns to read out your sentences. Your partner asks you one question about each of your sentences. Use phrases from Exercise D2 when you answer the questions.

Task

Pre-task: Brainstorm

Work in groups and brainstorm ideas.

1 Why would a company relocate from a city centre office to the city outskirts?
2 Why would a company want to replace face-to-face courses with online training?
3 Why would a company want to ban remote working?

Part 1: Preparation

Your company has decided to introduce the three ideas above. Prepare a 3–5 minute presentation to staff about one of the changes.

1 **Work in pairs. Read your role cards.**

Students A and B: Turn to page ix.
Students C and D: Turn to page xiii.
Students E and F: Turn to page xv.

2 Prepare your presentation. Think about these points.

Structure
Remember to include an introduction, a main body, an ending and a question and answer session.

Techniques and language
Organise the information in your ending:
- Signal the end.
- Summarise the main points.
- Give a conclusion.
- Thank the audience and invite questions.
- Try to anticipate the questions you may be asked.

Part 2

Give your presentation.

Presenters: Use the guidance in Part 1.
Audience: Make notes. Do you think staff will support the proposals? Why? / Why not?

F PEER REVIEW

Think about another presentation. Complete the sentences to give feedback.

1 You included these items at the end of your presentation: …

2 You used these techniques in the question and answer session: …

3 What I liked about your conclusion was …

4 One suggestion for improving your presentation is …

G SELF-ASSESSMENT

Look back at the lesson objectives and answer the questions.

1 What techniques did you use to respond to follow-up questions? To ask for confirmation of understanding?

2 What do you think you did well? What would you like to do better next time?

H PROFESSIONAL DEVELOPMENT AND PERFORMANCE GOALS

Write three sentences about ways you will improve your question and answer strategies in the future.

Interviews

Objectives

Speaking

- Can maintain professional etiquette in conversation using simple phrases and fixed expressions.
- Can provide a basic description of professional goals.

Listening

Can understand information about a job role presented during a job interview.

Lesson deliverable

To prepare and participate in an appraisal interview.

Performance review

To review your own progress and performance against the lesson objectives at the end of the lesson.

A SPEAKING 1

Work in pairs. Discuss the questions.

1 What are the main tasks in your job?

2 What have you done well this year?

3 What have been the main difficulties?

4 How could you improve your future performance?

B READING 1

1 Read the advert. What is an appraisal?

Appraisals are a simple tool to help employees do one thing: identify lessons learnt. Often, self-evaluation focuses on what went wrong in a situation, but successful individuals focus on what went right first. Visit my blog to see the five things you should do in every appraisal to get the best from your team.

Bob Hogg, Getting it right every time

2 Discuss what you think is important in a good appraisal.

C LISTENING

1 🔊 BSA4.2.19 Erin Conners works as the manager of strategic planning for a large American kitchen suppliers company. She is attending her annual appraisal meeting. Listen to the conversation and write the topics in the correct column in the table. Some topics may go in more than one column.

1 improving the range of products on offer

2 making changes to the way products are delivered

3 increasing sales

4 working relations with the delivery staff

5 one employee's performance

Achievements	Challenges	Objectives for next year

2 🔊 BSA4.2.20 Listen to three extracts from the conversation and complete the sentences. Notice how Erin gives bad news and discusses difficulties diplomatically.

1 We .... that to translate into increased sales by the end of the year. It .... so far, but I'm sure we'll see results next year.

2 With the new delivery system? Well, ..., the staff in the delivery room were against the changes from the start. I .... that they would cooperate more with this project once it was up and running, but they were very critical, and that didn't really help.

3 I have one member of my team, Jack, who's not really pulling his weight. I'm .... his appearance is sloppy and his social skills are quite poor.

D SPEAKING 2

Work in pairs. Role-play part of an appraisal interview. Use the language you have looked at to talk about problems and difficulties diplomatically and remember to describe your goals for the future.

Student A: Turn to page vi.   Student B: Turn to page viii.

Task

Pre-task: Research

It is time for your company's annual appraisal interviews. Turn to page xiv. Work in pairs and choose Scenario 1 or 2. Decide who is the appraiser and who is the employee. Read about your role and make notes.

Part 1: Preparation

Prepare for your appraisal interview. Think about the following points.

Employee
- your main tasks this year
- the things you have done well this year
- the things that have been difficult
- your objectives for the next year

Appraiser
- questions you want to ask the employee
- successes that you would like to be repeated
- areas that you would like the employee to improve on and how you can help them
- objectives for that employee in the next year

Part 2: Interview

1 Hold your interviews using the language you have learnt.

2 At the end of the interview, think about the points in the table in E below and make notes.

E PEER REVIEW

Use your notes from Part 2 of the Task and give feedback to your partner.

	Good points	One thing to change
the employee's answers to questions		
the employee's/appraiser's ability to understand the background information about a job or role		
the employee's/appraiser's ability to maintain professional etiquette		
the employee's description of their professional goals		

F SELF-ASSESSMENT

Write 50–80 words to assess your performance in the interview. Think about these points.

- your role in answering the questions
- the feedback from the appraisal interview
- the lesson objectives – Did you do well?
- what you think you need to do to get better

G PROFESSIONAL DEVELOPMENT AND PERFORMANCE GOALS

Think about the job would you like to do next and answer the questions.

1 What can you highlight in your professional profile?

2 What areas would you like to move into in future? What skills will that job require?

A16

Writing file

Letters

FAR EASTERN AIRWAYS COMPANY LIMITED

Regent House, 5th Floor
12/16 Haymarket London W1V 5BX
Administration: 020 7285 9981
Reservations: 020 7564 0930
Fax: 020 7285 9984

15 February 2011

Mr Roberto García
Universal Imports
28 Whitechapel Court
London
E10 7NB

Dear Mr García

Re: Roxanna Garbey

Roxanna Garbey has been accepted for a position as Passenger Service Agent with Far Eastern Airways at Gatwick Airport.

In order for Roxanna to work at Gatwick, she must have a special pass which would permit her to visit high-security areas. She has given your name as a reference.

I would appreciate it if you could complete the enclosed form and return it to us as quickly as possible. She is due to start work with us on 15 March, but can only do so after we receive your reference.

Thank you for your cooperation. I enclose a stamped addressed envelope.

Yours sincerely

J P Dent

J. P. Dent
Personnel Manager

Press releases

The aim of a press release is to draw a forthcoming event to the attention of the people who choose what is reported in the media. For commercial events like product launches, public relations agencies are often used to ensure good coverage in the relevant sections of the media.

Note that it's important to provide a contact name and address for further information.

Press release

For:	Business editors, national press; motoring press
Release date:	26 October
Subject:	Revolutionary new car to be unveiled at Motor Show

After weeks of rumour and speculation, ITS will unveil their revolutionary new concept car at the Tokyo Motor Show on 3 November. The vehicle requires very small amounts of petrol and instead uses a combination of solar energy and hydrogen to power it. Massive public interest is expected in this vehicle of the future.

For more information, contact:
Sarah Wells, High Profile Communications
sarah@hpc-centre.com

E-mails

Be careful to type in all e-mail addresses accurately.

Bcc means 'blind copy' (a copy will be sent to this person, but other people will not know this).

To:	tom.hunt@promoworld.com
From:	Harry King
Cc:	mary.fowler@audiovision.com
Bcc:	claudia.stahnke@audiovision.com
Subject:	Friday's meeting

Tom

Just to confirm that we will be able to attend the meeting next Friday. I'll be with our Sales Director, Mary Fowler.

Harry

To:	John Waters (John.Waters@sitco.com)
From:	Peter Lewis
Subject:	Extension of trading agreement

This style of e-mail is similar to a standard business letter. The ending can be the less formal *Best wishes* or *Best regards* or the more formal *Yours sincerely*, depending on how well the writer knows the recipient.

Dear Mr Waters

It was very good to see you again at our meeting in Paris on 16 July. I hope you had a safe journey home afterwards.

We agreed that your company will continue to represent us and to promote the full range of our services throughout Europe, the Middle East and North Africa for three years, with effect from 1 August. During this period, we expect to see an increase of at least 15% in the value of business we do in this region.

Full details of the payment we will make and the expenses we will cover are included in the attached agreement. Can you please check this and, if all is in order, sign and return one copy of the agreement to me.

We look forward to continuing to develop our business in the region in association with yourselves.

Best wishes
Peter Lewis
Managing Director
Mesnik Professional Services
397 City Lane
London EC2 3RW

Faxes

Information transmitted by fax may be presented in various formats, for example in letter, memo or note form.

Faxes may contain the following headings:
To / From / Date / Subject / No. of pages / Fax numbers

The style of a fax message may be formal, informal or neutral, depending on the subject and recipient.

FAX — Falcon Hotels

TO	Alice Wong
Fax No	00 852 7514329
FROM	Zofia Nadstoga
	Reservations Dept. Falcon Hotels
Fax No	00 (0)20 7945 2647
Date	5 July
No of pages	(including this) 1

Dear Ms Wong

This is to confirm your booking for a single room from 20 July to 27 July inclusive, at a rate of £150.00 per night (excluding sales tax).

As requested, we will hold your room until midnight on the day of your arrival.

We look forward to meeting you shortly.

Yours sincerely

Zofia Nadstoga

Zofia Nadstoga

Agendas

Always put the title, date, time and venue (place).

Larger meetings and committee meetings may also include the following:
a) Apologies for absence
b) Matters arising from last meeting
c) Correspondence
d) Date of next meeting

AOB means 'any other business'. This is for other relevant issues that were not included in the agenda.

Management meeting
AGENDA

Date: 1 March
Time: 14.00
Venue: Room 23M, Shaw House

1   Complaints about reception staff
2   New brochure
3   Price list for next year
4   New product presentation
5   AOB

Action minutes

For most business meetings, action minutes are more useful than full minutes.

Action minutes are intended to make sure that decisions of the meeting are understood and carried out.

There is a brief summary of the discussion for each item on the agenda.

The initials of the person responsible for carrying out any action required are given in the margin, along with any deadline.

Minutes of the management meeting

Date	1 March
Venue	Room 23M, Shaw House
Present	Chris Glover, Bill Brace, Gill Winstanley, Iwona Pawlowska, Gareth Massey

	Action	By
1 Guidelines for reception staff		
Following recent complaints about the attitude and professionalism of the reception staff, we all agreed that it is essential to produce a set of written guidelines.	IP	8 March
The Human Resources Department will also arrange additional customer service training to take place over the next two months.	IP	
2 New brochure		
The Marketing Department is speaking to all senior managers about this on an individual basis. A draft brochure will be circulated so that it can be approved and sent to the printers by 15 March to be ready for next month's trade fair.	BB	5 March
3 Price list		
We agreed that our new prices this year will be contained in a separate booklet, rather than as part of the New Product Brochure. An updated list is being compiled.	BB	15 March

Next meeting:	18 March, 11.00 a.m.
Venue:	To be confirmed

An action plan focuses on key events and is usually based on a timetable. Sentences are short, and verbs are usually imperatives (*complete*, *agree*, etc.).

Action plan

We plan to launch the new range in November. The following stages are all critical to the success of the launch.

January
Complete test marketing and report back findings to Research and Development.

April
Agree final specifications with manufacturers.
Book advertising space with media agency.

May, June
Manufacturing

July, August
Distribution of stock to key wholesalers

September, October
Advertising campaign, including media interviews and features

November
Launch at Milan Trade Fair

Reports

A report should be well organised, with information in a logical order. There is no set layout for a report. It will depend on:

a) the type of report

b) the company style.

The format used here is suitable for formal reports:

- title
- executive summary
- introduction
- findings
- conclusion
- recommendations

Business Software plc
Product report

The *executive summary* is a summary of the main points and conclusion of the report. It gives the reader a quick overview of the total situation.

Executive summary

We have been contacted by Lenz AG, a German manufacturer of mobile telephones, and asked about the possibility of a co-operation agreement. We would adapt our business software for use in their products. Tests show that their product is a very good one and popular with our target market.

The *introduction* shows the points that will be looked at.

Introduction

This report will look at:

- the hardware manufacturer and their equipment
- software that could be used on their mobile phones
- the advantages of working together
- recommendations for action.

The *findings* are the facts discovered.

Findings

1 Lenz has been developing cheap, small-scale electronic devices for 35 years. In the last five years, they have focused on more expensive mobile phones for businesspeople. These have been very successful. One in four mobile phones for the business market is a Lenz.

2 Our new Executive Organiser software has a lot of attractive features for the travelling businessperson (e.g. address book, e-mail, video and voice recorder, street-finder function, etc.).

3 Market research shows that there is a lot of interest in our products being used on machines apart from computers.

The *conclusion* is what you think about the facts and how you interpret them.

Conclusion

The two companies have products which fit well together.

Recommendations are practical suggestions to deal with the situation and ideas for making sure future activities run more easily.

Recommendation

We should have a meeting with representatives from Lenz as soon as possible to discuss a joint venture between our companies, with the aim of putting our software onto their mobile phones.

Tracy Cruickshank

Research and Development Director

19 October

Summaries

When you summarise something, you express the most important facts or points about something in a short and clear form.

Writing a summary involves:

- selecting the most important ideas or facts from a text
- rewriting those ideas/facts in a short, concise form, using your own language
- producing a text which is shorter than the original – usually at least half the number of words.

Here is an example of an original text and two sample summaries.

Hispanics are more influenced by advertising than other US consumers, suggesting that the growth of the Spanish-speaking population could prove beneficial to big corporate sponsors, according to two studies.

A Nielsen Media Research study released on Wednesday found that Spanish-language television viewers pay more attention to commercials and are more likely to base their purchasing decisions on advertisements than other US consumers. The report was issued after Euro RSCG, the marketing communication agency, released a study that showed Hispanics are more aware of brand names than other US consumers.

Taken together, the reports suggest that growing corporate interest in Hispanic marketing might involve factors that go beyond the mere size of the Spanish-speaking population. The US Hispanic population is estimated at about 39m.

The studies also suggest that Hispanic consumers offer big companies the chance to use the kinds of sales pitches that worked with US consumers in decades past, but which are now less popular with advertising-weary viewers.

Fifty-two per cent of Hispanics say they frequently get information for making purchase decisions from watching TV commercials in Spanish, compared with 7 per cent of non-Hispanics watching English-language television.

This summary is effective because:

- it contains the key ideas from the original text
- the language used to express the key ideas is different from the original
- the new text is much shorter in length.

Recent research has found that Spanish TV viewers are very influenced by television commercials when they buy products, and they also know more about brands than other people in the United States.

Another finding of the research was that conventional methods of advertising appeal to Spanish-speaking people, even though other viewers are tired of them. Some interesting statistics: 52% of Hispanics depend on TV commercials for information about what to buy, whereas only 7% of non-Hispanics do.

(96 words)

Sometimes a summary can be expressed in a series of short numbered statements.

1 The Spanish-speaking population in the United States is 39m. Research has been carried out into this group's buying habits. Spanish TV viewers are very influenced by television commercials when buying products.

2 They know more about brands than other consumers.

3 Spanish-speaking people respond to conventional methods of advertising, but other consumers do not.

4 52% of Hispanics use television commercials to help them choose products. Only 7% of non-Hispanics do so.

Notices

Notices are used to inform people about changes of plan, instructions or warnings.

A notice needs a clear heading.

Information must be presented in a clear, concise form.

The tone of notices is usually rather formal and impersonal.

It must have the name and position of the person who wrote it and the date.

AURIC BANK
CUSTOMER NOTICE

This branch will be closed until 10.30 a.m. on Tuesday 7 November for staff training.

We apologise in advance for any inconvenience caused.

Antonia Valdes
Branch Manager
2 November

The social-cultural game

1 You have forgotten the name of the person you are talking to. Find out his/her name politely.

2 Which of the following cultures are generally comfortable with interruptions?
a) Latin American
b) Asian
c) north American
d) north European

6 You are in a restaurant with an important client. The bill arrives, and you realise you have left your wallet/purse in the office

7 In which country is it quite normal to begin presenting your product straight away?
a) Qatar
b) the US
c) Venezuela
d) Kuwait

8 You are having dinner with a foreign colleague in his/her country. The food is unfamiliar to you, and you do not know what to choose.

12 Which country is likely to have the most informal meetings?
a) Italy
b) Germany
c) the UK
d) the US

13 At a conference, you meet someone you think you've met before.

14 Invite someone out to dinner.

18 You are in a restaurant with a guest. His/Her food arrives before yours. You want him/her to start eating.

19 Give your e-mail address.

20 In which country is chewing gum forbidden by law?
a) Iran
b) Iraq
c) Indonesia
d) Singapore

24 Give directions from your office to the closest station or airport.

25 In which country is it illegal to drink anything alcoholic and drive?
a) Sweden
b) France
c) the UK
d) the USA

26 Recommend a restaurant to a client.

30 In which country is it common to go out to eat after 10 p.m.?
a) the UK
b) Sweden
c) Japan
d) Spain

31 You arrive for an appointment. Introduce yourself to the person at the reception desk.

32 You spent a very pleasant evening with a client. Thank him/her.

How to play

1 Decide how many players per board (six maximum).
2 Place counters on **WHAT DO YOU SAY?**. The first player to throw a six begins.
3 Take turns to throw the die. When you land on a square, decide what you would say in that situation or answer the relevant question.
4 If the other players do not accept what you say, you must go back to the square you have just come from.
5 The winner is the player who reaches FINISH! first.

3 You are at a party. You want to get away from someone who will not stop talking.

4 You want to pay for the drinks which have just been ordered.

5 You should not point the sole of your foot towards your hosts. Which area does this refer to?
a) Arab world
b) West Indies
c) Scandinavia
d) Australia

9 You are at a cocktail party and the host/hostess has just handed you a glass of champagne. You do not drink alcohol.

10 In which country would it be a grave insult to touch someone on the head?
a) Thailand
b) Japan
c) Pakistan
d) Iraq

11 You have been invited to your colleague's house for dinner. He/She telephones you to ask if there is anything you don't eat.

15 In which country is it quite likely that you will be asked to sing a song?
a) Italy
b) Austria
c) Japan
d) Germany

16 You don't hear the name of the person you have just been introduced to.

17 A visitor wants advice on how to spend an evening in your town.

21 Talk about today's weather.

22 You are on the phone. Describe yourself to someone you are going to meet at the airport, so he/she can recognise you.

23 In which country is it not essential to arrive at business meetings on time?
a) Germany
b) South Korea
c) Vietnam
d) France

27 You are on a plane. Introduce yourself to the person sitting next to you.

28 In which country should you always use your right hand to hold a business card?
a) China
b) Japan
c) India
d) the UK

29 You are having a small dinner party. Introduce two of your friends to each other.

33 In which country should you greet everyone when entering a lift?
a) the UK
b) Japan
c) China
d) Saudi Arabia

34 You meet a business contact at the station. Offer to carry some of his/her luggage.

Finish

Activity file

1 Brands, Starting up, Exercise A, page 6

	INTERBRAND LIST 1999		INTERBRAND LIST 2007
1	Coca-Cola	1	Coca-Cola
2	Microsoft	2	Microsoft
3	IBM	3	IBM
4	General Electric	4	General Electric
5	Ford	5	Nokia
6	Disney	6	Toyota
7	Intel	7	Intel
8	McDonald's	8	McDonald's
9	AT&T	9	Disney
10	Marlboro	10	Mercedes-Benz

1 Brands, Skills, Exercise D, page 11

Student A

In your opinion, the Cecile products have sales potential, but the marketing strategy is wrong. You want:

- a new brand name. 'Cecile' does not suit this beautiful jewellery for sophisticated women.

- a new logo. The present logo (three wavy lines) is boring.

- a much wider range of products and designs – at present there are only five in the collection.

- a better slogan. 'Only for you' has not been successful.

- more colours.

2 Travel, Reading, Exercise B, page 16

FT

Business travel on a budget

by Roger Bray

The mere existence of business class and 'business hotels' tends to convey the impression that anyone travelling in connection with work has cash to spend. But this is untrue. UK-based John Cox, who runs his own publishing consultancy, is a perfect example: 'I mainly fly on Star Alliance carriers and do between 80,000 and 100,000 miles a year, mostly across the Atlantic with United. I always pay the lowest economy fare I can find, but, of course, I earn frequent-flyer points to get upgrades. Sometimes I even go on a Saturday to get the lowest fare.'

'I recently flew from London to Los Angeles, San Francisco and Washington and back – and saved £400 by travelling out on a Saturday rather than Sunday.'

For simple trips – three days in New York, for example – he suggests seeking a city break from a tour operator, which might incorporate a fare for midweek flights at the same sort of level otherwise available to passengers flying on Saturdays.

It is also possible to cut the air-ticket bill by booking in advance and avoiding peak travel. A recent study published by BTI UK showed companies could make the greatest savings by booking flights three to four weeks in advance. Mr Cox says he tends to use taxis only when burdened with heavy luggage. 'I'm probably the world's greatest customer of public transport. A taxi to or from JFK, for example, costs about $60 with a tip. On the AirTrain and subway, it's only $7. Not long ago, I went to Milan for the first time in 20 years, flew to Linate rather than Malpensa because it's much closer to the city, inquired at the airport about transport and took a bus which cost me a couple of euros.' Regarding hotels, Mr Cox says, 'I want a certain level of service, Internet access – preferably wireless – and a good-class laundry service.' High-speed, in-room Internet access is becoming available further and further down the price scale. In the UK, the 470 properties under the Premier Travel Inn brand have high-speed connections in all rooms.

Finally, remember that hotel groups have shifted to 'dynamic pricing', which is jargon for doing what airlines do: altering rates to reflect demand. Try to bear in mind that in city-centre hotels, Tuesday and Wednesday nights are generally the most popular for business travellers.

2 Travel, Case study, page 20

Head of Travel, NeoTech

You want to arrange a suitable time for a meeting with the Account Manger of BTS. Here is your diary for the week.

	Morning	Afternoon
Monday	All day at exhibition	
Tuesday	Free	Appointment at dentist 2 p.m.
Wednesday	Meeting	Free after 1 p.m.
Thursday	Training session all day and early evening	
Friday	Correspondence + interviews	Free after 2 p.m.

4 Organisation, Skills, Exercise F, page 41

Students A and B

Student A: You are attending the conference with your boss (Student B).

Student B: You are attending the conference with a junior colleague (Student A).

1   Decide together on the following:

- company name
- activity / area of business
- department you work for
- recent activities

2   Introduce yourselves to the people at the conference. Find out about them.
   Note: you both enjoy talking about your department

4 Organisation, Case study, page 43

Vice-President

You chair the meeting. You have not finally decided on the relocation. Listen to the opinions, then make up your mind. You have the following thoughts at present. Add any other points you can think of.

- You can understand that many staff may not want to leave a beautiful city where they have friends and relatives.
- Some staff will not be able to move because they are caring for elderly relatives.
- Overseas visitors would probably prefer to visit the Head Office in Paris, even though hotels there would be more expensive than in the Beauchamp region.

But ...

- The new purpose-built building will help to create a more loyal, less mobile workforce.
- The working environment in the new building will be good for communication and staff relations.
- Buying land for further expansion will not be expensive in the new location.
- Rising rental costs in Paris will make it difficult for InStep to expand in the city.

Business in brief

It was a bad day for the London market. Following disappointing results from FedEx in the US and fears of a credit crunch, the FTSE
5 100 fell 125 points or 1.8 per cent to 5,756.9, while the FTSE 250 fell 189.1 points or 1.9 per cent to 9,538. Only eight blue-chip stocks managed to make gains. The best
10 was Smith & Nephew. Shares in the medical devices group rose 2.9 per cent to 599p after UBS upgraded the stock to a 'buy' recommendation. S&N was also
15 supported by rumours of a bid approach from a Japanese company.

On the other hand, British Airways, down 5.2 per cent to 225^1/$_4$p, fell even further after Morgan Stanley
20 cut its target to 149p. This was because of worries about increasing fuel prices.

Tate and Lyle, the sugar and sweeteners group, lost 5.8 per cent
25 to 402^3/$_4$p after CityGroup lowered its forecasts because of rising corn prices. Following recent floods in the US, the cost of corn has risen 2.5 per cent.

Sculptures of famous people

Description

You make sculptures of famous people, e.g. Mohammed Ali, Michael Jackson, George Clooney, etc.

The average price of a sculpture is $30,000. A recent sculpture of Nelson Mandela was bought for $55,000.

The sculptures are aimed at all art lovers, but especially wealthy collectors.

Why you want the money

To finance and market exhibitions of 100 sculptures in New York and San Francisco art galleries next year.

Advantages for tycoons

The sculptures are very popular. The tycoons will be allowed to own nine of the sculptures at the end of the exhibitions.

Negotiating terms

You want the tycoons to invest $200,000 in 100 sculptures. You offer 10% of the total sales revenue.

You may invent any other information you wish. Note: it is likely that the tycoons will ask for a bigger stake in your business. You must decide if it is worth increasing your offer. Try to predict what questions they will ask you.

Alfresh lunch box with cooler

Description

You have your own company, WangLi Products. It makes a range of products for the leisure and food industries.

The lunch box has sections for food, such as cheese and fruit, and small and large pots for milk, yoghurt, fruit juice, etc. There's a space for cooler bags.

Alfresh is aimed mainly at schoolchildren, but will also be used by adults.

Why you want the money

You have cashflow problems at present. You need additional finance to launch and market the new product.

Advantages for tycoons

The unique design of the box, its shape and colourful appearance will ensure it will be a winner!

Turnover/profit projections

Year 1: $100,000/$20,000

Year 2: $500,000/$260,000

Year 3: $3.5m/$1.2m

Negotiating terms

You want the tycoons to invest $200,000 for a stake of 10% in your business.

You may invent any other information you wish. Note: it is likely that the tycoons will ask for a bigger stake in your business. You must decide if it is worth increasing your offer. Try to predict what questions they will ask you.

8 Human resources, Reading, Exercise A, page 76

Article B

by Alison Maitland

Nissan Motor's sales executives in Japan used to take cars to customers' homes for viewing, often late in the evening. Now the showrooms and salespeople operate more regular working hours.

The change of approach might sound like a decline in personal service. In fact, it is signed to be the opposite. Cars are no longer just 'boys' toys', even in conservative Japan. Nissan's research shows that women make a third of car purchases, and women and men jointly make another third. Female customers overwhelmingly would like there to be more women in the sales teams, but the late hours made the job unappealing to women in a country where there is still often a stark choice between work and family.

These findings prompted Carlos Ghosn, Chief Executive of Nissan and Renault, to adopt a strategy to hire and promote more women into the leadership ranks.

Since 2004, Nissan's 'Women in the Driver's Seat' initiative has more than doubled recruitment of female engineering graduates to 17 per cent this year and recruitment of female salespeople has jumped from 15 per cent to 34 per cent.

The number of women managers at Nissan, while still tiny, has risen from 2 per cent to 5 per cent. 'In an ideal situation, we should mirror the market we serve – 50 per cent – but there is a long way to go,' says Miyuki Takahashi, General Manager of the Diversity Development Office that runs the initiative to woo female employees and customers.

At a conference organised by Catalyst, which researches and campaigns for the advancement of women in business, Nissan was one of this year's two award winners, not least for having hit its initial target of women making up 5 per cent of its managers in an industry in which the average is just 0.6 per cent.

Nissan says that getting more women engineers into the company, in which 80 per cent of employees are engineers, is important to its success. 'Males are attracted by big pictures of cars and specifications about performance,' says Ms Takahashi, who was previously Marketing Director in Japan. 'We found most mothers were attracted by pictures of a family having a great time with the car.'

To prioritise female customers, three years ago Nissan launched the Serena people carrier, which was designed by and for women. Last year, it won the top-selling spot in Japan. Ms Takahashi says, 'I am convinced that this hit is closely related to women's advancement in Nissan in terms of marketing and sales.

8 Human resources, Skills, Exercise C, page 79

Human Resources Manager

You are the Human Resources Manager for the Dolphin Department Store. Before you start using the Omnia Employment Agency, you need the following information. Call the agency, identify yourself, state the purpose of the call and get the necessary information.

Ask about:

- introductory fees (If so, how much?)
- the hourly wage for temporary workers
- minimum period to hire a temporary worker (If so, what is it?)
- how much to pay if a temporary worker does overtime or weekend work
- work permits (Who arranges them?)
- travel expenses of temporary workers (Who pays them?)
- when to pay for temporary workers.

9 International markets, Skills, Exercise E, page 88

Student B

1 **You are a buyer for a department store.**

Because the market for handbags is very competitive, you want to:

- pay the same price this year as last year
- have a shorter delivery time of two weeks
- get a three-year contract with the supplier.

2 **You are the director of a kitchen equipment company.**

Because business conditions are difficult, you want to:

- continue to pay all your European agents a commission of 5%
- communicate with agents more frequently by phone and e-mail
- use as many different distributors as possible to sell your goods
- offer agents shorter contracts, with a maximum period of three years.

9 International markets, Case study, page 89

Information file: Pampas Leather Company

Models	You can supply three models: the Clubman, the Nightrider and the Look. The Clubman will be costly to produce, as it is hand-finished, made of high-quality leather and has a unique design.
Quality	To reduce costs of production, you will outsource the manufacture of the cheapest model, the Look, to a Chinese firm.
Quantity	You want WCA to place an order for at least 3,000 jackets. You need a large order to cover the costs of the additional workers you will have to hire to deal with the order. Try to persuade WCA to buy a large number of the Clubman model, as you make most profit from this model.

Prices	Unit cost of production	Prices quoted to WCA
Clubman	$110	$380
Nightrider	$100	$280
Look	$80	$150

Payment	By bank transfer as soon as the goods have been despatched.
Discounts	Your policy is to offer new customers a 2% introductory discount on list prices for a first order, and 3% for further orders.
Delivery	Prompt delivery within one week of the agreed date.
Guarantee	Three years.

Working across cultures 3, page 90

The six mistakes were:

1 Hospitality is a matter of honour in the Arab world. It is polite to accept at least one cup of coffee or tea.

2 Al-Jabri was probably surprised that Collins hadn't bothered to see at least something of Riyadh, a city that Al-Jabri was proud of.

3 Collins shouldn't have been upset that Al-Jabri interrupted the meeting to take telephone calls. This is usual practice in the Arab world.

4 If a guest admires something belonging to an Arab host, the host may sometimes offer it as a gift.

5 Collins did not prepare properly for his presentation.

6 He misinterpreted Al-Jabri's comment 'if God pleases'. This did not mean that Al-Jabri had agreed to place an order.

11 Leadership, Case study, page 111

Director 1

In your opinion, the company should do the following:

- Agree to be taken over by the French retailer Universelle, so that the company will become stronger financially.

- Focus on other sports, such as golf, rugby and ice hockey, where the competition is less fierce.

- Reduce the company's dependence on the football and athletics market.

- Concentrate more on lifestyle and fashion products, e.g. trainers and footwear for informal occasions.

- Introduce a more open style of management, giving responsibility for some decision-making to lower levels of management. This will improve staff morale.

Prepare your presentation. You may add any other ideas of your own for improving the company's performance.

---

11 Leadership, Case study, page 111

Director 3

In your opinion, the company should do the following:

- Bring out collections of footwear and clothing by famous international designers, aimed at the top part of the market. The profit margins on such products will be high.

- Go upmarket and aim to build a strong image for making luxury sports goods. Source all materials from Europe rather than from the Asia-Pacific region. This will help to keep both prices and quality high.

- Make more customised shoes, bags and sports accessories aimed at the top end of the market. This will help to attract consumer attention to the brand.

- Restructure the company into a series of business units, each with its own management reporting to the CEO. This will increase competition within the company, leading to greater efficiency.

Prepare your presentation. You may add any other ideas of your own for improving the company's performance.

---

12 Competition, Case study, page 119

Buyers

- You each meet one of the suppliers.

    - Buyer 1 meets Rashid Singh Enterprises.

    - Buyer 2 meets Pacific Traders.

    - Buyer 3 meets The Artisans Co-operative.

- Get details of the missing information and negotiate to get a good offer to bring back to your company. You would like the following:

    - delivery by 15 November

    - a discount of at least 5% on all goods ordered

    - to be able to return all unsold goods, with the amount credited to your account

    - a two-year guarantee, if possible.

12 Competition, Starting up, page 112

Key

1	a) 3	b) 2	c) 1		6	a) 3	b) 2	c) 1
2	a) 3	b) 2	c) 1		7	a) 1	b) 2	c) 3
3	a) 1	b) 2	c) 3		8	a) 1	b) 2	c) 3
4	a) 1	b) 2	c) 3		9	a) 3	b) 2	c) 1
5	a) 1	b) 2	c) 3		10	a) 3	b) 2	c) 1

Over 26

You are extremely competitive. You have high standards and expect a lot from yourself and other people. You are probably an impatient person. You like to win at all times and get upset if you lose. You perform well under pressure and enjoy a challenge.

18–26

You are fairly competitive. You are competitive in areas that are important to you. You don't always have to be the best. You are pleased when other people are successful, such as members of your family or your colleagues. You don't believe that 'winning is everything'.

12–17

You are not very competitive. You believe it is more important to take part than to win. You enjoy working in a group rather than individually. You try to avoid pressure as much as possible.

11–10

You are not at all competitive. You are probably a good team player. You want to enjoy life and be as relaxed as possible. You don't like being the centre of attention. You try to avoid working under pressure or having to meet tight deadlines.

1 Brands, Skills, Exercise D, page 11

Student B

In your opinion, the product is the problem. The jewellery is fairly fashionable, but not a lot different from competing products. You want to:

- take the Cecile range out of the market and stop selling it.
- develop new jewellery which fills a gap in the market and which has an obvious USP (unique selling point).
- invest more money in research for new jewellery products.
- carefully study rival products to find out why they are so successful.
- market more unusual designs from young Asian and Indian designers.

2 Travel, Case study, page 20

Account Manager, BTS

You agree to a meeting with NeoTech's Head of Travel. Suggest that you meet at NeoTech's head office. Here is your diary for next week.

	Morning	Afternoon
Monday	All-day meeting to discuss new business developments	
Tuesday	Presentation to the Board of Directors. You may be available late in the afternoon, after 5 p.m.	
Wednesday	All-day meetings with clients	
Thursday	Medical check-up	Free
Friday	Writing a report	Flight to New York 6 p.m.

4 Organisation, Skills, Exercise F, page 41

Student C

You are a colleague of Students A and B from a subsidiary. You met Student A at the same conference last year.

1 Decide on the following:
- company name
- activity / area of business
- department you work for
- recent activities

2 Greet Student A and introduce yourself to the other people at the conference. Note: you enjoy talking about yourself and your free-time activities.

4 Organisation, Case study, page 43

Manager A

You are strongly against the relocation. Listen to the opinions of the other members of the committee. Try to persuade them to oppose the relocation. These are some of your reasons. Add any other points you can think of.

- The open-plan office in the new building will be unpopular with staff. Most people like to have their own office.
- Young, talented graduates will not want to work in Beauchamp. They will prefer to be in Paris, so there will be a recruitment problem.
- Some workers may choose to stay in Paris, but travel 120 kilometres each day to the new building. They will be tired and stressed, which will affect their work.
- The move will have a bad effect on the work-life balance of most staff.
- Overseas visitors enjoy coming to the European Head Office in Paris. Will they enjoy staying in a small, northern, industrial town?

6 Money, Case study, page 59

New Formula XF anti-wrinkle cream

Description

The anti-wrinkle cream is based on a secret formula. You visited a tribe in the Amazon jungle last year. The women had beautiful skin because of a cream they put on their faces. They taught you how to make the cream. The product will be aimed at women over 30.

Why you want the money

To manufacture the product, launch and market it.

Advantages for tycoons

You tested the cream with 200 women volunteers; 90% said the cream smoothed their skin and got rid of their wrinkles. The product should be a world-beater.

Turnover/profit projections

You do not have a business plan or turnover/profit projections. You want the tycoons to provide you with expertise in these areas.

Negotiating terms

You want the tycoons to invest $400,000 for a 30% stake in your business.

You may invent any other information you wish. Note: it is likely that the tycoons will ask for a bigger stake in your business. You must decide if it is worth increasing your offer. Try to predict what questions they will ask you.

8 Human resources, Skills, Exercise C, page 79

Employment agency consultant

You will receive a call from the Human Resources Manager of Dolphin Department Store. The manager will ask you some questions. Here are the details:

- An introductory fee is charged: 25% of worker's first pay cheque.
- The hourly wage for temporary workers is €12.
- There is a minimum charge of four hours per day for all temporary workers.
- Overtime: company pays time and a half; Saturday/Sunday rates: double the hourly rate.
- Agency is responsible for work permits.
- Travel expenses of workers paid for by the client.
- The agency bills clients each week for the total hours worked by temporary staff.

9 International markets, Case study, page 89

Information file: West Coast Apparel

Models	You are interested in ordering all three models – at the right price.
Quality	You will emphasise in your marketing that all the models in the collection have been made in Argentina – a guarantee of their quality. You do not want any of the manufacture of the models to be outsourced.
Quantity	You want to place the following first order:

Model	Quantity
Clubman	500
Nightrider	1,000
Look	800

You are sure that the Nightrider and the Look will sell well. However, you are not certain that you can sell large quantities of the Clubman. Americans are very price-conscious at the present, due to the current economic situation.

Prices	Pampas Leather have quoted these unit prices:

Clubman	$380
Nightrider	$280
Look	$150

Note: prices include all delivery costs to your specified US port.

Payment	By bank transfer. You would like to pay 50% of the order immediately and the remaining 50% one month after receiving the goods.
Discounts	As you are such a large company and have placed a substantial order, you expect an introductory discount of at least 5%.
Delivery	Prompt delivery within five days of the agreed date.
Guarantee	Three years for all the models except the Clubman. You would like a guarantee of five years for this model.

11 Leadership, Case study, page 111

Director 2

In your opinion, the company should do the following:

- Buy smaller specialist companies and build them up, e.g. firms making golf bags and balls. There will be less competition in selling these products.

- Reduce the company's endorsements of top sportspeople. Instead, it should pay well-known sportsmen and women to advise the company on new products. This will lead to more product innovation.

- Focus more on developing products with revolutionary designs and higher prices. This will help to improve profit margins.

- Keep the present style of management and introduce a cost-cutting programme, with the aim of reducing costs by 20% in the next year to help profitability.

Prepare your presentation. You may add any other ideas of your own for improving the company's performance.

12 Competition, Case study, page 119

Supplier 1

You represent Rashid Singh Enterprises. These are the terms you can offer.

- Delivery: by sea; 1,000 necklaces and bracelets immediately on receipt of an order, remaining 4,000 by 15 November; earrings: 3,000 by 30 November – products not available from stock, as important customers have already placed orders.

- Trade discount of 2% off list prices

- Returned goods: unsold goods may be returned within one month and the amount credited to the customer's account.

- Guarantee: one year (bracelets, earrings), but two years for necklaces

1 Brands, Skills, Exercise D, page 11

Student C

In your opinion, the Cecile line has a lot of sales potential. You think the products and brand name are excellent. However, you believe the products are not promoted in the right way and not sold in places which reflect the high status of the jewellery. You want:

- to pay a famous film star to endorse the jewellery and wear it as often as possible.

- to spend a lot of money on a creative television commercial to advertise the jewellery.

- to sell the jewellery only in a limited number of high-class jewellery and department stores and at airports.

- to have a new slogan which reflects the upmarket status of the jewellery.

- a top designer to create a new range of jewellery which can be sold under the Cecile brand. You think the present range is too limited.

4 Organisation, Skills, Exercise F, page 41

Student D

This is your first time at this conference. You don't know anyone.

1 Decide on the following:

- company name
- department you work for
- activity / area of business
- recent activities

2 **Introduce yourself (and your company) to people at the conference. You enjoy talking about your company. You are looking for new business contacts.**

4 Organisation, Case study, page 43

Manager B

You are in favour of the relocation. Listen to the opinions of the other members of the committee. Try to persuade them to agree to the relocation. These are some of your reasons. Add any other points you can think of.

- Relocation will reduce costs and boost profits in the long run.
- Having everyone on one site will improve communication.
- Excellent facilities in the new building will motivate staff. For example, there is a top-floor café, fitness centre and a swimming pool in the basement.
- Relocation grants and tax incentives will be available from the local authority in the area.
- Overseas visitors will enjoy the surrounding countryside.
- There are several cheap hotels in Beauchamp and the surrounding area.

---

4 Organisation, Case study, page 43

Independent Management Consultant

You have advised many companies on relocation. You think the relocation would be good for the company. Add any other points you can think of.

- The new building will have a large, open-plan office, which is very good for communication and staff relations.
- Teamwork should improve in the new building because there is a spacious lounge where staff can relax and share ideas.
- InStep will help staff to relocate. The company will provide:
  - vans to help them move their belongings;
  - subsidised meals in the canteen;
  - childcare facilities (crèche);
  - petrol subsidies;
  - flexitime working hours for staff with young children.

---

6 Money, Case study, page 59

On-the-Spot car cleaning

Description

Two years ago you started up a business, hiring and training unemployed youngsters to clean cars in car parks and garages in Atlanta. You provide modern, high-powered equipment. This enables your workers to clean car interiors and exteriors quickly and to a high standard.

Why you want the money

To expand your cleaning service to other cities in Georgia.

Advantages to tycoons

The business is providing work for unemployed people. This would be good for the tycoons' image.

It is a very successful local business. Last year's turnover was $1.5 million. Profit: $0.3m.

Turnover/profit projections

Year 1: $2.5m/$0.5m   Year 2: $4m/$0.8m   Year 3: $6m/$1.4m

Negotiating terms

You want the tycoons to invest $500,000 for a stake of 20% in your business.

You may invent any other information you wish. Note: it is likely that the tycoons will ask for a bigger stake in your business. You must decide if it is worth increasing your offer. Try to predict what questions they will ask you.

6 Money, Case study, page 59

Tycoons

The entrepreneur(s) will give a short presentation of their product/service, then they will answer your questions. You decide whether to invest in their project and on what terms. You normally ask for a bigger stake than the amount the entrepreneurs offer.

Here are some suggested questions. Try to add three questions to the list.

- Tell us about your background.
- Where did you meet?
- Do you have a business plan?
- How would you describe the market for your product?
- What is special about your product/service? What are its USPs (unique selling points)?
- Do you have a patent for it?

- How much of your own money have you spent on it?
- What about competitors?
- What are your forecasts for (a) turnover and (b) profit?
- What do you want from us, in addition to money?
- Who will make your product?
- How will you market your product/service?

Note: If you are working with another tycoon, you may wish to offer the whole of the stake yourself in order to make as much profit as possible. You don't have to divide the stake between the two of you!

11 Leadership, Case study, page 111

Other members of the board (not presenting)

1 As one group, discuss the three strategies. What are the advantages and disadvantages of each one? Which will be a) the most risky, b) the most expensive?

2 Prepare some questions to ask after you have heard each presentation by the three directors.

12 Competition, Case study, page 119

Supplier 2

You represent Pacific Traders. These are the terms you can offer.

- Delivery: by sea; 3,000 necklaces and bracelets within 30 days of receipt of order; 2,000 necklaces and bracelets by 15 November; earrings should be available by the end of November.
- Trade discount of 5% off list prices
- Returned goods: no returns unless the goods are faulty.
- Guarantee: three months

12 Competition, Case study, page 119

Supplier 3

You represent The Artisans Co-operative. These are the terms you can offer.

- Delivery: normally 30 days by sea after receiving an order, but there have been problems with delivery recently. Your company has just appointed a new shipping agent, who should be more reliable.
- Trade discount of 10% for new customers
- Returned goods: no returns except for faulty or damaged goods
- Guarantee: six months

Grammar reference

1 Present simple and present continuous

Present simple

We use the present simple:

1 to give factual information, for example about company activities.

   *Unilever **makes** a wide variety of consumer goods.*

   ***Does** it **market** these goods globally?*

   *It **doesn't sell** in every sector.*

2 to talk about routine activities or habits.

   *I always **buy** the supermarket's own brand of detergent.*

   ***Do** you usually **pick up** groceries on the way home?*

   *He **doesn't choose clothes** with designer labels.*

3 for actions and situations which are generally true.

   *Many consumers **prefer** well-known brands.*

4 for timetables and scheduled events.

   *We **launch** the new range on 15 January.*

Present continuous

We use the present continuous to:

1 talk about ongoing situations and projects.

   *We**'re developing** a completely new image for the brand.*

   ***Are** you still **working** with those designers?*

   *They **aren't saying** anything to the press this time.*

2 describe temporary situations.

   *We**'re testing** a new logo at the moment.*

   ***Are** they **offering** a good discount during the launch period?*

3 describe trends.

   *The number of people shopping online is **growing**.*

4 talk about personal arrangements and plans.

   *I**'m meeting** Frau Scharping next week.*

2 Talking about the future

1 We use *going to* to talk about what we intend to do or what someone else has already decided to do.

   *I'm **going to** buy a new car.*

   *She's **going to** tell us about the ideas they've come up with for the ad campaign.*

   Both *going to* and *will* are used for predictions.

   *There's **going to** be a flight of capital from the West towards India and China.*

   *The Fortune Garment Company **will** continue to lose market share unless it solves its problems.*

2 We use *'ll* to make a spontaneous promise or offer to do something.

   'I haven't got time to do this myself.'
   *'Don't worry. I**'ll** give you a hand.'*

3 We use the present continuous to talk about fixed plans or arrangements.

   *I**'m meeting** Mrs da Silva next week.*
   *She**'s arriving** on Wednesday.*

4 We use the present simple to talk about a schedule.

   *The flight **leaves** at 15:50 tomorrow.*

   In time clauses, we use the present simple to refer to future time. It is incorrect to use *will* in a time clause.

   *We won't start until everyone **gets** here.*

   *I'm going to go round the world when I **retire**.*

   *As soon as I **have** the results, I'll give you a ring.*

   *Come and see me before you **go**.*

3 Past simple and present perfect

Past simple

1 We use the past simple to refer to events that took place in the past.

*A pharmacist called John Pemberton **invented** Coca-Cola.*

*'**Did** you **go** to Berlin last week?'*
*'Yes, and I **met** Herr Gnuchtel.'*

2 We frequently use a time adverb to situate the event in finished past time.

*Rolls Royce went bust **in 1973**.*

***A few years ago**, the City Plaza hotel was a leader in its segment of the market.*

*Many people lost a lot of money on the stock market **during 2008 and 2009**.*

3 We use the past simple in annual reports to describe the company's performance over the last year.

*Last year **was** a good year for our group. Sales **rose** by more than 11%, and we **made** substantial gains in market share in a number of countries.*

Present perfect

1 We use the present perfect to say that a finished past action is relevant now.

*They **have developed** a new brand of toothpaste.*

*The Chairman **has** recently **resigned**.*

2 We use the present perfect when we are thinking of a period of time continuing up to the present.

*For over 50 years, Stirling Cars **has developed** classic sports cars.*

*Calvin Klein **has been** one of the leading fashion designers since the mid-1970s.*

3 We often use this tense to talk about our life experiences.

*She **has had** a number of interesting jobs.*

*He**'s worked** for a variety of firms.*

4 Noun combinations

1 We use *'s* to express a relationship between a person or organisation and another person or thing.

*Mr Blake**'s** secretary*

*her husband**'s** car BA's employees*

*Volvo**'s** reputation*

The *'s* very often means that the relationship can be expressed using *have*.

*Mr Blake **has** a secretary.*

*Volvo **has** a reputation.*

2 When two nouns are used together, the first noun functions as an adjective and describes the second noun.

a business card   *a job description*

an office complex   *a travel agency*

Sometimes three or more nouns occur together.

a company credit card (a credit card issued by a company)

a management training programme (a training programme designed for management)

3 Two nouns are joined by *of* when the ideas are more abstract.

*the cost **of** living*

*independence **of** mind*

*the joy **of** working and lifelong learning*

4 Some compound nouns are written as one word.

database   *answerphone*

letterhead   *headquarters*

5 When compound nouns are used with a number in expressions of measurement, the first noun is singular.

*a six-**lane** motorway*   *a four-**day** week*

5 | Articles

The indefinite article: a/an

We use *a/an in the following ways*:

1 before unspecified singular countable nouns.

*She works in **an** office.*

2 with the names of professions.

*She's **an** executive and he's **a** manager.*

3 in expressions of measurement.

*We charge $500 **an** hour.*

*It sells at €1.75 **a** litre.*

4 before a noun to mean all things of the same type.

***A** loss leader is **an** article that a store sells at a low price to tempt customers to buy other goods.*

The definite article: the

We use *the*:

1 when it is clear from the context what particular thing or place is meant.

*I'll meet you in **the** reception area.*

2 before a noun that we have mentioned before.

*They had a villa in Cannes and a chalet in Innsbruck, but they sold **the** villa.*

3 before adjectives to specify a category of people or things.

***the** rich, **the** poor, **the** French, **the** unemployed, **the** World Wide Web*

Zero article: (Ø)

We do not use an article before:

1 mass nouns used in general statements.

***(Ø)** Money is the root of all **(Ø)** evil.*

2 the names of places and people.

***(Ø)** Poland, **(Ø)** Japan, **(Ø)** Dr Spock, **(Ø)** President Obama*

6 | Describing trends

1 To describe changing circumstances, we can use verbs of movement.

improve   increase   recover   rise   (↗)
decline   decrease   drop   fall   (↘)

A dramatic movement may be expressed by:

rocket   soar   (↗)

dive   plummet   (↘)

A slight movement can be indicated by:

edge up   (↗)

edge down   dip   (↘)

The amount of increase can also be indicated using these verbs:

halve   ($1/_2$)

double   (x2)

triple   (x3)

quadruple   (x4)

increase tenfold   (x10)

Or with a preposition:

*Our business grew **by** 15% last year.*

*Sales have increased **from** €5 million to €5.8 million.*

2 Changes which have not reached their end-point are expressed using *-ing*.

*Profits are fall**ing**.*

*Unemployment has been ris**ing**.*

If the change is complete, we use a perfect tense.

*The government **has privatised** the rail network.*

*Sales **have increased**, and that has meant higher profits.*

7 Modal verbs

Advice

1 We can use *should* and *shouldn't* to give or ask for advice.

*You **should** always learn something about a country before visiting it.*

***Should** I invite our agents out to dinner after the meeting?*

*He **shouldn't** ask so many personal questions.*

Should often follows the verbs *suggest* and *think*.

*I think we **should** find out more about them before signing the contract.*

2 For strong advice, we can use *must* or *mustn't*.

*They **must** pay their bills on time in future.*

*You **mustn't** refuse if you're offered a small gift.*

Obligation/Necessity

1 We often use *must* when the obligation comes from the person speaking or writing.

*We **must** ask them to dinner when they're over here.*

2 We use *mustn't* to say that something is prohibited, it is not allowed.

*You **mustn't** smoke in here.*

3 We often use *have to* to show that the obligation comes from another person or institution, not the speaker.

*You **have to** renew your residence permit after three months.* (This is the law.)

Lack of obligation / Lack of necessity

We use *don't have to* when there is no need or obligation to do something.

*You **don't have to** wait for your order. You can collect it now.*

Compare the uses of *must not* and *don't have to* here.

*We **mustn't** rush into a new partnership too quickly. We **don't have to** make a decision for at least six months.*

8 *-ing* forms and infinitives

1 We sometimes use one verb after another verb. Often, the second verb is in the infinitive form.

*We **are continuing to cut** our manufacturing costs.*

*Management **agreed to offer** generous redundancy terms to all staff affected.*

The verbs below are often followed by the infinitive.

intend	attempt	promise	plan
mean	try	arrange	offer
want	pretend	hope	forget
seem	fail	wish	expect
claim	guarantee		

2 Sometimes, the second verb must be in the *-ing* form. This depends on the first verb.

*The decision **involves reducing** our heavy losses.*

The verbs below are usually followed by the *-ing* form.

admit	appreciate	contemplate
give up	involve	deny
enjoy	consider	carry on
mean	mind	justify
can't stand	don't mind	remember
resent	detest	recommend
risk	delay	miss
suggest	avoid	put off
look forward to		

Some verbs can be followed by the *-ing* form or the infinitive form without a big change in meaning.

*She **started loading** the software. / She **started to load** the software.*

Sometimes, however, the meaning changes.

*She **stopped to read** the manual.* (She stopped what she was doing in order to read the manual.)

*She **stopped reading** the manual.* (She no longer bothered to read the manual.)

9 Conditions

First conditional

1   We use conditional sentences when discussing the terms of an agreement, making hypothetical proposals, bargaining and making concessions.

*If you order now, we **will** give you a discount.*

*We **will** reduce the price by 10% **if** you give us a firm order in advance.*

*If we give you 90 days' credit instead of 60, **will** you give us the interest you would have paid?*

The use of *if* + *will* + base form of the verb suggests that the acceptance of the condition is the basis for a deal.

2   We use *unless* in conditional sentences to mean *if not.*

*We **won't** be able to start construction **unless** you train our personnel.*

3   *As long as* and *provided that* are also used to state conditions.

*We **will** sign the contract **as long as** you guarantee prices for the next 18 months.*

*We can reach agreement on a joint venture **provided that** our firm has a representative on your board.*

Second conditional

If the proposal is more tentative and possibly less certain, we use past verb forms.

*If we **said** we were prepared to deliver in March, **would** you make a firm order?*

*If you **agreed** to create more jobs, we **might** think about a productivity deal.*

*If the government **found** some extra money, **would** you be prepared to create a subsidiary in our country?*

10 Narrative tenses

1   The past simple is common when we describe a sequence of events or tell a story in chronological order about events that happened in the past.

*On Monday 3 December 1984, a poisonous cloud of gas **escaped** from a pesticide plant in Bhopal, India. Eye witnesses **described** a cloud in the shape of a mushroom which rose above the plant and then **descended** over the town.*

2   We use the past perfect to situate an event that happened before another past event.

*By the end of the week, 1,200 people **had died** and at least 10,000 **had been affected** very seriously.*

3   The present perfect is used to describe past events of current significance.

*A major problem for doctors in Bhopal was lack of information on how to treat the chemical's effects. A pathologist said: 'Why **hasn't** Union Carbide **come forward** to tell us about the gas that **has leaked** and how to treat it? Is it not their moral duty? They **have not come** forward.'*

4   We use the past continuous to describe unfinished events which were in progress around a particular past time.

*By Monday 10 December, the death toll had risen to 2,000, and American lawyers representing Indian families **were suing** Union Carbide for $12.5 billion in compensation. Meanwhile, journalists **were asking** the company difficult questions about its safety procedures, and the share price **was dropping** sharply, as investors became worried about the billions of dollars of compensation that the company might have to pay.*

(Adapted from Ian Marcousé, *Business Case Studies*, Longman 1990)

11 Relative clauses

1 We use *who* or *that* in a relative clause to identify people.

*The people **who/ that** we employ are very highly qualified.*

As *people is* the object of the clause, the relative pronoun can be left out.

The people we employ are very highly qualified.

If the relative pronoun defines the subject of the sentence, it must be included.

*A counterfeiter is a person **who** copies goods in order to trick people.*

2 We use *that* or *which* in a relative clause to identify things.

*Have you read the report **that/which** I left on your desk?*

If *that* or *which* identifies the object of the clause, it can be left out.

Have you read the report I left on your desk?

If *that* or *which* defines the subject of the sentence, it must be included.

*Organisations **that** are flexible can respond to change.*

3 Non-defining clauses provide extra information about the subject or object of a sentence. The extra information is separated by commas.

*Philip Condit, **who was** Chairman of Boeing, wanted the airline to become a global company.*

Note that it is not possible to use *that*.

*The Dorfmann hotel, **which** is situated 30 km outside Vienna, charges US$ 1,400 per person.*

Again, it is not possible to use *that* in a non-defining clause.

12 Passives

1 We use a passive structure when we are not interested in who carries out an action or it is not necessary to know.

*The company **was founded** in 1996.*
*Some changes **have been made**.*
*He **has been promoted** to the post of Sales Director.*
*A new low-alcohol lager **is being developed**.*

2 If we also want to mention who performs the action, we can use a phrase beginning with *by*.

*The self-extinguishing cigarette was invented **by Kaj Jensen**.*

*The prototype is being checked **by the design team**.*

3 In a passive sentence, the grammatical subject receives the focus.

***You will be met** at the airport by a company driver.*

(You receives the focus of attention.)

Compare with:

***A company driver will meet** you at the airport.*

4 The passive is often used to describe processes and procedures.

*First of all, an advertising agency **is contacted** and the aim of the campaign **is discussed**. Then, a storyboard **is created** and, if acceptable, the TV commercial **is filmed** and **broadcast** at prime time.*

5 We also use the passive in a formal or impersonal style.

*It **was felt** that our design should be more innovative.*

*Company procedures **must be respected** at all times.*

Audio scripts

UNIT 1 BRANDS

CD1 TRACK 1 (I = Interviewer, R1 = Respondent 1; R2 = Respondent 2)

I Do you buy brands?

R1 Yes, I do. I am basically pro-brands. If you buy a branded product, it's a guarantee that the quality is fairly good and the product is reliable. Another reason is you attract a bit of attention if you buy something stylish, and branded products are usually stylish and have a good design. Let's face it, most people buy brands because they want to impress other people. They want to show that they have style and good taste.

I Do you buy brands?

R2 No – well, not actively, anyway. I don't want to give free advertising to companies. I hate all the advertising hype around brands. And I don't want other people to think I'm trying to impress them with lots of logos. And I also get fed up with seeing the same things wherever you go. If you buy a suit from a famous brand, you'll see five people with the same suit that month. It's so boring. Oh, another thing – am I buying the genuine product or an illegal copy? Basically, I want value for money – I won't pay inflated prices for a name, a fancy logo and packaging. However, I do buy brands for my kids – especially sports goods and trainers. It's always Nike, Adidas or Reebok.

CD1 TRACK 2 (I = Interviewer, CC = Chris Cleaver)

I What are the qualities of a really good brand?

CC Strong brands – really, you know, brands that you would say have, er, a real traction in the marketplace, um, will have a number of important qualities. Obviously, the first is, they will have high levels of awareness, so people will know about them and recognise them when they see them, and that might be the physical product, or it might be the visual identity, the design manifestation. Um, but obviously recognition is not enough. What needs to happen also is that people, you know, the target customer or consumer, needs to know a lot about that brand, so a strong brand will also immediately communicate a set of appealing and persuasive ideas, er, and perceptions, that enable the end user, er, you know, the target audience, to know whether or not this is a brand for them, um, or whether it's a brand that they, perhaps, are not attracted to.

CD1 TRACK 3 (CC = Chris Cleaver)

CC Brands are really useful ways of firstly conveying all that information instantly, so – think of any brand you like, any brand that you can imagine, say BMW or British Airways or in any sector, and immediately your head is filled with, er, a raft of important information about what the brand does, but as much as that, what it's like and how it appeals to you and connects with you. And so its function, therefore, is to enable you to choose one thing from another – often in markets where there is very little actual difference between, you know, the product. So a BMW – I'm sure BMW would probably be horrified for me to say this – but, you know, a BMW is a car like an Audi is a car like a Mercedes is a car – they've all got four wheels and an engine and, you know, air conditioning and all that type of thing, but the way people feel about them, because of the information and awareness and perception that they have, enables them to decide whether or not one is better for them or right for them or says the right things about them than another.

CD1 TRACK 4 (I = Interviewer, CC = Chris Cleaver)

I Can you give us an example of a brand you have helped?

CC One I can think of is Nokia. Nokia is, you know, a well-known brand, um, it's by far the biggest mobile phone manufacturer – I think it has about a third of the market, so it's way bigger than anybody else. It's also been, um, in the market – it was, kind of, invented the market in a way, so for many people, particularly people of my generation, Nokia equals mobile phones. We've helped them in a couple of important ways. Firstly, um, in a market that's changed and a brand that's expanded hugely in terms of what it offers, we helped them with, er, the question of what is it that Nokia is about, and how does it relate to its customers, its broad range of customers, in ways in which its competitors don't. So to give it that, um, element of choice, you know, so why I should choose a Nokia over a Motorola, um, in addition to what it looks like and what it does. So, what the brand is about – um, so that on what you might call technically the master brand.

And we've also helped them with, um, developing certain parts of their offer in order to, um, react to the market and also to keep the brand fresh. So we worked with Nokia on their N series, which is one of their more technological phones, multimedia phones – although they don't like to call them phones any more because they do so much more – um, in order to satisfy, er, the needs that that emerging customer group has, primarily younger consumers who want to be able to do all sorts of things with their phones – or devices. Um, but also, in order to sharpen Nokia's brand image as a technology leader, it was important that it had products in, in those areas.

CD1 TRACK 5 (D = David, J = Joy, N = Natasha, M = Mario)

D Joy, we know our client doesn't want to be linked to football any more. It seems the club they sponsor is asking for too much money. And in any case, they're looking for something more exciting, something that'll give their brand a bit more punch. Any ideas?

J Well, there are several possibilities. How about ice hockey? It's an incredibly fast, exciting sport, it's very popular in America and in a lot of European countries.

D OK, that's a possibility. What do you think, Natasha? Would ice hockey be a good choice?

N Mmm, I'm not so sure. It's not really an international sport, is it? Not in the same way as baseball, for example, or … tennis.

D That's true – baseball's got a lot more international appeal, and it's a sport that's got a good image. I don't know about tennis – I'm not sure it would be suitable. Mario, how do you feel about this?

M In my opinion, motor racing would be perfect for our client. It's fast, exciting, and the TV coverage of Formula One races is excellent. They would get a lot of exposure, it will really strengthen their image.

D That's a great idea, Mario! Why don't we get in touch with Larry Harrington's agency and see if he's interested? Harrington's young, exciting – he'd probably jump at the chance to work with our client. They're a perfect match. But first I must check with our client and make sure they're happy with our choice.

CD1 TRACK 6 (C = Cornelius, D = Diana, R = Ruth, T = Tom)

C OK everyone, we'll be getting a report soon from the consultants we've hired, European Marketing. But let's think a bit about the problems we may face entering the European markets. Diana, what do you think?

D Well, one thing's for sure, we're going to have to do a lot of advertising to establish our brand, and that's going to be expensive. And we may need to adapt a lot of our luggage for European consumers – that could be very costly, too.

C Yes, but we've allowed for that in our budget. Ruth, what difficulties do you think we'll have?

R Well, we'll need to get the pricing of our products right. But European consumers aren't as price conscious as we are back home, so pricing may not be too much of a problem. I know for a fact people in Europe will pay high prices for luxury goods if they like the design and it gives them status. So, I think we have to develop the Hudson brand as an exclusive 'Made in America' product … that'll mean high prices and a strong message that our luggage is high quality and great value for money.

C Mmm, that makes sense to me. Tom, what do you think?

T I don't agree at all. I just don't think Ruth's right. I think we should go downmarket, sell at very competitive prices, and aim to achieve high-volume sales. To do that, we'll need to look carefully at our manufacturing costs. So, it's probably time we stopped manufacturing in the US. The costs are just too high.

C Thanks, Tom, that's an interesting point of view. I think we all feel that we need to position Hudson right in European markets. Should we go upmarket or downmarket? That's an important decision we'll have to make.

R/D/T Yeah. True.

C My feeling, too, is we may need to increase the range of our products and stretch our brand, put it on other products – the right products, of course, ones that fit with our brand image. We certainly need some new thinking if we're going to succeed in Europe. And our consultants, European Marketing, will have plenty of advice for us, I've no doubt.

UNIT 2 TRAVEL

CD1 TRACK 7

1 What I really don't like is the way airlines treat people on the plane. There are far too many seats on most planes, so there's not enough legroom, and I'm not even particularly tall! I always try and get the seats near the emergency exit for that reason – you get much more room. Also, the poor-quality food and drink you get on airlines annoys me. It's all so processed and packaged, I just can't eat it. I prefer trains!

2 I like flying, but I really don't enjoy being at airports. Things like long queues at check-in irritate me. Also, when I have a lot of luggage and there are no baggage trolleys around, it's really inconvenient. What's even more frustrating is when I do find a trolley and then see that the departure board is full of flight delays and cancellations.

3 I must be really unlucky because it seems I'm always a victim of lost or delayed luggage. It usually turns up, but never with an apology. I don't like the attitude of the airlines, and I'm sorry, they're all the same. They seem to treat passengers like just another piece of luggage to be moved around the world. They seem to forget that we're people. For example, they overbook seats and just expect people to be able to get the next flight if their flight is full. What I really hate, though, is jet lag. It's a big problem for me, as I travel a lot to the Far East on business.

CD1 TRACK 8

My last overseas business trip was a nightmare from start to finish. First of all, there was a delay on the way to the airport, as there was an accident on the freeway. When I got there, I found the lower level of the airport parking lot was flooded. Next, my carry-on baggage was too big and heavy, so I had to check it in. When we arrived, the subway was closed, and there were no cabs at all. After a long time trying to figure out the schedule and waiting in line for 40 minutes, we finally got a bus downtown and found the hotel. Then there was a problem with our room reservation and, would you believe it, the elevator wasn't working, and our rooms were on the fifth floor.

CD1 TRACK 9 (I = INTERVIEWER, SS = SHOLTO SMITH)

I What are the main needs of business travellers, and how do your hotels meet them?

SS A key point would be the location of our hotels, um, good links with um subway underground networks, close to the airport, um, and obviously close to an office that the guest would be working in while they're staying in the hotel. Um, technology is also a key feature, and nowadays it's expected because obviously people have, um, great technology at home and therefore if it's also available in a hotel, that's also, um, a key feature. Um, Internet, a business centre, um, obviously translation services and that kind of facility is also, is paramount, and guests also expect an area where they can, er, go to a gymnasium, they can exercise, um, and also that kind of thing. These would be the key features.

CD1 TRACK 10 (I = INTERVIEWER, SS = SHOLTO SMITH)

I And how have rising travel costs affected the hotel business?

SS Er, they have affected business, but it's made the hotels more savvy in that they are being more competitive and looking at ways of adding value to the guests' stay, and that can take in anything from, um, including breakfast, um, on a daily basis, membership to, to the health club, er, including newspapers or possibly looking at, um, you know, transportation to and from the airport, a shuttle service to the local department store or a shuttle service to the offices in which the client, um, works in, um and that kind of, that value-add benefit, as opposed to just directly dropping the rate, which really doesn't benefit either party.

CD1 TRACK 11 (I = INTERVIEWER, SS = SHOLTO SMITH)

I What future developments do you foresee in the business travel market?

SS Future developments in the business travel market? I think … technology is still a hot topic as is, um, the obviously

environmental policies because that really is, um, is obviously still a buzzword, so to speak. We went through, um, healthy eating, we've gone through gymnasiums in hotels and the like, and now really there's such a huge focus on, um, on the likes of the environment – so whether it be water conservation, low-energy lighting in bedrooms, um, and the likes thereof, that, that kind of thing. Um, but obviously it's high-speed Internet, it's television on demand, it's, um, lower-cost telephone calls from the rooms, because obviously people now travel with BlackBerry and with mobile phones, so they're not actually having to use hotel telephone services – um, and these are the ways forward for hotels.

CD1 TRACK 12 (R = RECEPTIONIST, JN = JENNIFER NORTH, CV = CRISTINA VERDI)

R Good morning, The Fashion House. How can I help you?

JN This is Jennifer North here. Could you put me through to extension 4891, please?

R Certainly. Putting you through now.

CV Hello, Cristina Verdi speaking.

JN Hello, Cristina. It's Jennifer North from Madison in New York.

CV Hi, Jennifer, how are things?

JN Fine, thanks. I'm calling because I'll be in London next week and I'd like to make an appointment to see you. I want to tell you about our new collection.

CV Great. What day would suit you? I'm fairly free next week, I think.

JN How about Wednesday? In the afternoon? Could you make it then?

CV Let me look now. Er, let me check the diary. Yes, that'd be no problem at all. What about two o'clock? Is that OK?

JN Perfect. Thanks very much. It'll be great to see you again. We'll have plenty to talk about.

CV That's for sure. See you next week, then.

JN Right. Bye.

CV Bye then.

CD1 TRACK 13 (R = RECEPTIONIST, JN = JENNIFER NORTH)

R Good morning, The Fashion House. How may I help you?

JN I'd like to speak to Cristina Verdi, extension 4891, please.

R Thank you. Who's calling, please?

JN It's Jennifer North from Madison.

R Thank you. I'm putting you through … Hello, I'm afraid she's engaged at the moment. Will you hold or can I put you through to her voicemail?

JN Um, would you be able to take a message for me, please? I'm in a bit of a hurry.

R Yes, certainly.

JN The thing is, I should be meeting Ms Verdi at 2 p.m., but something's come up. My plane was delayed, and I've got to reschedule my appointments. If possible, I'd like to meet her tomorrow, preferably in the morning. Could she call me back here at the hotel, please, to confirm?

R Certainly, what's the number?

JN It's 020 7855 3814, and I'm in Room 611. I'll be leaving the hotel soon, so if she can't call me back within the next half an hour, I'll call her again this morning. Is that OK?

R Right, I've got that. I'll make sure she gets the message.

JN Thanks for your help. Goodbye.

R Thank you. Goodbye.

UNIT 3 CHANGE

CD1 TRACK 14 (I = INTERVIEWER, AD = ANNE DEERING)

I How do you advise businesses which are planning to change?

AD The two important things to take into account when advising businesses is, first of all, help them understand what does success look like – what are they going to change, how are they going to measure that change, and how will they know they've been successful?
And I think the second key point is to make sure people are fully engaged in the change, that they feel this is something they are doing for themselves and not something which is being done to them.

CD1 TRACK 15 (I = INTERVIEWER, AD = ANNE DEERING)

I What are the typical problems that businesses face when they're going through change?

AD Change is a very difficult process. There are many problems, but I would say the two, perhaps most important, ones are, first of all, what we think of as change fatigue. Organisations have often faced wave after wave of change, programme after programme. Organisations become very cynical about programmes' ability to deliver real change and change that's sustained over time, so it can be very hard to bring people along and create passion, enthusiasm around change when they've seen it again and again.

And the second big area that I see is the ability to get leaders engaged and aligned around the change, so that leadership speaks with one voice, leadership provides a role model for the organisation, and very importantly, helps the organisation stay focused on the change throughout what is sometimes a long and difficult process.

CD1 TRACK 16 (I = INTERVIEWER, AD = ANNE DEERING)

I Can you give us an example of an organisation that you have helped to change?

AD We work with a wide range of organisations around the world. One we helped recently was Nokia and Siemens when they merged their networks business. That was a very exciting change programme at a time of trying to create better value for the organisation. We helped NSN create a future for the organisation, so we had 8,000 people involved around the world in a conversation over 72 hours in which they constructed the values of the future organisation and, following that, then put changes in place that would make that future organisation a reality for them.

CD1 TRACK 17 (P = PETRA, E = EDUARDO, M = MITSUKO, W = WILLIAM)

P Good morning, everyone, I take it you've received the agenda and the minutes of our last meeting. Does anyone have any comments?

E/M/W No/OK.

P Right. The purpose of this meeting is to discuss our smoking policy. As you know, people are complaining that our staff have been smoking just outside the door of the building and leaving cigarette ends everywhere on the pavement. That's not acceptable. Eduardo, you're a smoker, what do you think we should do about it?

E Well, I think we should be able to smoke outside the restaurant, on the balcony. It's big enough for plenty of people to sit there, it's in the open air, and we smokers would be happy. We wouldn't bother to go outside the building.

P Mmm, interesting. How do you feel about that, Mitsuko? Do you agree with Eduardo?

M Not at all. Our policy has always been 'no smoking on company premises'. I think we should keep it that way. Non-smoking staff often go out on the balcony to relax, they don't want to breathe in a lot of filthy smoke. No, it's not at all—

W Come on, Mitsuko, I'm not a smoker, but I do think you should be a little more open-minded, more tolerant …

P I'm sorry, William. What you say is very interesting, I'm sure, but could you let Mitsuko finish, please? You'll get your turn to give your opinion.

W Sorry for interrupting you, Mitsuko. Please go on.

M I just wanted to say, I don't think we should provide places in the building for people to smoke. It's setting a bad example, especially to younger staff.

P William, what do you want to say?

W I just think we have to try to understand smokers. They're addicted to smoking, they find it very hard to give up, so we should provide them with somewhere to enjoy their habit. Or, if we can't do that, give them a longer break during the morning, say at 11 o'clock, so they can go to the park near here and have a cigarette.

M I think that's a good idea, Petra. It would show smokers that we want to help them, you know, that we're a tolerant, open-minded company.

P Not a bad idea. It's definitely worth considering, too. But I think we should move on now. Can we come back to the smoking issue at our next meeting? I want to get the opinion of staff about our smoking policy. So they'll be getting a questionnaire about it from our HR department …

***

OK everyone, thanks for your comments. To sum up, then, on the smoking policy, we'll consider whether we want to give smokers a longer break in the morning. And we'll discuss the matter again at next week's meeting. OK, any other business? … Right, thanks everyone for your contributions. Have a good lunch.

CD1 TRACK 18 (I = INTERVIEWER, SH = SCOTT HENDERSON)

I First of all, Mr Henderson, what was your main reason for the acquisition?

SH Well, it'll benefit our group in many ways. Obviously, we expect the deal to boost our earnings. It's bound to be good for our bottom line – not immediately, but the year after next, we're hoping …

I Hold on, it sounds to me, from what you're saying it'll be bad for your bottom line, won't it?

SH Look, like all acquisitions, the reorganisation will involve additional costs, so these will affect earnings in the early stages – all mergers are costly at the beginning.

I Mmm, I suppose there'll be savings as well.

SH What exactly do you mean?

I Well, savings in terms of personnel, staff cuts, redundancies …

SH I'd rather not comment on that, if you don't mind. We're in the early stages at present, nothing's been decided yet.

I So what are the synergies? What are the main benefits, apart from boosting earnings in the long run?

SH Well, we plan to expand the TV channels, offer more variety and sell more entertainment products. Also, we'll import a lot of Australian films for Asian audiences. I want to make our new group a strong force in Asia.

I I see. Are you worried about the cultural differences between the two organisations?

SH Not really. There'll be some initial problems, no doubt, but our managers have an understanding of Chinese culture, and don't forget, I'm a fluent Mandarin speaker. But of course, the working language in the group will continue to be English.

I Right. Thanks very much, Mr Henderson. I hope your company will be very successful in the future.

SH Thank you.

WORKING ACROSS CULTURES 1: SOCIALISING

CD1 TRACK 19 (AS = ANTONIO SILVA, JW = JAMES WHITFIELD)

AS Hi, I'm Antonio Silva, nice to meet you.

JW Nice to meet you, too. I'm James Whitfield. Call me James.

AS Where are you from, James?

JW I'm from Atlanta, Georgia. How about you?

AS I've come a long way. I'm from Belo Horizonte in Brazil. I'm Sales Manager for an office equipment group, Techko. Maybe you know us?

JW Yeah, I've certainly heard of your company. I work for New Era, in New York. I'm a systems analyst.

AS Right. How is business going for you? Is it a bit tough, like for most people?

JW No, not so far. Actually, our sales were up last quarter, but it's early days, I suppose. To be honest, we're all worried about the future, no doubt about that. How about your company?

AS Things are not too good at all. We've had quite a few redundancies lately. All departments have been told to cut costs this year. It's not going to be easy, but we've got to do it.

JW Mmm, doesn't sound too good.

AS No, but these are difficult times for everyone. How was your journey here? I suppose you came by air, did you?

JW Yeah, it was quite a long flight, a bit turbulent at times, but the food and service were OK, so I'm not complaining. How about your journey?

AS Pretty exhausting. But I stopped over at Los Angeles and did some business there. So I did get a rest before coming here. Are you staying at this hotel?

JW Actually, I'm not. I'm lucky, I'm staying with my daughter. She lives downtown, not far from here, and she insisted I stayed with her. It's fine by me. She's a fantastic cook!

AS Woah, you're lucky. I'm staying in a pretty cheap hotel a few blocks away to cut costs, and I'm not at all happy.

JW How's that?

AS Well, the room's very small, and the hotel doesn't have many facilities. It would be nice if there was a pool or gym, so I could have a workout. I couldn't use their business centre yesterday. Apparently, there was no one to run it. It was really annoying!

JW Maybe you should change your hotel.

AS I don't think I'll bother. The main thing is the conference. If the speakers are good, I can put up with a bit of inconvenience at the hotel.

JW Yeah, you're right. We all want to enjoy the conference and listen to some good speakers.

CD1 TRACK 20
(J = James, K = Klaus, A = Antonio, L = Ludmila, N = Nancy)

J Hi, Klaus, please join us, there's plenty of room.

K Thanks, we'd love to … I don't think we've met.

J Let me do the introductions. I'm James Whitfield, I'm from Atlanta, Georgia, and I'm a systems analyst for New Era. This is Antonio Silva from Brazil. He's a sales manager with an office equipment firm.

A How do you do.

K Pleased to meet you. I'm Klaus Liebermann, I'm a colleague of James's. I'm the Managing Director of New Era's Frankfurt subsidiary. And this is Ludmila Poigina from St Petersburg. She's a director of an engineering company.

L How do you do.

K And this is Nancy Chen from Beijing. She's a senior official in the Chinese Department of Environment.

N How do you do.

J So … have any of you had time to visit the city yet? I suppose you want to explore it a bit.

N Well, I'd love to, I've never been to Seattle, and I've heard a lot of good things about it. But I just don't have the time. I'm only here for two days, and I want to go to as many talks as possible.

K That's not much time, but you should try to see a few of the sights here, like the famous Space Needle. It's a real landmark. And if you go to the market area, you can see where the first Starbucks store was located, back in the early 1970s.

N OK, well, I might try to sneak away for a few hours if possible. What about you, Ludmila, are you going to check out the local area?

L Actually, I've already done that. I came here early so I could look around a bit. I've seen the Space Needle and visited the civic centre. I was really impressed with the Columbia Centre – it's a massive skyscraper, much bigger than the ones I saw in New York.

K What about the conference? Anyone special you want to see, Antonio?

A I'll definitely go to Mark Carlson's talk. He's always worth listening to. I don't know much about the other speakers, though. Can anyone recommend a good speaker?

L Well, I've registered to go to David Broadus's presentation. He's written a lot of books on information systems. I think he'll be the star of the conference. He's a very stimulating speaker.

K Yes, I can confirm that. I went to one of his talks in Munich last year, and the questions afterwards went on for over half an hour. He went down really well with the audience because he was obviously so knowledgeable about his topic.

N Yes, I want to go to his talk, too, if it's not already booked up. Another good speaker is Jerry Chin. He's an expert on management software. He's another speaker who shouldn't be missed.

UNIT 4 ORGANISATION

CD1 TRACK 21
1 Stock levels have been low for two weeks now.
2 Why do we always have to check with the parent company before making decisions?
3 Yes, that's fine. If you could just hold on a minute, I'll need to transfer you to a supervisor.
4 We need to deliver this consignment on Friday.
5 The production line is operating at full capacity.
6 The Board of Directors has fixed the Annual General Meeting for Tuesday the second.
7 Can you e-mail head office as soon as possible and find out about the designs for the new window displays?
8 I'm afraid all our engineers are out working on repairs at the moment.

CD1 TRACK 22
1 Well, in some ways, it's quite a conservative company, so some of the systems are a bit old-fashioned. There's still a lot of paperwork, so I suppose you could say it's very bureaucratic. I seem to spend a lot of time looking in files, both on the computer and in our paper archives.
2 Our department seems to be busy all the time. We're always getting enquiries from journalists and dealing with the broadcast media. I guess it's because we have such a high-profile boss. Although the company itself is quite hierarchical, our department is actually very democratic – everyone is an equal member of the team.
3 It's a big department, and we deal with a lot of employees. It's everything from recruitment and running training courses through to dealing with retirement. It's quite a progressive company, so everything is open plan – which is a bit difficult if I need to have a private meeting. There are meeting rooms, but they always seem to be busy.

CD1 TRACK 23
1	bureaucratic	7	centralised
2	decentralised	8	dynamic
3	impersonal	9	professional
4	caring	10	conservative
5	democratic	11	hierarchical
6	market-driven	12	progressive

CD1 TRACK 24 (I = Interviewer, RR = Richard Rawlinson)

I How do you analyse a company's organisation?

RR Well, we take a fairly broad view of organisation. We start with the formal structure of lines and boxes – who reports to who, what their official responsibilities are. But it's mu-, very important to go beyond that and think first about their decision rights – what does the position actually have the authority to decide? Who do they need to consult, who do they need to keep informed, who do they need to have approvals? Third area is information flows. If you want to understand how a company works, you need to know who knows what, so we look at communications, information, the sort of data that is provided and who gets it. And then the final area is the rewards, the performance management – not just who gets bonuses and what they're based on, but how do you get promoted and how do people get rewarded in all the other ways that provide incentives in an organisation?
We put all those four things together – the formal organisation, the decision rights, the information flows and the incentives – and we call that the 'organisational DNA'. So we put a lot of emphasis on understanding that.

CD1 TRACK 25 (RR = Richard Rawlinson)

RR If you want to start an analysis, we have a survey tool – it's on a website, orgdna.com, where you can answer just a small number of questions about your organisation and then we compare that to answers from about 40,000 other executives and we can recognise patterns, and that helps us to say that your organisation is like these other organisations, and so we can get some learning from comparable organisations. And we call that the 'orgdna profiler'. It gives you a superficial view and it's a good place to start the conversation. But then we have to go much deeper. And we usually organise both workshops with the executives and probes into particular aspects that seem to be particularly interesting. So, for example, we might take a single major controversial decision and look at how that was actually made, and really you often find that the reality is quite different from the theory.

CD1 TRACK 26 (I = Interviewer, RR = Richard Rawlinson)

I Can you give us an example of how you've helped a company with its organisation?

RR I recently did a major piece of work for a very large, global American company that was organised by function. So Manufacturing had responsibility for all the plants around the world, Marketing ran all the brands in every country. It was a very efficient organisation, but it wasn't very good at responding to the local markets, and so they decided that they wanted to move to a geographically based organisation. So we had to figure out, first of all, what were the right geographies – was every country a separate geography or are we going to put some together? What are you going to do for Europe as a whole, as well as what you are going to do for Germany and for Spain? Um, so we did a lot of looking at how the business operated, where products were made, where they were shipped to, how competitors were organised. And we also had to spend a lot of time thinking about whether we needed regional organisations or whether every single business unit would report back to the headquarters, er, in the US.

CD1 TRACK 27 (M = Maria, A = Alex)

M Hello, Alex, great to see you again.

A Hi, Maria. How are you?

M Fine, thanks. I haven't seen you for ages. We last met at that trade show in Geneva, didn't we? How is everything going with you?

A Yes, we did … er great … pretty well at the moment, thanks. I'm still in the same department, but I got promoted last year, so I'm now Head of Marketing. I'm in charge of 50 people.

M Fantastic!

A How about you? Are you still in sales?

M Actually, no. I changed my job last year. I'm in finance now. I'm really enjoying it.

A That's good.

M Yes, but the big news is, Alex, I finally passed my driving test! It took me three attempts, but I finally did it and now I am going to get a sports car.

A Really? That's great! Well, congratulations!

CD1 TRACK 28 (B = BOB, K = KARIN)

B Hi, my name's Bob Danvers.

K Hi, good to meet you. I'm Karin Schmidt.

B Which part of the group are you working for?

K I've just joined MCB. We provide all the market research. What about you?

B I'm with Clear View.

K I don't know much about Clear View. What sort of projects do you work on?

B Well, we're basically an outsourcing business. We supply companies and organisations with various services, including IT, office equipment, travel and even cleaning services.

K I see. And is it a new company?

B No, we're well established. The company was founded in the mid-1980s, and we've been growing rapidly ever since. It's organised into four divisions. We have over 7,000 employees; we've got our headquarters in London and offices in New York, Cape Town and Sydney – so we're pretty big.

CD1 TRACK 29 (F = FRANK, N = NATHALIE, C = CHRISTOPH)

F Christoph, I'd like you to meet Nathalie. She's joining us from the Italian subsidiary. She'll be with us for the next 12 months.

N Nice to meet you, Christoph.

C It's a pleasure.

F Nathalie speaks fluent Spanish, so she could be very useful when you're dealing with our South American customers. She's also very keen on sailing, so you two should have plenty to talk about.

C Oh, that's interesting. I'm sure you're much better than me – I'm a beginner, really, but I do love it. Let me show you where you'll be working. It's over here. By the way, would you like a coffee?

CD1 TRACK 30 (C = CARL, F = FRANÇOISE, JP = JEAN-PIERRE, P = PAOLO)

C I suppose you've all seen the Vice-President's message on the notice boards. What do you think, Françoise?

F Huh, it's pretty typical, isn't it? It's all about how the company will benefit. What about us? Don't we count?

ALL Yeah/Right/Exactly.

F I mean, why should we leave this beautiful building, on one of most famous avenues in the world? We love it here. The move's not convenient for me at all. If we go to Beauchamp, my husband will have to drive 120 kilometres every day to get to work. He'll soon get tired of doing that. And what about my children's education? Will the schools be any good in Beauchamp? I have no idea. How about you, Jean Pierre?

JP Well, to be honest, it doesn't bother me. I'm really tired of living in Paris. It's so stressful here, everyone rushing around, trying to make money. I wouldn't mind moving to a quieter area. Beauchamp sounds quite nice, and the countryside outside the town is pleasant, I believe. What about you, Paolo? Do you think the move will be good for us?

P I am absolutely against it. It will upset families and cause a lot of problems for some staff. I will have to sell my apartment if we move. I only bought it last year, so I will probably lose a lot of money – I don't think I will get any compensation for that, do you? You don't agree, Jean Pierre, I can see that.

JP Well, you're right, Paolo, it'll cause a lot of problems, there's no doubt about that. But the company will benefit a lot, and that's important, too. In the long run, the move will increase our revenue, make us more competitive and keep us in jobs. That's a good reason for moving, isn't it, Carl? What do you think?

C Maybe, but I feel pretty depressed at the moment. I hope they'll postpone the proposal. There's a lot of bad feeling about it. I tell you one thing, a lot of our best staff will refuse to relocate. They can easily get another job here in Paris, they won't want to move. They've got a really good lifestyle, and they won't want to give it up. The management will get a big shock if the relocation goes ahead.

UNIT 5 ADVERTISING

CD1 TRACK 31 (I = INTERVIEWER, MR = MARCO RIMINI)

I What are the key elements of a really good advertising campaign?

MR When I answer the question of what ['s] really makes a good advertising campaign, I always go back to the beginning and ask the question, what is the person who's paying for the campaign trying to achieve? What is that person's objectives, what is it that that person wants to happen as a result of spending money on this advertising campaign? So in order to decide whether it is good or bad, it is first of all most important to understand what it is that the campaign must try and achieve. Some people might say, well that's obvious – to sell more goods, to sell more services, to sell more bottles of Coca-Cola or jeans – and often, of course, it is simply to sell more of a product. But not always. Sometimes it is to change the image of a company. Sometimes it is to change people's views of an issue. Sometimes it is to get people to drink less alcohol, to do up their seat belts, to change the way in which they use energy. So a good or bad advertising campaign depends on what it is there to achieve.

CD1 TRACK 32 (I = INTERVIEWER, MR = MARCO RIMINI)

I Can you take us through the typical planning and launch stages of a campaign?

MR So, when we look at the different stages of a campaign, we tend to start always with the briefing. The first stage is to identify the brief from the client and to agree the brief with the client. It is at this stage that we tend to agree the objectives I referred to earlier – what will make the client happy after this campaign has been aired?
The second stage is then to take that brief and articulate it for the people in our organisations who have to make recommendations and have ideas about the campaign itself. At this stage, we brief creative people to come up with ideas and media people to ask, to have ideas about which channels those ideas will be seen in.
The third stage will be the presentation of those ideas to the client. There is then some debate … that debate process can go on for quite a long time until there's agreement. At that point of agreement, we get into the execution phase. The execution phase is where we then produce the creative material and buy the space and the places in the channels of distribution for that material.

CD1 TRACK 33 (I = INTERVIEWER, MR = MARCO RIMINI)

I Can you give us an example of a successful new media campaign?

MR One of the most successful new media campaigns, from one of the clients that uses new media best, is Nike. Nike, of course, have a young audience who are very literate about the new media and therefore live their lives in that media. And so rather than simply use advertising on television to talk to this youthful audience, what Nike does is they start seeding viral campaigns. And viral campaigns are pieces of film or pieces of content which they hope will be picked up by individuals who see it – perhaps on YouTube – and passed on to their friends with comments to say, 'Look at this piece of film. Isn't it fantastic?'
Perhaps the most famous piece of Nike viral was Ronaldinho, the footballer, appearing to be able to, er, lob the ball directly onto the goalpost – er, goal bar – and it bouncing back to him, ten times – a piece of outrageous skill which is just about believable, and then the viral campaign actually became about was it real or was it faked? So it was not only an entertaining piece of film, but it generated its own PR, public-relations exercise, it generated its own gossip on the web. The answer was, it was fake.

CD1 TRACK 34

1 Could I have your attention, please? Right, good morning, everyone. On behalf of Alpha Advertising, I'd like to welcome you. My name's Marc Hayward, I'm Creative Director. This morning, I'd like to outline the campaign concept we've developed for you. I've divided my presentation into three parts. Firstly, I'll give you the background to the campaign. Secondly, I'll discuss the target markets. Finally, I'll talk you through the media we plan to use. I'd be grateful if you could leave any questions to the end. So, first of all, let me give you some of the background …

2 Right, let's get started. Hi, everyone, I'm Marc Hayward. As you may know, I'm Creative Director of Alpha Advertising. Great to see you all. Anyway, I'm here to tell you about the ideas we've come up with for the ad campaign. My talk is in three parts. I'll start with the background to the campaign, move on to the target markets, and finish with the media we plan to use. If there's anything you're not clear about, feel free to stop me and ask any questions. Right, so, the background …

CD1 TRACK 35

… and particularly in Germany, where this is very important. Just to give you a specific example: if you look at the next slide, we can see from the chart that the key age group is 18 to 25, but that this will become less, not more, important as the product matures in the market. As I say, this is reflected across all the markets.

Right, that's all I have to say about the target markets. Let's now move on to the final part, and the media we plan to use. We'll start in a month's time with a viral campaign on the Internet to generate interest, of which more later. Then there is the new TV commercial, which I'll be showing you in the form of a storyboard at the end of the presentation. Finally, we intend to use images from the commercial for outdoor advertising on hoardings and public transport. This will be linked to a co-ordinated press campaign, starting in June.

So, to sum up, then, before we go to the storyboard: the key points again are that firstly, the product already has wide appeal, so we're really just developing the brand and trying to keep it fresh. Secondly, that we will need to bear in mind the younger sections of the market for the future; and finally, the key to getting the campaign started is the viral advertising campaign. Thank you very much. Now, are there any questions?

UNIT 6 MONEY

CD1 TRACK 36

And now the business news …

There was a further downturn in the economy this month as the recession in the United States and Asia-Pacific region continues. Yesterday was another day of heavy trading on the stock market with big losses in share values. The forecast for the near future is not good, as market confidence remains low.

Paradise Lane, the struggling luxury hotel group, is seeking new investment to try and avoid bankruptcy, following the announcement of disastrous interim results. It currently has a debt of nearly $5 billion. There are rumours of rivals GHN taking a large equity stake in the troubled hotel group.

Phoenix Media announced a 15% increase in pre-tax profits on an annual turnover of $4.5 million. Added to the strong performance in the last quarter, this is likely to result in an increased dividend of over 14 cents per share, well up on last year, which will certainly please shareholders. Following a rise in sales in the emerging markets of …

CD1 TRACK 37 (I = Interviewer, DM = Darrell Mercer)

I   Could you tell me what your role is as an investment director?

DM   The aim of the business is to provide investment solutions for private individuals who have, er, capital that they wish to employ to achieve a certain level of return. Um, my role as the Investment Director is to both design the strategy for the client with the intention of meeting that aim, that return, and also then manage that strategy on an ongoing basis.

CD1 TRACK 38 (I = Interviewer, DM = Darrell Mercer)

I   What are the main areas that you invest in?

DM   We invest in a number of different areas … to try and, as I said earlier, to keep the overall spread of investment right. And they really start from the lowest risk asset, which is cash, and then we introduce other asset classes that have different risk and return profiles. So as one is prepared to take on a bit more risk, then obviously one is going potentially to get some more return. So, moving up the scale of risk we go from cash to fixed-interest securities, where in effect the client will be lending their money to either a government or a company in return for a fixed rate of return, with the view that capital will increase over a period of time. We then look at, um, index-linked – i.e. linked to the rate of inflation – securities. Equities will be the next level of risk – an equity being a stock or a share – where you're buying part of a company, and obviously as the company performs better, the price of that share should increase. We then look at slightly more esoteric or different areas of investment to give some return that's not linked to equity returns … to share returns … for instance, commercial property is an area where one can achieve a fairly good income return, but you're investing long term into bricks and mortar – something that you can see … something that's slightly more safe. We also look at, er, commodities … so looking at precious metals either gold or platinum. We look at agriculture, which has become an interesting area of development over the last 20 years. And then we have the final asset class we call our alternative investments, and they can be either hedge funds, which invest in lots of different areas, or something that's called absolute return funds, where the manager will invest money across a whole wide range of areas with the view to giving small incremental elements of return over a reasonable period. And as I said earlier, we try and combine those asset classes to get the best level of risk and return.

CD1 TRACK 39

(I = Interviewer, DM = Darrell Mercer)

I   In difficult economic times, what would you suggest are attractive areas for investment?

DM   There are a number of attractive areas, and I think I've touched on one earlier with the bond investments. But perhaps I'll develop that a little bit further. A lot really depends on where we are within that economic cycle. If we're at the very bottom of an economic cycle, then the best form of recovery is probably going to be in companies who are going to recover as the economy recovers. So when prices are very low, you can invest in equity of a company where you saw they would benefit from that reduction in interest rates that you've seen. If it's in the early stages of an economic depression, or recession shall we call it, then with interest rates likely to be cut aggressively, then obviously the fixed-income area of the market is perhaps the most appropriate place to be. Another area which I think has traditionally been a very safe haven has been gold, and I think over the last 15 years or so, gold has been through a number of different cycles and in particular, I think, as a recovery play, it will always be perceived as a store of value. At the same time, as the emerging markets keep continuing to grow, there's a lot of interest … appetite … for people to invest in gold in terms of their jewellery, as well as wishing to own … to own that asset. So, I think gold, fixed-income securities and early cycle equities would be my answer.

CD1 TRACK 40

Business in brief

It was a bad day for the London market. Following disappointing results from FedEx in the US and fears of a credit crunch, the FTSE 100 fell 105 points or 1.8 per cent to 5,756.9, while the FTSE 250 fell 189.1 points or 1.9 per cent to 9,534.8.

Only eight blue-chip stocks managed to make gains. The best was Smith & Nephew. Shares in the medical devices group rose 2.9 per cent to 595 $^1/_2$p after UBS upgraded the stock to a 'buy' recommendation. S&N was also supported by rumours of a bid approach from a Japanese company.

On the other hand, British Airways, down 5.2 per cent to 225 $^3/_4$p, fell even further after Morgan Stanley cut its target to 149p. This was because of worries about increasing fuel prices.

Tate and Lyle, the sugar and sweeteners group, lost 5.2 per cent to 402 $^1/_4$p after CityGroup lowered its forecasts because of rising corn prices. Following recent floods in the US, the cost of corn has risen 25 per cent.

CD1 TRACK 41

So, to summarise, our product is a storage device with a modular design. It's very flexible, very versatile. It can be divided up, added to and shaped to fit any space in a house or apartment. You can put bottles, flowers, magazines, fruit, nuts, lots of other things in it. It's lightweight, durable and very stylish, and made out of a special, recyclable material.

We're looking for an investment of $200,000 from you in return for a stake of 25% in our business. The name of our product is MultiStore.

CD1 TRACK 42 (T1 = Tycoon 1, T2 = Tycoon 2, E1 = Entrepreneur 1, E2 = Entrepreneur 2)

T1   OK, another question I'd like to ask you. Have you taken out a patent for the device?

E1   Yes, we have. The product is fully protected against copying.

T1   Excellent. And what's your profit margin on each 10-module unit?

E1   It's approximately 80%.

T1   Mmm, quite good. And how about your forecasts for the next three years, turnover and profit?

E1   In year one, we forecast a turnover of $150,000 and a profit of approximately $120,000. Year two, turnover of $600,000 and a profit of $480,000. And in year three, a turnover of $3 million and a profit of $2.4 million.

T2   Now I'd like to ask a question. How many of the 10-module units have you sold, and who have you sold them to?

E2   I can answer that question, as I'm the sales person in our team. We've sold about 2,000 units, mainly to major department stores and specialist shops for household goods in New York and Chicago.

T2   OK, thanks for all the information. Now, I'll tell you what I think. I like your product, it's definitely got sales potential, and I'd like to make you an offer. I'll give you the full amount, $200,000, but I'd want a stake of 50% in your business. The market for this sort of product is very competitive, there's a lot of risk involved, and marketing and promoting it could be very expensive. So that's the deal I'm offering you.

E1 Mmm … we'll have to think about that. OK, thank you. How about you? Are you interested as well?

T1 Yes, I like the product as well, but I also think it'll need a lot of marketing to get established, and you may have to change the packaging. So … I'll offer you the full amount, $200,000, for a stake of 45%.

E1 OK, so we seem to have two offers on the table. Could I ask each of you, what business expertise you could bring to our business? How much help could you give us, apart from money?

T1 Well, I have a company which sells household products to the retail trade, and it's very successful. You would be able to use our sales force to build up sales and develop the brand. And I would be very hands-on in developing your product.

T2 In my case, I have a very good track record investing in start-up businesses like yours. Basically, I invest in people, and I've been impressed with your presentation. I think we could work well together.

E1 Thanks to both of you. Could we have a break and consider your offer?

T1&2 By all means/certainly. Take your time..

WORKING ACROSS CULTURES 2: INTERNATIONAL MEETINGS

CD1 TRACK 43

The culture we come from or live in influences what we see, do, believe and say. It affects our expectations and behaviour, and we need to be very aware of it. The simple fact is that what's normal or appropriate for us may seem very strange or even rude to someone from a different culture.

I'll look at three of the key areas of culture which may affect communication in international meetings, causing confusion and frustration. Firstly, time: not all cultures or people are ruled by the clock. There are some cultures, it's true, where the feeling is indeed that 'time is money'. They will often have strict approaches to this aspect of meetings, such as starting and finishing times and the duration of discussion. Other cultures, however, have a completely different approach and see the starting time as a guide only and the finishing time as not fixed. Other stages may be surprisingly flexible, and you may find that there is little attempt to stick to the agenda. Secondly, the idea of hierarchy in a culture, and therefore in meetings, can be very significant. By this, we mean the relative levels of importance and seniority which people have in a company. Someone from a very hierarchical culture is likely to feel very uncomfortable saying what they think or criticising the ideas of others, especially if the person being criticised holds a higher position. They are also unlikely to openly disagree or report a problem in front of a boss or manager. Criticising the ideas of a superior could be seen as a loss of face for both people involved. Another key area to think about is the objective of the meeting. In many cultures, there's an attitude that meetings should have very clear purposes and 'get down to business' pretty quickly … using a structured, pre-planned agenda is important. In such cases, there's very little in the way of small talk – maybe just a couple of comments about the weather, football, etc. However, other cultures see meetings as the place for relationship building and developing trust, so the meeting may be a lengthy discussion, and actual decisions may often be made outside the meeting. Again, the idea that the purpose of a meeting is to make a decision may be alien to some cultures. It's important to bear this in mind, as it can be quite a surprise if you're not used to it.

Finally, some advice on successful international meetings. Clarifying is key in any international meeting. Different cultural assumptions mean that sometimes spoken language, body language, including gestures, and written symbols can be misunderstood. Constant checking and feedback is crucial. At the end of a meeting, it's vital to summarise the main areas of agreement and disagreement and ensure that everyone's happy with them to avoid confusion and frustration later.

Overall, any international meeting requires planning, organisation and thinking about if it's to succeed. We must consider how cultural differences may affect mutual understanding and we should try to predict any areas open to misunderstanding before they happen.

UNIT 7 CULTURES

CD1 TRACK 44 (I = INTERVIEWER, JT = JEFF TOMS)

I Can you give us some examples of culture shock that people have experienced?

JT There are many, many examples of culture shock, and, er, many of those really come about because people haven't prepared themselves well enough. So examples of that might be timing, where in some cultures the concept and perception of timekeeping is very different, and I guess the obvious one that people always use is the example of the Middle East. The Middle Eastern clock really revolves around two things really – the prayer times and of course, because they were desert travellers, about the movements of the sun and the moon, er, during periods of the day.

Um, other examples is where, again around time, where, perhaps from a Latin culture's perspective, um, it's about building relationships before you actually get down to, to business. Now very often Western, and particularly American, businesspeople find that very frustrating. For Americans, time is money, and so they'll be very keen to actually … er, the salesman will be very keen to get out his sales literature and start exalting the virtues of the product he's trying to sell you, er, they'll try to get on with the agenda as quickly as possible, whereas, particularly in Latin cultures and also in people like Chinese cultures, relationship building is very important. They'll want to entertain you for sure, and very often invite you back to their home, and all this before they actually want to sit down and do business with you because, in the Latin culture, they are making judgements about you as an individual, as to, as to whether you're the kind of person that they want to do business with.

CD1 TRACK 45 (I = INTERVIEWER, JT = JEFF TOMS)

I Are some people better suited for international business than others?

JT Absolutely – er, what companies still tend to do is select people for international business and business assignments, er, purely based on their skill set. So if you're the best civil engineer or you're the greatest IT consultant in the business, it is often thought that this fully equips you to be the best person to conduct that business internationally. Clearly those skills are very important, but they have to be underpinned by, I think, a number of personal traits that make you a more effective international businessperson.

Some of those traits – um, adaptability: you have got to be prepared to adapt the way that you do business or adapt your expectations or your needs, to meet the needs of the culture of the people that you're doing business with – so, adaptability; flexibility is obviously very important. Er, you've got to be prepared to actually change the parameters with which you were intending to do business.

CD1 TRACK 46 (JT = JEFF TOMS)

JT Very important – and you'll know from this course in communication – um, you've got to be a good listener. Er, you've got to pay more attention than you would when speaking to somebody in your own culture to make sure that you have understood quite clearly what is being said. And one of the things that we always say to people is that, to be very sure that you've actually heard what you think you've heard. There are some steps you can take. It's always a very good idea to get the individual, if you're not clear, to repeat what they've said. It may seem tedious to you, but actually it's very important to make sure that you haven't made mistakes.

I think also one of the key features of the successful international businessperson is to be non-judgemental. For instance, if you're coming from an Asian culture, er, to try and do business with, er, a Western culture, er, for certain the way that people do things will be fundamentally different – er, the hierarchy, the structure, the decision-making process, the seniority and the influence of the people you're doing business with – will be fundamentally different. Er, you may not agree, you may not approve of the way that business is done in another culture; but the way that people do business in that culture is as a result of many, many years of, of development and so you have to be accepting, er, that it may be not to your liking and it may be different, but it is not wrong.

CD1 TRACK 47

1 Small talk is one way to break the ice when meeting someone for the first time.

2 I was thrown in at the deep end when my company sent me to run the German office. I was only given two days' notice to get everything ready.

3 We don't see eye to eye with our US parent company about punctuality. We have very different ideas about what being 'on time' means. It's a question of culture.

4 I got into hot water with my boss for wearing casual clothes to the meeting with the potential Japanese customers.

5 I really put my foot in it when I met our Spanish partner. Because I was nervous, I said 'Who are you?' rather than 'How are you?'.

6   I get on like a house on fire with our Polish agent; we like the same things and have the same sense of humour.

7   When I visited China for the first time, I was like a fish out of water. Everything was so different, and I couldn't read any of the signs.

8   My first meeting with our overseas clients was a real eye-opener. I hadn't seen that style of negotiation before.

CD1 TRACK 48

A   So where did you go on holiday, then?
B   Italy.
A   Did you have a good time?
B   Yes. It was OK.
A   And which part of Italy did you go to?
B   Sicily.
A   I've been to Sicily – Taormina. I really enjoyed it. What did you think of it?
B   Nothing special.
A   Oh, right. So … How's it going at work?
B   We're busy.
A   That's really good, isn't it?
B   I don't know about that.

CD2 TRACK 1

1   I'm sorry. I didn't quite catch your name.
2   I'm really sorry – I'd love to, but I'm afraid I'm going to the theatre on Wednesday night.
3   Not for me, thanks. I'm not keen on seafood.
4   I'm sorry, but I really do have to be going. It was really nice talking to you.
5   Welcome to our headquarters. It's a pleasure to meet you. I'm James Clayton.
6   Katrina, can I introduce you to Greg? Greg's over from the States. Greg, this is Katrina Siedler, my boss.
7   Please, let me get this.
8   Here's to our future success.
9   I'm very sorry to hear about what happened.
10 I'm sorry I'm late, the traffic from the airport was terrible.

CD2 TRACK 2

A   Is this your first visit to the region?
B   No, I come here quite a lot, but usually to Hong Kong.
A   Oh really! What do you do?
B   I'm an Account Director for a marketing company.
A   How long have you been there?
B   Nearly five years now.
A   Have you been to Tokyo before?
B   No, this is my first trip.
A   Business or pleasure?
B   Business, I'm afraid.
A   How long have you been here?
B   Six days.
A   And how long are you staying?
B   Until tomorrow evening.
A   Where are you staying?
B   At the Metropolitan Hotel.
A   What's the food like?
B   It's very good, but eating at the Metropolitan can be quite expensive.
A   So, what do you think of Tokyo?
B   I really like it. There's so much to see and do.

CD2 TRACK 3 (R = Rosana, E = Enrique)

R   So, Enrique, what can you tell me about Germany?
E   Well, I don't think there'll be any language problem for you. Most German businesspeople are pretty fluent in English, and they'll use English with you, as you don't know any German. They're pretty formal in business, so don't be surprised at how they address each other. They tend to use family names, not first names, when they talk to each other.
R   I see. What about when you first meet German managers? How do you greet them?
E   Well, generally they shake hands.
R   OK. How about topics of conversation, say, if I'm asked out for dinner or whatever? What are good topics of conversation in France?
E   Oh, that's easy. French people love talking about food – they're very proud of their cuisine, so you can't go wrong if you introduce that topic into the conversation. The French are like the Spanish and Portuguese, they'll go on for hours talking about local dishes.

R   That's good to hear. I love talking about food, too. But I like food a bit too much, so I'm always worrying about my weight. What about safe topics of conversation in Russia? You've spent quite a lot of time there, haven't you?
E   Yeah, Russians like food, too, so it's a good topic. But you could try asking Russians you meet about the state of the economy. That'll get them going. Most Russians love talking about the economy and the problems they're having. It's a really good subject. And Russian men like to talk about ice hockey – it's a very popular sport there. By the way, plenty of Russians speak English well, so you won't have any problems understanding them. But you may have difficulty reading the name of streets, because they're all in Cyrillic script. It can be very confusing for visitors.
R   Oh, thanks. What about Germany? What do Germans like talking about?
E   If you're with men, just bring up the subject of football. They're as keen on football as we are in Portugal. Germans expect to win any match they play, and they often do, except when they play the Brazilians or the Italians! Yeah, football's a great topic of conversation with men. I'm not sure what subjects German women like talking about.
R   OK, thanks very much. What about gifts? Supposing I'm invited out to dinner, what do I bring with me to give my host?
E   Well, in France, most visitors bring flowers for their hostess – everyone loves to receive them. And in Russia, too, flowers are very acceptable. They'd also be a great gift in Germany.
R   Yeah, flowers are the answer in most countries, I'd say. But what else would be a good gift? Chocolates? Something typical from my country, would they like that …?

UNIT 8 HUMAN RESOURCES

CD2 TRACK 4

Well, what usually happens is that an employer will advertise a vacancy or new post – sometimes both inside and outside the company. Then, after they have received all the applications, they will screen them – go through and shortlist the candidates for interview – choosing those who appear to meet the criteria for the job. Next, they will assemble an interview panel, which is perhaps as many as four or five people in some cases, and then call the candidates to interview. Some employers choose to check references at this stage to avoid delays later, while others wait until after the interview when they have chosen one of the candidates. Provided the panel is happy, the employer will make a job offer, and the successful candidate starts work. Often he or she will attend induction sessions or be given a mentor who helps to train new staff.

CD2 TRACK 5

A enthusiastic   B adaptable   C methodical   D reliable
E ambitious   F objective   G creative   H analytical
I authoritative   J practical

CD2 TRACK 6 (I = Interviewer, CO = Carys Owen)

I   How do you help people to find the right job?
CO As a specialist recruiter, our role is to assist job seekers in finding the perfect role for them. Er, we do that predominantly via our network of offices globally. Er, candidates will have the opportunity to come in, meet with a Hays consultant, and the Hays consultant will work with them to gain an understanding of what type of role they're looking for, what type of organisation they would like to work for, and really anything else that they feel is appropriate for them finding the right role for them. In addition, we'll also work with them on how they present themselves – your CV, for example. We will work through a CV, perhaps give tips and hints as to how best to present that, so that the candidate has the best possible opportunity of being represented in the right way to the client.
We also use our Hays.com website, which is a jobseekers' website. Candidates can apply online for roles that we advertise – um, they will also have the opportunity to get advice from that website, as well as to how they should structure their application. There's quite often more information about prospective employer[s] on there so that you can really see, straight from the website, what type of role is best for you.

CD2 TRACK 7 (I = Interviewer, CO = Carys Owen)

I   Is there any particular preparation you recommend before a job interview?
CO Preparation is absolutely key for any job interview. Your Hays consultant can assist you prior to that in getting that interview and presenting your CV, but ultimately, at the end of the day, during that

meeting with an employer, it's really down to you. We advise all of our prospective jobseekers to … certainly look at their appearance. You need to look your best for an interview. The other aspect of preparation which is absolutely key is to research your employer. Most organisations have websites, so we always recommend that people conduct a lot of research into that company's website – anything that's going on, any press clippings, any information that you can use to prove to the employer that you have actually made an effort to research them before attending the interview.

From the point of view of the actual vacancy, we would always recommend that you look at the duties within that vacancy and have a think about where in your previous experience you might be able to demonstrate your ability to do that job.

CD2 TRACK 8 (I = Interviewer, CO = Carys Owen)

I What recent changes have you noticed in the job market?

CO I think probably the most unique change in the job market, in the – most recently, is the intervention of online recruitment and web-based recruitment and websites. For us as a global business, it means that we can truly act in that way – we can recruit roles in the UK that are based wherever, equally we can recruit roles from India that are based wherever. It also means that the candidate or job seekers do have a huge amount of choice. You can go onto your website at home, sitting at home, and look at roles and jobs that are advertised globally, worldwide, so it's an absolutely unique opportunity for both candidates and employers.

Equally, um, in terms of the recruitment market, we have seen in the last years … few years, a development in the need for interim employees and temporary employees. Lots of organisations now are going through periods of change, and I think it's an accepted fact that organisations will continue to go through change, and quite often, specialist people will need to be brought in on project bases, to undertake specific projects in areas such as IT, human resources … project management generally will be very sought after.

CD2 TRACK 9 (CT = Cindy Tang, LP = Li Ping)

CT Good morning, my name's Cindy Tan. I'm calling about your advertisement in the China Post for a Marketing Assistant. I was wondering if you could give me a little more information.

LP Certainly, what do you need to know?

CT Well, first of all, am I still in time to apply? I only saw the advert today, and the newspaper was two weeks old. So, I was thinking, maybe it's too late …

LP No, don't worry, you're not too late, but you must hurry because the closing date for application is this Friday, so you haven't got a lot of time.

CT I see, that gives me just a couple of days. Well, I see there's an application form on your website, so I'll complete it right away and e-mail it to you.

LP Good, I look forward to getting it.

CT Just one or two more questions. I'd also like to know when the successful candidate has to start work with you. I mean, if I get the job, will I be able to give my present employer sufficient notice?

LP OK, that's a good question. How much notice would you need to give?

CT Well, I think my contract states that I have to give a month's notice.

LP Oh, that's no problem at all. We wouldn't expect anyone to join us immediately. In fact, if you were offered the job, I believe you'd start after the New Year – that would give you plenty of time.

CT OK, so, just to get this clear, I probably wouldn't have to start working until February, and maybe even later?

LP Exactly.

CT One last question. Could I ask you what the salary is? It wasn't given in the advert.

LP You're right. It would depend on a lot of things: qualifications, experience, personal qualities, that sort of thing.

CT Are you saying you can't give me a figure?

LP That's right. The salary's negotiable. But I can tell you, we pay very competitive salaries. I don't think you'll be disappointed by the starting salary we offer.

CT OK, I think that's everything. Thanks very much for your help.

LP Not at all, and good luck if you get an interview.

CT Thanks very much.

CD2 TRACK 10 (I = Interviewer, SW = Sean Wilder)

I Could I ask you, Mr Wilder, why you want to leave your present job?

SW OK, well, I really enjoy teaching languages, but I'm 52 now, and I feel I need a new challenge, something to really motivate me. It's not about money – we're very well off as a family – but recently I've felt teaching really wasn't enough, wasn't stretching me. I wasn't going to work with a good feeling inside me, let me put it that way.

I So, basically, you were bored?

SW Exactly.

I OK. Now, what would you say is your main weakness, in terms of this job?

SW Mmm, that's a tricky question. Let me think … well, I seem to get on well with most people, you know, I'm very easy-going – everyone says so – and someone has to do something really bad to me before I get angry. In fact, I can't remember the last time I got angry. I try to avoid confrontation with people. What's the point? I mean, for example, a lot of people say to me, you seem to have such a happy marriage, you two, you never seem to argue, and I say, well, actually, we never do! I hope that answers your question.

I Well … er … perhaps. A final question: why should we offer you the job?

SW Well, I've got a background organising sports, I'm very fit, as you can see, and I think teaching's just like running a health and leisure centre. You need the same skills, to get on well with people, have good communication skills and plenty of common sense. I'll find lots of ways to make money for you and increase the profits of the business. Also, don't forget I have a very good academic background. Yale is one of the best universities in the world, and my Master's in Sports Management is ideal for the job, even if I did get it years ago.

CD2 TRACK 11 (I = Interviewer, PG = Paolo Goncalves)

I My first question, Mr Goncalves, is why do you want to leave your present job?

PG Well, my present job's OK, I suppose … but I think I can do better. Who doesn't? I'm well known in São Paulo because of my movie career, and I think it's time for me to use my image to make more money. Actually, my agent suggested I apply for this job – he thought my background in martial arts would appeal to your organisation.

I OK, thanks. Now, what about your weaknesses? What would you say is a weakness in terms of the job we're offering?

PG Well, I suppose I don't have a lot of educational qualifications … probably the other candidates have more to offer in that area. But the teachers did try to widen my horizons when I was training to be an actor at RADA in London. I don't have qualifications in business, but it seems to me you need other qualities for the job you are offering, like a strong personality, a charismatic person, with good people skills, and I've certainly got all that.

I Mm-hm. Finally, why should we offer *you* the job?

PG Offer me the job because I'm famous in Brazil, and that will attract lots of customers for you. And I've got a load of ideas for improving your clubs. I could send you a report if you like, by the end of the week, showing what I would like to do to raise Fast Fitness's profile in São Paulo. I'm a very enterprising man, a risk-taker, and that's what you want at the moment.

CD2 TRACK 12 (I = Interviewer, MG = Martha Gómez)

I Could I ask you, Ms Gómez, why you want to leave your present job?

MG OK, it's a good question. I really enjoy working for Superfit, but it's rather a small centre, and the equipment is mostly out of date. I don't think I'm using all my skills at the moment, and to be honest, I don't get on at all with my boss.

I Oh, what's the problem?

MG Well, for one thing, I don't think he really values the work I do with people suffering from disease. I think he's a bit jealous of me, especially when I won that award. But what really bugs me is that he doesn't appreciate the fact that I manage Superfit most of the time. He's always away visiting the other centres, and then I'm in charge – it's a lot of responsibility, but he never gives me a word of thanks.

I What would you say is your main weakness, in terms of this job?

MG Well … my friends say, um, I need to be more assertive. I just don't like upsetting people, so I often do what they want, instead of saying 'no'. I suppose I'm a little shy, but I'm becoming more self-confident as I get older. Actually, I went on an assertiveness course a few weeks ago, and it really helped me a lot.

I A final question: why should we offer you the job?

MG Well, I've got lots of energy, and I really believe I can persuade people to have a healthier lifestyle. That's the key, I think, to building up a good fitness centre. Also, I'm a creative person and I will come up with other ideas for serving our local community and bringing more customers into Fast Fitness clubs.

CD2 TRACK 13 (I = Interviewer, SC = Silvia Cominelli)

I First, Ms Cominelli, why do you want to leave your present job?

SC That's easy to answer. To be honest, I'm not being paid enough for my qualifications and experience. I'm looking for a really big job that is well paid and will enable me to meet a lot of people and challenge me in the years to come.

I OK. Now, what would you say is your main weakness, in terms of this job?

SC Main weakness … I speak my mind, and that can sometimes upset people. I'm not a diplomatic person, but staff and students know where they are with me, and they like that. I don't talk about people behind their back, I say it to their face or not at all.

I A final question: why should we offer you the job?

SC Look, let me put my cards on the table. You're looking for someone who'll boost your profits and meet some very tough targets. I can do that for you. I expect a lot from people working with me, I set high standards, and staff have to achieve those standards. That's the bottom line. I believe in rewarding people who do well and getting rid of those who don't. And that's the kind of general manager you need at the moment. So that's why you should offer me the job.

UNIT 9 INTERNATIONAL MARKETS

CD2 TRACK 14 (I = Interviewer, IM = Ian McPherson)

I Perhaps you could summarise for our listeners the points you've made so far, Ian. You started by telling us what free trade is.

IM Right, I defined it as a situation in which goods come into and out of a country without any controls or taxes. Countries which truly believe in free trade try to liberalise their trade, that's to say, they take away barriers to trade, they remove things which stop people trading freely. They have open borders and few controls of goods at customs.

CD2 TRACK 15 (I = Interviewer, IM = Ian McPherson)

I OK … then you gave us several examples of barriers to trade.

IM Yes, I said that there are two main barriers: tariffs and subsidies. Tariffs are taxes on imported goods, so that the imports cannot compete so well against domestic products. Subsidies are money paid to domestic producers so that they can sell their goods more cheaply than foreign competitors. Tariffs and subsidies are barriers to trade because when people are given a choice, generally they will buy the cheapest product.

I You mentioned other barriers – less important ones, perhaps.

IM Uh-huh. I talked about quotas, which limit the quantity of a product which can be imported, and I discussed other restrictions on trade, such as expensive licences for importers, which add greatly to costs; and regulations relating to documents which a company must have to export its goods to certain countries. The documents can be very complicated and difficult to complete, so they slow down trading.

CD2 TRACK 16 (I = Interviewer, IM = Ian McPherson)

I I asked you if free trade was always a good thing.

IM And I answered, in principle, yes, it is a good thing, it's beneficial to countries.

I Why?

IM Countries which open their markets usually have a policy of deregulation, that's to say, they free their companies to compete in markets, without government control or subsidies. Because of this, consumers in free-trade areas are offered a wider range of high-quality products at lower prices. People in those areas can move to the most productive parts of the economy and get better jobs with higher wages or salaries. OK?

I So why do so many countries protect their industries and not allow free markets?

IM I gave three reasons, if you remember. Firstly, some people say, why should we practise free trade if other nations compete unfairly? For example, dumping is fairly common in international trade. When companies dump goods in overseas markets, they sell goods at very low prices, usually for less than it costs the company to produce the goods. Companies can usually only do that when they are heavily subsidised by their governments.
Secondly, many people believe that strategic industries must be protected. These are industries that are very important to the economy: steel, power, communications and so on. In the United States, many Americans think that the steel industry should be protected against cheap imports from Brazil and other countries. If the US depends too much on foreign-made steel, they argue, this could be bad in a time of war.

Finally, some say that in developing countries, industries need to be protected until they're strong enough to compete in world markets. This is the 'infant industry' argument: certain industries have to be protected until they can stand on their own feet, as it were.
My final point was that, throughout the world, there is a trend towards liberalising trade and removing trade barriers. The most successful economies tend to have open markets, and most of their industries have been deregulated.

CD2 TRACK 17 (NN = Naoko Nakamura, LB = Li Bai)

NN If I order 30,000 silk scarves, what discount will you offer us?

LB On 30,000, nothing. But if you buy 50,000 scarves, then we'll offer you 10%.

NN OK, I'll think about that. And tell me, if we placed a very large order, say, er, 80,000 units, would you be able to despatch immediately?

LB We can normally guarantee to despatch a large order within three weeks. But if you order at a peak time, like just before the Chinese New Year, it will be impossible to deliver that quickly.

NN I take it your price includes insurance?

LB Actually, no. Usually, you'd be responsible for that. But if the order was really large, that would be negotiable, I'm sure.

NN What about payment?

LB To be honest, we'd prefer cash on delivery, as this is our first contract with you. If you were a regular customer, we would offer you 30 days' credit, maybe even a little more.

NN That's all right. I quite understand.

LB Look, how about having some lunch now, and continuing later this afternoon? Then we could meet for an evening meal. I know an excellent restaurant in Wanchai.

NN Yes, let's continue after lunch. If I had more time, I would love to have dinner with you, but unfortunately my flight for Tokyo leaves at eight tonight, and I need to be at the airport by six.

CD2 TRACK 18 (I = Interviewer, AS = Andy Simmons)

I How do you train people to be good negotiators?

AS There are three things that are important in negotiation training. Number one is to create an environment where people can do. Using case studies and the use of video, people are able to see how they behave on video. They can look at what's appropriate and they can look at what is inappropriate. What I mean by that is, where they're effective and where they are ineffective. Using feedback, people are then able to change their behaviour – rather than just telling people about negotiation or reading a book. So the experience is vital.
Number two: it's about keeping the learning fresh. Using different vehicles and different formats, whether that be, er, e-learning, watching videos online – or recently podcasts – or whether it be through a series of different activities following on the workshop to keep it live, keep it fresh, and to stop people falling into those old habits.
The third thing that's very important indeed is to look at the feedback from the negotiations themselves. And at The Gap Partnership, we use a ROI system – which means 'return on investment'. We measure the effectiveness of those negotiations for many months after the training, and this enables us to tweak and change the training and make it more customised. But it also allows the client to see the effects of that training, to measure it, and that provides them with a degree of investment for the future.

CD2 TRACK 19 (I = Interviewer, AS = Andy Simmons)

I Do the same techniques work with every type of negotiation?

AS Yes, this is a good point. Um, there is no one way to negotiate. There are many different ways to negotiate. The common misnomer is that people find one way of negotiating and they don't change. In fact, this concept of appropriateness – that's what we teach – says that there is no one way, there are many different ways, ranging from the very competitive, very high-conflict negotiations that are generally win–lose, all the way through to the very, very co-operative negotiations, which are deemed as win–win. And there's no right or wrong, or there's no good or bad, it's just what's appropriate to the circumstances that you either find yourself in as a negotiator or, better still, the circumstances that you put yourself in, if you're really in charge of that negotiation and if you're really well prepared.

CD2 TRACK 20 (I = Interviewer, AS = Andy Simmons)

I What makes a really good negotiator?

AS There are many behaviours that make a good negotiator. And, er, when I say 'good negotiator', it's the word 'appropriate' – appropriate in being able to change – and so the overriding thing is to be versatile, to be adaptable, to be able to change your behaviour according to those circumstances. And the behaviours that are appropriate are everything from being able to manage conflict, be able to, er, manage the pressure in a face-to-face negotiation, right the way through to being able to plan effectively, to be analytical, but at the other end of the spectrum, to also be open-minded and creative, in other words to come up with ideas on how to repackage the negotiation, and to have the self-discipline in being able to communicate that with the right use of language.

And when I say 'the right use of language', er, effective negotiators are able to watch for when there is more scope for negotiation. What I mean by that is, the ability to be able to look out and listen for what we call 'soft exposing give-aways'. These are the small bits of language around proposals that will tell you that your counterpart, the person on the other side of the table, has more negotiation room. And these are words like 'I'm looking for … roughly … in the region of … around about … I'd like … I'm hoping for … currently … right now … er, probably'. Er, these are words that negotiators spot to help them understand just how movable the other side is. And so language itself is very important and the control of that language; but also the ability to listen. Because the more information you have, the more powerful you become, because information is power.

CD2 TRACK 21 (B1 = Buyer 1, B2 = Buyer 2, S = Supplier)
Extract 1

B1 OK, let's go over our objectives again. What do we really want from this deal?

B2 Well, price is the main issue, I'd say. We want Pierlucci to supply us with some top-quality men's wallets, but we don't want to pay the prices listed in his catalogue.

B1 I agree, they're too high for our market, the wallets would never leave the shelves. So we need to get a substantial discount from him, at least 20%.

B2 Yeah, we should be able to do that. There's a recession in Italy at the moment – money's tight – so he's not in a strong bargaining position.

B1 Exactly. But he won't admit that!

Extract 2

S I have never been to your store in Moscow. Can you tell me a bit about your customers? What sort of leather products do they buy? Are they very price conscious? Will they pay a higher price for really top-quality products? How many men's wallets do you sell each week?

Extract 3

B1 If you can give us a discount of 25% for our first order, we can accept a later delivery date, say the end of June. But I do understand it won't be easy for you to get your new range of wallets to us by then.

S Twenty-five per cent? I'm afraid that's far more than we usually offer new customers, even a store like yours, which I know is very prestigious. We could possibly send half your order by that date. Would that help?

B1 It certainly would, as the peak buying months are July and August. Let's come back to the discount later.

Extract 4

S How about if we send the first consignment by express delivery? We will probably use UPS or TNT as the carrier, they are very fast and reliable. And we'll send the remaining part of the order by regular airmail – that will take a little longer.

B2 That's OK, as long as you get the first part of the order to us by the end of June – that's vital.

S Trust me. I can guarantee delivery by that date.

Extract 5

S Normally, we only supply our top-of-the-range wallets in two colours, black and brown – most customers ask for those colours. If you wanted other colours …

B1 What? You mean the wallets would be even more expensive?

S Well, we would have to charge a little more, because the quantities we produced in that colour would be small, but we could do it.

Extract 6

S Great, we agree on prices, discounts, the items you want to buy, delivery and method of payment. I will send you an e-mail confirming what we have agreed, and enclosing a draft invoice.

Extract 7

S OK, I think we have covered everything. If there are any points we have forgotten, just give me a call.

B2 Excellent, that was a very good meeting. I'm sure we'll do a lot of business in the future.

S I hope so. Now, about dinner tonight – what time would be convenient for you?

WORKING ACROSS CULTURES 3: DOING BUSINESS INTERNATIONALLY

CD2 TRACK 22

Martin did the right thing when he arrived for the meeting on time. The Japanese value punctuality greatly. He shouldn't have been upset by the number of Japanese staff at the meeting. The Japanese are used to working as a group. But he made a mistake with the business card. When you receive a business card from a Japanese person, you should examine it carefully and then put it on the table in front of you during the meeting.

Martin asked a direct question about exclusivity. Matsumoto, like many Japanese, didn't want to say 'no', so he used an expression that Martin had to interpret. Martin may also have had to interpret Matsumoto's body language. Non-verbal communication is important in understanding Japanese businesspeople.

The Japanese believe in consensus and harmony. They want everyone to support an important decision, so many staff may be involved in decision-making, and the process may take longer than in the Western world.

Martin made a mistake when he gave white water lilies as a gift for Matsumoto's wife. White flowers remind the Japanese of death.

CD2 TRACK 23 (JF = John Fisher, SS = Sven Selig)

JF So, Sven, how did it go, your trip to São Paulo?

SS Mmm, not too well. I felt a bit out of my depth while I was there. And I'm not sure I can work with Pedro Oliveira, we're very different.

JF What happened?

SS Well, I set up the appointment with Pedro two weeks before and when I got to São Paulo, I confirmed by phone. There was a heavy thunderstorm that day. I arrived on time, but Pedro wasn't there. He turned up over an hour later, said something about traffic delays because of the storm, then shook my hand warmly, grabbed my arm and led me into his office.

Next thing, he offered me a cup of very strong coffee. I thanked him, but said no, I'd already had two cups of coffee at my hotel. Then he said, 'We're very proud of our coffee here in Brazil.' I wondered if I'd made a mistake to refuse his offer.

JF Maybe.

SS Anyway, instead of getting down to business, he called three colleagues into the office. During the next hour, we talked about everything except business – football, the thunderstorm – and they asked me lots of questions about my family, life in Denmark and so on.

JF I suppose you got a bit frustrated.

SS Of course! I was impatient to start, maybe I showed it a little. Anyway, it was lunchtime, so we went to a local restaurant. Great food, but no talk of business. So I asked them about the crime rate in Brazil, the Amazon rainforest and what sort of government they had at the moment, but I'm afraid the topics didn't generate much discussion. They just didn't seem to want to talk about those things. But we did have a more lively discussion when we started comparing food in our two countries.

JF Ah, interesting. Food is always a good topic of conversation when you're abroad.

SS Yeah. We left the restaurant over two hours later, and then we all went to a business club. We played snooker until about six o'clock. It was very enjoyable, I must admit. As I was leaving to go back to my hotel, Pedro put a hand on my shoulder and said he hoped I'd enjoyed the day.

JF So nothing happened on the first day?

SS No! If we're talking about business, it was a wasted day.

CD2 TRACK 24 (JF = John Fisher, SS = Sven Selig)

JF Tell me about the second day. Things went better, I hope.

SS Not really. I was meant to give my presentation at ten in the morning. But his secretary phoned and told me the meeting was put off until two in the afternoon.

JF That must have been annoying.

SS It certainly was. Pedro invited quite a few of his colleagues to attend the presentation. That was OK, but they kept on interrupting me during my talk, asking lots of questions – I became very impatient. I suggested they ask their questions when I'd finished. I don't think that went down well because they didn't ask many questions at the end.

In the meeting afterwards, Pedro didn't stick to the agenda. The government had just announced a new tax policy, and they spent most of the time discussing this and getting quite emotional.

At times, they raised their voices to each other. I was really shocked. It was late in the afternoon when Pedro was ready to talk about the first item on the agenda. But I had to leave, as I'd arranged an appointment with someone at the embassy. I apologised that I had to rush off.

Pedro just said to me, 'You know, Sven, meetings in our country can last a long time.' Then he put his arm around my shoulder and said, 'You must come to dinner tomorrow night at my home. My wife is a wonderful cook.'

JF So that was it. Did you enjoy the meal?

SS It was a lovely meal, and they made me very welcome, but I'm not sure I can work with Pedro. He's a nice guy, but our ways of doing business are so different. I felt constantly frustrated during the visit, and after going all that way, I don't feel I accomplished anything.

UNIT 10 ETHICS

CD2 TRACK 25

1	bribery and corruption	6	tax fraud
2	price fixing	7	counterfeit goods
3	environmental pollution	8	money laundering
4	sex discrimination	9	animal testing
5	insider trading	10	industrial espionage

CD2 TRACK 26 (DH = David Hillyard)

DH EarthWatch is an international research and conservation and education organisation, and we have over 100 field research projects around the world. That involves, er, scientists looking at how animals and plants are coping in their natural environment. So all these 100 projects are supported from offices that we have in the US, in the UK, in India, in Melbourne, and in Japan and China. And the purpose of our work is to provide the scientific data about what's happening to animals and plants in the world as climate change and as human population expands and the environment is degraded. All our field research projects are designed in a way that members of the public, company employees, teachers, youth, young scientists can join our researchers in the field as field assistants and collect real data that is contributing to understanding what is happening.

CD2 TRACK 27 (I = Interviewer, DH = David Hillyard)

I What role can corporate sponsors play in helping the environment?

DH Companies have a huge role to play. Er, our global economy is based on the companies operating and producing goods and services that we consume. So, fundamentally, businesses need to change the way they operate in order to help and reduce the environmental impact of their operations. I think many companies are able to set leading examples, to innovate and to find new solutions to the environmental problems we have. So, erm, most people in the world work for a company, so the opportunity for companies to educate and engage their employees and get their employees inspired and motivated to do something in their own communities or in their workplace with respect to the environment is a big opportunity that … that EarthWatch certainly believes in, and EarthWatch works with many companies to try and promote environmental change and promote good practice so that those leading companies can then influence other companies to follow, and also influence government.

CD2 TRACK 28 (DH = David Hillyard)

DH So, for example, we work with HSBC, the global bank, on a climate partnership which is in collaboration with other key conservation organisations such as WWF and the Smithsonian Institute, and through that, we're providing a learning opportunity online for every single HSBC employee around the world and also setting up five climate-change research centres around the world, and 2,000 HSBC employees over the next five years will join our field researchers in India, in Brazil, in the US, in the UK and in China to carry out data collection to understand how forests are, are coping with climate change and what is happening and what, what, how animals and plants are being affected.

So that's a very important programme, and it's a very important way of getting company employees involved in our work, understanding what the issues are and then taking that back into their workplace and becoming, we call them climate champions, ambassadors for, for environmental change, so that they can then influence their colleagues and also the way that HSBC operates as a business.

So that's an example of a very important programme for us, erm, and a demonstration of how a company can, erm, can and should make a difference in terms of these issues.

CD2 TRACK 29

A There have been a number of cases of résumé dishonesty in the papers recently.

B That's right. And unfortunately, it happened to a really good friend of mine.

A Oh? What happened?

B Well, she got a really good job – Head of Sales at a prestigious company. She was over the moon. Everything was going really well. She was getting on with all her sales staff, she was receiving strong performance reviews and she was exceeding all her sales targets. She was getting a bit of a reputation as a rising star. Then suddenly, after four years in the job, her company fired her.

A Was it her CV?

B Yeah. She had lied on it. She had claimed she had a Master's degree – and she had also made up a fictitious previous employer.

A Do you know why she had done it?

B She said she had felt desperate because she had been unemployed for a few months.

A And how did they find out?

B An HR initiative. It required employees to show all college transcripts. And they found out she didn't have a Master's degree after all. It wasn't the lack of the degree that cost her her job. It was her dishonesty. Since then, I've advised everyone to be honest on their CV.

CD2 TRACK 30

A OK, let's talk about Tom. We all know he's become a real problem. And we can't turn a blind eye to what's going on any longer. He's sending in sales reports saying he's met various customers and we find out it's not true. And worst of all, he's putting in expense claims we know to be false. He claims he's had meals with customers, and then we find out they haven't met him for ages. These are serious matters, we can't ignore them. But also he's upsetting the other people in the department. They say he's really rude and unco-operative, a real nightmare to work with.

B Yeah, the problem is, he's a really good salesman – in fact, he was our top salesman last year – but I agree he needs tighter control. He isn't behaving professionally and he's not being a good team player. We can't let it go on.

A Exactly. But what are we going to do about it? It won't be easy; he's a really difficult character. Incredibly independent … he hates rules and regulations.

B I'd say there are two ways we could deal with this. We could have a chat with him about his sales reports. Also we could mention that we're checking all expense claims very carefully in the future. If we do that, he may come to his senses and start behaving professionally. Or we could take a strong approach. Tell him if he doesn't change his ways, we'll be sending him a warning letter, and that could lead to him being dismissed. What do you think?

A Mmm, both those options have advantages. But if we just have a friendly chat with him, he may not take it seriously. To be honest, I doubt whether he'll change much with that approach. But if we take a firm approach, there's a risk he may get upset and look for another job. We don't want that either.

B No, we certainly don't want to lose him. OK, let's look at it from another angle. I'm wondering if he has personal problems and they're affecting his work. Why don't we have a friendly talk with him and find out if that's the real problem? He might respond well to that approach.

A Mmm, maybe you're right. It might be the best way to deal with the problem. One thing's for sure, he's a brilliant salesman and he's making a load of money for us, so we certainly don't want to lose him unless we have to.

B OK, let's see if we can sort this out. I'll arrange for Tom to meet us. How about next Wednesday? Is that a good time?

A OK with me – I'm free that morning.

CD2 TRACK 31 (I = Ingrid, E = Ernesto)

I Ernesto, I've just had an interesting conversation with our Head of Research. She's been telling me about a new drug they've done some initial work on. It's for treating a disease which causes blindness.

E Oh yes, I've heard about that one. I think it's called river blindness or something like that. Millions of Africans are dying from it every year.

I Most of the people at risk are poor and can't afford expensive medicines to treat the disease. Anyway, it seems that the drug we're working on has had very promising results. It could well provide a cure for the disease.

E   That's good news. So how much money is needed to put it on the market, and what's the timescale?

I   Well, that's the problem. It'll cost about 100 million dollars to develop the drug, and it'll probably take 10 years or so to bring it to the market.

E   Mmm, that's a lot of money to invest. Is it worth it?

I   Well, that's the question. Should we spend that amount on a drug which will certainly help our image but may not make us much money? I mean, most of the people suffering from the disease probably won't have enough money to pay a realistic price for the drug.

E   I see. So the question is … should we spend time, money and resources on a drug which may not make us much money? Of course, we'll probably get some financial help in the beginning – a subsidy of some kind – but developing the drug is bound to require a huge investment on our part.

I   Yes, that's the problem. And remember, we're not a charity. The bottom line is, we're in business to make money.

E   Exactly. Anyway, we'll be hearing more about this one, because I see it's the first item on the agenda for next week's management meeting. Let's see what the others have to say about it.

UNIT 11 LEADERSHIP

CD2 TRACK 32 (I = Interviewer, EJ = Elizabeth Jackson)

I   What are the qualities of a good business leader?

EJ I'm going to highlight five, um, areas which I think are important, and I don't think that they are as complicated as many people believe. The first that I would highlight is, erm, a sense of direction. A business leader needs to know where they're planning to go to and how they're planning to get there. The second point I would want to highlight is courage. You need to have the courage to understand, um, when to make the right decision and how to, to push yourself forward – otherwise indecisiveness floods in. Thirdly, communication, um, because without that, you have no ability to take people with you, um, and there's no point at all in plotting a course, arriving there and finding that you've left the troops behind. The next point that I would highlight is respect. The communication with the people that you are, um, working with and the respect that you have, whether those are people within the top level of individuals or indeed other people lower down within the organisation, is very important in order to take people with you and to carry everything through.
The last point that I would highlight is emotional intelligence, and that's the sensitivity that you have with the people around you. So that you are able to, um, understand where they are in the organisation, how they behave in the way that they do within the organisation, and yet have the, um, the coldness of head to be able to bring the shutters down if you need to.

CD2 TRACK 33 (I = Interviewer, EJ = Elizabeth Jackson)

I   Do you think great business leaders are born or made?

EJ Well, there's a, um, … It's a very big question, that. Er, there is plenty of evidence to suggest that there are natural born leaders in life. And yet equally, there is, um, there's a lot of evidence to suggest that one can learn a great number of those skills. What I would say is that, when um, you're competing against a natural born leader, the person who has acquired the skills will, I think, fail every time. And the things that a natural born leader possesses, erm, are things like charisma, intelligence, the ability to influence other people – those are very difficult skills to learn. Um, and I think it's perhaps interesting as an anecdote to say that I believe 20 of the first 23 astronauts in America were all first born. Now, it may be a huge coincidence, but my, um, sense is that it probably isn't a coincidence and there is something about natural born leaders which, as I say, can be learnt from, and people can improve their skill set, but they're unlikely to compete and win against them.

CD2 TRACK 34 (I = Interviewer, EJ = Elizabeth Jackson)

I   Which leaders have impressed or influenced you, and why?

EJ The first of them is, is actually my husband. I've been privileged, um, to share a business life alongside a home life, and my husband is a few years older than me and therefore has paved the way if you like, um, in terms of his business successes. But what I've seen in him is, um, is a tremendous tenacity, and the ability to fight like a cornered rat when he needs to, and that's, that's really rare and very, very powerful when you see it.
Um, I also see in him the ability to, um, to strike a chord with people, just by walking in the room. He possesses, um, a level of natural leadership and and power, if you like. He also has an innate ability for inspired thinking, he works ahead of the pack, um, and I've learnt a lot from that, so I probably am not a natural born leader, but I have learnt an awful lot of skills from the likes of the individuals I've worked with, particularly my husband. And his strategic thinking and being able to work outside the box, I think, has been very, very powerful.

CD2 TRACK 35

Good morning, everyone, thanks for coming to my presentation. I know you're all very busy, so I'll be as brief as possible. OK, then, I'm going to talk about our new range of rackets, which we're selling under the brand name Excel. I'll tell you about the test launch we carried out in Croatia a few weeks ago.
I'm going to divide my presentation into four parts. First, I'll give you some background to the launch. After that, I'll tell you how things went during the launch. Next, I'll assess its effectiveness. Finally, I'll outline our future plans for the product. I'll be glad to answer any questions at the end of my talk.
Right, let's start with some background about the launch. As you know, it's taken almost two years to develop the Excel range. The rackets are targeted at enthusiastic amateur players, and thanks to some technical innovations, Excel rackets give a player great control over their shots and more power. So, everyone who uses the racket should immediately improve their game. The rackets were thoroughly tested in focus groups, and modifications were made to their design and appearance. OK, everyone? Yes, Manfred, you have a question …
So, that's the background. Right, let's move on to the test launch. How successful was it? Well, in two words, highly successful. We think the racket will be a winner. If you look at the graph, you'll see the racket's actual sales compared with forecast sales. Quite a difference, isn't there? The sales were 20% higher than we predicted – in other words, a really impressive result. Well above all our expectations. The results show that we got the pricing right. And it suggests the Excel range will make a big impact nationwide.
To sum up, a very promising test launch. I believe the new range of rackets has tremendous potential in the market. Right, where do we go from here? Obviously, we'll move on to stage two and have a multimedia advertising and marketing campaign. In a few months' time, you'll be visiting our customers and taking a lot of orders, I hope, for the new rackets.
Well, that's all I have to say. Thank you for listening. Are there any questions?

UNIT 12 COMPETITION

CD2 TRACK 36 (I = Interviewer, RT = Rory Taylor)

I   Can you tell us about the work of the Competition Commission?

RT The Competition Commission is a public body which carries out investigations into particular mergers and markets in the UK, as well as other matters related to what they call the regulated industries, erm, such as, er, water and energy and the communications sector. One of our most high-profile investigations at the moment is one we're carrying out into the ownership of airports in the United Kingdom. Currently, seven of the UK airports are owned by a company called BAA – that's the British Airports Authority. Um, we've been asked to look into that, their ownership of those airports and whether that ownership structure is in the interests of consumers or whether, er, an injection of greater competition, er, would benefit the users of those airports.

CD2 TRACK 37 (I = Interviewer, RT = Rory Taylor)

I   In some business sectors, there may be very few competitors. How can you ensure fairness in such cases?

RT It's actually a matter of not so many, not so much looking at the number of competitors or providers in a particular market so much as looking at the dynamics of that market. It's equally possible for what you could describe as a concentrated market – one with, say, just three or four major suppliers or providers – um, to be very competitive, but equally so, you can have a market with the same level of concentration, the same number of players, erm, which is relatively static. There's little competition going on between the players, customers aren't switching, and the companies concerned aren't reacting with each other in, in the way that you'd like to in a competitive market.

For example, one of our recent enquiries was into the groceries market in the UK. Um, that is quite a highly concentrated market, in the sense that there are, sort of, four or five major grocery companies in this country, erm, and they control something in the region of 80 per cent of the market. However, um, our–, after in-depth investigation, it was clear that this is a market where these companies are competing actively with each other. Um, customers have a choice and they're exercising that choice and, as a result, the companies concerned are competing with each other, which brings the benefits in terms of, um, lower prices, innovation and greater choice for consumers.

CD2 TRACK 38 (RT = RORY TAYLOR)

RT We could contrast that with another enquiry that we did, completed about two years ago, into what's known as liquid petroleum gas for domestic users. Essentially, this is for customers who are not supplied for energy through pipes – they live in remote areas, and therefore they need the gas, which is also known as propane, propane, delivered to their house and put in a tank. Again this is a market with only four major players in it, concentrated in the same way in nominal terms like the groceries industry, but we found a far more static market. Er, we found that customers were not switching between the companies, the companies were not competing with each other, erm, and consequently we were finding higher prices, less innovation and less choice.

CD2 TRACK 39 (M = MANUFACTURER, A = AGENT)

M OK, perhaps we could start, as we agreed, by discussing the kind of relationship we want.
A OK.
M Usually with a major distributor or agent, we don't offer an exclusive agency agreement, because they don't want it. They like to use and distribute the products of most of the top companies. They make more money that way.
A Yes, a non-exclusive contract would be perfect for us, too. As you know, we represent many famous brands and will be happy to add your product lines to our list.
M Right. Now, prices: we like to recommend prices for each overseas market – we advise on minimum and maximum prices for each of our models.
A No, that's no good for us. We prefer to set the prices for all the products we offer. We know the market conditions far better than you … we would set the correct prices to maximise profits, of course.
M OK, it is not really a problem if you prefer it that way – I won't argue with you. Now, the commission: I suggest a rate of 15 per cent on all the revenue you obtain, either directly or indirectly. Is that OK?
A Fifteen per cent is too low. We want at least 20 per cent. The market is very competitive. We'll have to spend a lot on advertising and promoting your products.
M Yes, but we could help with this.
A How much will you pay us?
M Well, we might go 50:50 up to an agreed limit. We can talk about the exact figures later.
A I'll have to think about it. We'll talk about the commission later.
M Let's discuss the length of the contract. Normally, we offer two years, and to be honest, with a new distributor, we prefer a shorter period. Either side can terminate with 60 days' notice.
A Well, it must be at least three years for it to be profitable for us.
M Well, we can talk about it later. I suggest we break for lunch now.

CD2 TRACK 40

1 A non-exclusive contract would be perfect for us, too.
2 No, that's no good for us.
3 We know the market conditions far better than you.
4 I suggest a rate of 15 per cent on all the revenue you obtain.
5 Fifteen per cent is too low. We want at least 20 per cent.
6 We could help with this.
7 How much will you pay us?
8 We'll talk about the commission later.
9 To be honest, with a new distributor, we prefer a shorter period.
10 It must be at least three years.

WORKING ACROSS CULTURES 4: COMMUNICATION STYLES

CD2 TRACK 41

How close do you like to be when speaking with a business colleague?
How much eye contact are you comfortable with? Are you comfortable
with long periods of silence? And how do you feel about interruptions?
These are some of the questions we will be looking at in today's workshop on communication styles and cultural awareness. My name's Patrick Keane and I'm the Managing Director of our office in Caracas, Venezuela.
So why should you listen to me? Well, I've had 12 overseas postings, including Brazil, Russia, China and India, and I speak four languages. By the end of the workshop today, you'll have a better understanding of communication styles in your own culture and an introduction to those styles in other cultures … and this is the starting point for learning how to deal with cultural differences.
It's worth bearing in mind that 60 per cent of people in this company get an overseas posting.
Let me tell you briefly what we are going to cover today. I'll get the workshop going with a brief talk. Firstly, I'm going to talk about some ways in which we use verbal communication and I'll look at two areas. Then I'm going to look at non-verbal communication, again looking at two areas. And after that, we'll do some activities looking at communication styles in your own culture.
Let me ask you a question: can you put up your hands if you've already had an overseas posting? Thank you. Now, we know that the majority of you will have an overseas posting at some time in your career. One of the challenges we face when we go into a new cultural environment is the communication style.
I'm going to begin with verbal communication. My first example is silence, and how comfortable people are with silence … when people don't say anything. East Asian and Arab cultures are generally quite comfortable with silence. However, Anglo-Saxon cultures don't feel happy with long pauses in the conversation.
My second example is the acceptance of interruption between speakers. This is seen differently among different cultures. Generally, we can say that East Asians, Americans and Northern Europeans are not comfortable with interruption. They prefer to have as few interruptions as possible during conversations. Now, I'm not saying that people in these cultures don't interrupt. However, in these cultures, people who interrupt frequently are regarded as rude. But if we look at Southern Europeans and Latin American cultures … well, they're quite comfortable with interruptions. They even see it as positive engagement. They can see cultures which remain quiet as being rather formal or cold.
Let me move on to non-verbal communication – body language and gestures which can provide challenges for staff not used to working abroad. Again, I have two examples. First, I want to talk about proximity, or how close you stand when talking to people. Now, this really does vary between cultures. There's been some research into this, and apparently East Asian cultures prefer the space between people in conversation to be approximately one metre. However, the Latin cultures of Europe and Latin America … they prefer less than half a metre. This can cause some strange situations where people from different cultures try to get comfortable during the conversation by moving forwards or backwards. As I said earlier, I'm based in Caracas, Venezuela. In fact, Venezuelans like to talk to each other standing about 12 centimetres apart. And they like to touch each other to show trust, or to show that the other person is what they call simpático.
My second example of non-verbal communication is the level of eye contact – how much eye contact is normal and when to break it. Some cultures may feel that the other side is not engaging with them and not showing enough eye contact. Other cultures may feel that they are being stared at. Well, Arab and Latin cultures usually have the most eye contact, while East Asians have the least. North Americans and Northern Europeans are somewhere in the middle. Before we move on to the workshop, I'd like to ask you which cultures you feel you know well.

Market Leader Extra: Business skills
Audio script Intermediate

1.1 MEETINGS

BSA1.1.1

Right, let's make a start. Good morning, everyone. I hope you've all received today's agenda. The aim of this meeting is to understand why our hotel chain has performed so poorly over the last 12 months and to assess how we can improve the situation quickly. The meeting will last 45 minutes. First, we'll discuss the results. Then we'll look at what our guest surveys have shown and finally, I'll ask you to suggest changes to our business strategy. Oh, and before we start, as we are now an international team, please could we all remember to speak slowly and clearly?

BSA1.1.2 (E = Emi, A = Amita, M = Mike)

E OK, I'll hand over to you, Amita.

A As you can see from the table, the figure for guests staying with Magnum Hotels has dropped by just over 10 per cent in 12 months. That is 270,000 room nights over the 12-month period up to this month, compared to 300,000 in the previous 12-month period. Income from bookings has dropped even further, from 15.2 million pounds to 12.1 million pounds.

M That bad? Well, you all know that my view last year was to focus less on the holidaymaker. I thought we should concentrate on the business traveller. If we had done that, maybe we wouldn't …

E Fine, Mike, but please let Amita finish her analysis first.

A The effect on profits of lower demand has been worse because we've had to sell off empty rooms at lower prices, so the average room rate has dropped, too. This quarter, the gross profit margin has just dropped to an all-time low of 16 per cent.

BSA1.1.3 (M = Mike, A = Amita, J = Jon)

M Well, as I was saying earlier, last year I suggested focusing more heavily on the business customer. Global trade is still on the increase, isn't it?

A Yes, absolutely. But long-distance business travel has actually been going down lately. People are being more economical about their business costs and travelling less these days. I don't think changing our marketing focus to the business customer is a good idea. In my opinion, it wouldn't improve our results. What's your view, Jon?

J I agree with Amita. What's more, conference calling is having a negative impact on business travel these days – especially long-distance travel. I don't think changing the customer mix is the right strategy.

BSA1.1.4

OK, shall we make a start? Unfortunately, I've just been informed that the big wedding party due to arrive a week on Friday for two nights has cancelled its booking due to unforeseen circumstances. Our task for this meeting is to decide how to resell all the rooms on the second floor, not to mention the bridal suite, very quickly! That's 22 double or twin rooms. So, first we need to identify which type of customer would be most likely to book a room at short notice. Then we need to decide on the most effective way of marketing to that group. After that, I'm afraid we might all have to do overtime to make this happen. I'll assign responsibilities. Well, actually, I'm rather hoping that you'll volunteer for them!

1.2 TELEPHONING

BSA1.2.5 (R = Receptionist, AW = Angela Wight, AC = Alex Chang)

R Global Relocation Consultants, good morning.

AW Good morning. Does a Mr Chang work for your company?

R Yes, Alex Chang. He's our manager for the Far East. Shall I put you through to him?

AW Yes, please.

AC Alex Chang speaking.

AW Good morning. My name is Angela Wight. I'm the Human Resources Manager at PBS Security Systems in Bristol. I got your name from a business advice centre in Bristol.

AC I see. How can I help you?

AW We're opening an office in Japan at the end of this year. Two of our staff are moving to Tokyo. Can you offer help with finding accommodation and learning the language?

AC Yes, we can. We have an office in Tokyo. Can you give me some details about the employees, please?

AW Yes. Tom Hill will be in charge. He is married and has two children. Alison Sanders is single.

AC I see. So that means you need two apartments – a one-bedded one and one with three bedrooms for the family. Is that right?

AW That's right.

AC What about schools? We can put you in touch with some very good international schools in Japan. How old are the children?

AW That's good. The Hills have got a girl aged 12 and a boy of nine.

AC OK. What about language training? Is that for the employees only or also for Mrs Hill and the children?

AW I'm not sure. What do you suggest?

AC Well, moving to a different country is often difficult for wives and children. Language training usually helps them adapt to the new country more quickly.

AW OK, then I need information and prices for training for all of them, please.

AC What about a cultural induction programme?

AW I'm sorry, what do you mean by a cultural induction programme?

AC It is a training programme about life in Japan. We teach people what things are polite or not polite. And we tell them about Japanese customs and habits. We can do that at our office here in London if you like.

AW That sounds useful. Can the language training also start before they go to Japan?

AC If you want a short intensive course here in London, yes.

AW What about in Bristol? A couple of evenings a week, perhaps?

AC I'm not sure if we have any Japanese teachers in that area. I can check and let you know. I'll also prepare a proposal for language training, in Britain and in Japan.

AW And for the cultural training you mentioned before?

AC Ah yes, in London, before they go. That's what you'd prefer, isn't it?

AW Yes, please.

AC OK, so it'll take a few days to get all the information together and to prepare a proposal for you. In the meantime, I can send you our general information pack about living and working in Japan. What's your postal address, please?

AW	Human Resources Department, PBS Security Systems, PO Box 275, Bristol BS32 9XZ.
AC	Can you repeat the postcode, please?
AW	BS32 9XZ.
AC	OK, and you are Angela White.
AW	Yes. Sorry, but can I check how you've spelt my surname?
AC	Yes. W-H-I-T-E. Is that not correct?
AW	No, it's W-I-G-H-T.
AC	I'm sorry about that. And your phone number, please?
AW	01179685734.
AC	OK, I'll call you when the proposal is ready and my secretary will put the information pack in the post this afternoon.
AW	Excellent. Many thanks for your help. Goodbye.
AC	Goodbye.

2.1 SMALL TALK

BSA2.1.6 (MB = Magda Beckman, GC = Grant Corbin), DS = Dao Sun

MB	Hello, Grant. Great to see you again.
GC	Hi, Magda. How are you?
MB	Very well, thanks. And you?
GC	Fine. I haven't seen you in ages. Since you visited the company in Melbourne, I think. Are you still in Sales?
MB	Yes, I am, but I had a promotion. I'm now Sales Director.
GC	That's fantastic, well done! And how's business?
MB	We're not doing too badly, actually. We met all our targets last year. And you? How's it going with your company?
GC	Well, last year was tough, but things are looking better for this year.
MB	That's great to hear.
DS	Excuse me, Ms Beckman?
MB	Oh hello, Doctor Sun. Can I introduce you to Grant Corbin? He's the project director from the Australian office in Brisbane. Grant, this is Doctor Sun, Vice President of the group.
DS	Very pleased to meet you, Mr Corbin.
GC	Pleased to meet you at last, Mr Sun.
MB	It's Doctor Sun, Grant.
GC	My apologies, Doctor Sun.
MB	I believe you two have something in common. Doctor Sun's a big tennis fan.
GC	Really? Do you play?
DS	Yes, every weekend. And you, Mr Corbin?
GC	As often as I can. By the way, I hear you're visiting the Australian company next month, is that right?
DS	Yes, it is. I'm looking forward to it.
GC	You'll be in Australia while the Open Tennis Championship is on. Would you like me to arrange tickets for you?
DS	That would be wonderful. Thank you.
GC	No problem.
DS	Oh, er, excuse me ...
GC	What was all that about? What did I do wrong, Magda?
MB	You patted him on the back. In Chinese culture, touching someone is not very polite.
GC	Oh dear! I'd better get him the best tickets I can for the tennis next month, then.
MB	Yes, you had!

BSA2.1.7 (DK = Dietger Kappel, MB = Magda Beckman, GC = Grant Corbin)

DK	Hello, I'm Dietger Kappel from the XBL GmbH in Germany. Which company do you work for?
MB	Hello, I'm Magda Beckman, from Etlo International, a Swedish company.
DK	I don't think I know anything about your company.

MB	We manufacture aircraft parts. And what about XBL? What business are you in?
DK	We're in manufacturing, too. Car parts, in fact, although we're looking to move into aircraft parts as well, so we'll be direct competitors.
MB	Right. That should be interesting. Oh, Grant, have you met Dietger Kappel from Germany?
GC	Hello, Dietger. We met at the conference last year, didn't we?
DK	Did we? I don't remember.
GC	Oh well, never mind. Nice to see you again.
DK	Hmm.
GC	I'm glad I've met you. I'm flying to Frankfurt at the end of the week to see some suppliers. Any advice you can give me about doing business in Germany?
DK	Well, firstly, we don't like to spend too much time chatting. We like to get down to business as soon as possible.
GC	Oh. Right, I'll remember that.
DK	Yes, well, excuse me ...
MB	A cultural clash, I think.
GC	He's a really serious guy, isn't he? Doesn't seem to have a sense of humour.
MB	Oh, he does. It's just that business will always come first.
GC	But isn't chatting informally part of business?
MB	In most cultures, yes. But some like to do less rather than more!
GC	I see that. Let's see who else is here ...

BSA2.1.8 (MB = Magda Beckman, GP = Govind Patil, GC = Grant Corbin)

MB	Ah, Mr Patil, pleased to meet you, at last. Magda Beckman from ...
GP	Yes, Ms Beckman, I know who you are. Very pleased to meet you finally, too. We did that video conference last month, didn't we?
MB	Yes, we did. How are you?
GP	I'm very well, thank you, Ms Beckman. And you?
MB	Fine, thanks. I think you might be able to help me. Grant Corbin from Australia is looking for a new supplier and I thought that maybe your company is just what he's looking for.
GP	I'm happy to talk to him. Is he here?
MB	Yes, over there. I'll call him over. Grant, I'd like you to meet Mr Patil. He might be able to solve your supplier problem.
GC	Oh, how do you do, Mr Patil? Nice to meet you.
GP	And you, Mr Corbin.
GC	Where are you based in India?
GP	Mumbai. We're a long-established family business. The company was founded over a 100 years ago.
GC	Wow, that's amazing!
GP	I hear you're looking for a new supplier. I think we may be able to help each other as I'm hoping to expand into Australia.
GC	Ah! Have you ever been there?
GP	Oh yes, I visited with my family last year on holiday.
GC	Where did you go?
GP	We travelled up and down the Gold Coast. We had a lovely time. Where are you based, Mr Corbin?
GC	Melbourne. But we've got subsidiaries in Brisbane and Perth. Let me give you my business card. Call me and we can arrange to meet to discuss potential business.
GP	Thank you. And here's mine, Mr Corbin. Look forward to hearing from you.
GC	You too. See you later. Bye for now, Magda.

2.2 PRESENTATIONS

BSA2.2.9

This has been a disappointing year, but most of our competitors have reported similar difficulties. Unfortunately, net profit has fallen from 2.47 million US dollars to 2.39 million, and net revenue is also down. It has decreased by three per cent over the same period. Our revenue has fallen from 12.5 to 12.3 million. Rising costs and increased competition have accounted for a large part of the problem this year.

BSA2.2.10

So, as we've seen, our net profit is down from 2.47 million in 2014 to 2.39 million this financial year. That's a fall of around three per cent. Our net revenue is also down this year, from 12.5 million to 12.3 million. There are three main reasons for the changes.

The first reason is a change in drinking habits. As you know, carbonated drinks have represented around 55 per cent of our total sales. Overall, the sales volume of carbonated drinks stayed flat, but sales in Europe and the United States started to fall in April last year for the first time since 1996. It seems that people in those regions are making healthier choices.

The second reason is a rise in commodity prices. Juices are our second biggest sellers – around 25 per cent of our total sales. However, the price of fruit and sugar rose. We increased the price of our juice products, but despite those higher prices, profits were still lower this year than last year.

On a more positive note, we invested heavily in restructuring our operations in China and India. The cost of this appears in our year-end accounts, but we'll make savings from these changes next year.

OK, let's look in more detail at this year's trends. Looking at the next slide – can everyone see that? – OK, well, this slide shows the volume of juice that we've sold this year and as you can see, there's been a four per cent increase in the number of cartons we've sold.

BSA2.2.11 (C = Carolyn, S1 = Speaker 1, S2 = Speaker 2)

C OK, let's look in more detail at this year's trends. Looking at the next slide – can everyone see that? – OK, well, this slide shows the volume of juice that we've sold this year and as you can see, there's been a four per cent increase in the number of cartons we've sold.

S1 Sorry, Carolyn, I thought you said that the volume of carbonated drinks was the same last year and juices are up; so why has revenue fallen?

C Well, the reason is that more of our sales are coming from other markets, that is, markets outside the USA and Europe, where the prices are lower. We don't believe that carbonated drinks will ever become as popular again in the USA as they were.

S2 Carolyn, you mentioned other markets. Which ones?

C Well, we've had some good results from our emerging markets. Sales of all products are up by 11 per cent in India and 10 per cent in China, and we expect this to continue.

S1 Could I just ask, isn't that lower than in previous years?

C Yes, it is. Uh, we've seen higher increases in the past, but these markets are much stronger now and this is still very healthy growth.

3.1 NEGOTIATIONS

BSA3.1.12 (RD = Rahul Darzi, LT = Luca Tessaro)

RD Would you like some more tea, Luca? More chai, please, Deepak!

LT Thanks. They say it's good to drink tea when it's hot.

RD Ah yes, I think it was Oscar Wilde who said, 'Tea is the only simple pleasure left to us.'

LT Well, as an Italian, I prefer coffee. But you know the saying, 'When in Rome, do as the Romans do!' So, as I was saying, we'd like to reach a deal with you, Rahul. And I like working with you …

RD But?

LT To be honest, we're worried about the quality of your materials. There are two issues, really: the quality of the silk and the faulty zips. The silk is not up to standard, I'm afraid. It tears easily and we've had complaints from our store managers. We've also had problems with your zips – the ones we use on our handbags. When the zip breaks, you can't use the bag …

RD I'm sorry to hear that, Luca. Let's try to solve these problems. First, if you need stronger zips for handbags, that's no problem. I'll show you some samples and you can choose the ones that are best for your designs.

LT Fine.

RD Second, can you tell me more about the kind of silk you need and I'll find you the right quality fabric.

LT Right, so the silk tears easily – like this – and we can't use it for our dresses and sleepwear. Our factories have problems when they're making the garments.

RD You know, silk is a complicated material. I can sell you better quality silks, Luca, but at a higher price.

LT That would be difficult for us.

RD Yes, but if you went to one of your Italian suppliers, they would charge you 10 times more than we do!

LT So, what do you have in mind, Rahul?

BSA3.1.13 (RD = Rahul Darzi, LT = Luca Tessaro)

RD We can sell you our high quality silk at five euros a metre.

LT Five euros? But the one we usually buy from you costs 1.50 a metre.

RD But I understand you need a superior material. Look at this sample, Luca. Do you feel it? Compare it to this one that you're buying from us now.

LT Five euros … that's much more than we usually pay. I'll have to consult head office.

RD Look, if you order more than 500 metres, I'll give you a 20 per cent discount.

LT So that'll be four euros per metre.

RD That's right. Do you see how it's stronger? Pull it.

LT OK, it feels good, but can you do the same colours?

RD The colours are better! There's a bigger range. These lighter colours, pink, grey and blue, will work very well with your sleepwear. And these darker colours, the green, red and purple, will go well with the evening dresses.

LT I'm not sure. We can't buy this silk unless we order smaller quantities and adapt the design. Or we just use man-made materials like our competitors.

RD We'd be prepared to offer you a good price on man-made fabrics if you increased your order. And you could order less silk, but better quality silk for your quality products.

LT I'll buy your silk as long as you can guarantee the quality.

RD No problem. How much do you need?

LT I need to think about the quantities. I'll have to talk to the product manager. Let me make a few phone calls and we'll talk later.

RD   Take your time. But let me suggest something: my assistant can measure you and we'll make you some silk pyjamas in this superior silk. If you wear them tonight, you'll be able to test the material yourself.

LT   Sure, provided they're ready by 7 p.m. this evening!

RD   Of course! Deepak! Take this gentleman's measurements for some pyjamas, please!

BSA3.1.14 (RD = Rahul Darzi, LT = Luca Tessaro)

RD   What do you think, Luca?

LT   Mmm, they feel very cool and comfortable.

RD   You see, that's Indian silk. Did you speak to your head office?

LT   I spoke to the product manager. We'll order the same quantities as before, but 75 per cent man-made fabric – that's imitation silk – and 25 per cent of your quality silk for our luxury sleepwear collection. That represents over 1,000 metres each season. So, if we ordered 1,000 metres, we'd buy it at 3.50 per metre, not four.

RD   So that's 3.50 per metre for quantities of over 1,000 metres. Yes, I can do that.

LT   Good, we agree on price, quantity and discounts.

RD   And how about terms and conditions?

LT   Provided that the silk is sent by air, the consignment will reach us in time. You can ship the other fabrics as usual.

RD   That should be OK.

LT   Let me know if it isn't. We need the silk to arrive in very good condition and we can't take any risks shipping it.

RD   Yes, yes.

LT   The silk has to be sent by air, Rahul. We also need it in time for the campaign for our luxury collection.

RD   I understand.

LT   Good. Well, I think we've covered everything. Was there anything else?

RD   Just one question: do the usual terms apply? Is it still 90 days credit?

LT   Yes.

RD   But if we send the silk by air, will you give us 60 days credit?

LT   60 days credit? But 90 days are our usual terms.

RD   Luca, we've been doing business together for years. And now all this hurry, and the additional costs for us ...

LT   I'll have to consult my boss.

RD   Sure, but remember to show him your Indian pyjamas!

LT   I don't think I'll wear them to the office!

RD   I can guarantee we'll send the silk by air if you pay us in 60 days.

LT   All right. So, to sum up, you'll supply us with stronger zips for bags, but if we have any more complaints, we'll have to renegotiate.

RD   No problem. If you're not happy with the new zips, feel free to return them.

LT   And if we buy over 1,000 metres of your quality silks, we'll pay 3.50 per metre.

RD   Correct. And 75 per cent of your orders will be for man-made fabrics and twenty-five per cent will be quality silk.

LT   And you'll send the silk consignment by air.

RD   As long as we have 60 days credit term.

LT   Exactly. If there's anything else, I'll e-mail you when I get back to Milan.

RD   It's good doing business with you. Those Indian pyjamas really suit you!

3.2 E-MAILS

BSA3.2.15 (R = Richard, O = Olivia)

R   Olivia, can I have a quick word?

O   Yes, of course.

R   I just spoke to Petra, and the board wants some sales data for the meeting next week.

O   OK, what data? They have all the figures so far for this year from all the countries.

R   No, they want to see some rough forecasts for next year. Just for the top five customers and top five products. Main numbers, basically, and net of discount, not gross. I think they have some investment decisions to make and they just want to check expectations on sales for next year before they commit.

O   OK, so when do they need the figures?

R   Yes, that's the problem. They want them by the end of this week. Really short notice, I know.

O   You know people hate these requests ...

R   I know. But if the board asks, then the board gets. Can you write an e-mail to heads of sales in each of the countries? Tell them not to put too much work into the analysis, but the numbers need to be realistic.

O   OK, will do.

R   And be sensitive with the language in the e-mail. This is going to cause a bit of a problem because people won't have time. So, try to ask in a nice way. You know what I mean. And check if they need any help with this. I think e-mails are always a bit more reader-friendly if you offer support.

O   OK, sure. I'll be extra polite.

R   Thanks, Olivia.

O   No problem.

4.1 PRESENTATIONS

BSA4.1.16

So that brings me to the end of my presentation. To sum up, as I've demonstrated today, there are three very good reasons to outsource our manufacturing to Asia.

Firstly, the figures I presented earlier clearly show that the cost savings would be huge given the supply of cheaper labour and the more flexible working conditions in countries like China.

Secondly, our competitors are outsourcing, so how can we possibly be competitive without doing the same?

Thirdly, by shifting production to Asia, it will also help us to expand and gain access to new markets in the region.

In conclusion, I think you'll agree that off-shoring production makes excellent business sense. Thanks very much. Are there any more questions?

BSA4.1.17 (R = Ruben, L = Lynne, S = Sandra, A = Angelo)

R   Thanks very much. Are there any more questions?

L   Yes, can I ask you when exactly do you plan to outsource production? Do you have a date?

R   That's a good question, but I don't have the answer right now. It's very early days, Lynne. At the moment we're still investigating options.

L   I see. But what are the implications for our production staff here if, or should I say, when this proposal goes ahead?

R   So, your question is: how many redundancies will there be? Is that right?

L   Yes, that's right, how many jobs will be lost.

R   I'm sorry, I'm not in a position to answer that at this stage. As we all know, this is a very sensitive issue. You see, it isn't confirmed yet, so I can't say. It's still highly confidential. Have I made myself clear?

L   Very! But rumours have already started and it's affecting morale.

R   I understand your concerns and I will get back to you with an answer as soon as I can.

S   Ruben, I have another question for you: if we off-shore our production, will we have to pay import duty on our electrical goods?

R   Sorry, Sandra, I didn't catch that. Could you repeat the question, please?

S   Yeah, sure. Will the company have to pay import duty if we shift manufacturing to Asia? And if so, what is the rate for electrical goods?

R   OK, the answer to your first question is yes, we will have to pay duty on imported goods. And, erm, to answer the second, if I remember correctly, the rate is 3.7 per cent. Yes, that's right, 3.7. But we will still make huge savings despite the import duty. Does that answer your questions?

S   Yes, thanks.

A   Ruben, will some of the savings we make on the production side be dedicated to expanding the marketing and sales department?

R   Erm, I know this is important for you, Angelo, but I'm afraid that's not part of my objective for today. Perhaps we can talk about your department's needs another time.

A   But you said one of the objectives was to expand and gain access to new markets. That will need a marketing budget.

R   I see your point, but we need to move on. Are there any other questions about this proposal? No? OK, well, just to conclude, I believe outsourcing production is the right decision. In fact, it's the only option we have if we want to be competitive in the future. Thank you.

BSA4.1.18

So, your question is: how many redundancies will there be? Is that right?

Sorry, I didn't catch that. Could you repeat the question, please?

That's a good question.

I understand your concerns.

I know this is important for you.

I see your point.

Have I made myself clear?

Does that answer your questions?

I'm not in a position to answer that.

4.2 INTERVIEWS

BSA4.2.19 (D = Dan, E = Erin)

D   Hi, Erin. Come on in, sit down. I appreciate you coming in this morning.

E   I can't believe it's been a whole year.

D   Well, you've shown good work this year and I know the team really value you.

E   Thank you.

D   It's been a busy year, with a lot of changes. I wanted to start by asking you what you feel are the most important tasks you've performed this year.

E   Well, I think that my main goals for the year were, firstly, to strengthen our range of products and secondly, to put the new strategic delivery plan into action.

D   How well do you think you did with those tasks?

E   Well, the new products we introduced have received positive reviews from customers. They like them. We were expecting that to translate into increased sales by the end of the year. It hasn't happened so far, but I'm sure we'll see results next year.

D   We're very excited about the new range. You chose well and with the advertising campaign, we could see record sales next year.

E   I guess the other big task this year was the new delivery system. It's working well now after a few problems at the start.

D   Uh huh. So what were the main difficulties with that project?

E   With the new delivery system? Well, to be honest, the staff in the delivery room were against the changes from the start. I was hoping that they would cooperate more with this project once it was up and running, but they were very critical, and that didn't really help. They just didn't seem to understand that competition is tough at the moment and our ability to deliver faster than our competitors is a major selling point.

D   I understand how you feel – faster deliveries are key – but our delivery drivers are also one of our main contacts with clients. We need them to feel part of the team because they're out there representing us as a company. How do you think you could improve on this issue and work with them better in future?

E   Well, I suppose I could involve them in new decisions at an earlier date. They may want to put forward ideas of their own on how to improve delivery and customer relations.

D   Do you think I could see this in your next meeting with them?

E   Sure.

D   Now then, what action do you need from the company in the coming year to help improve your performance?

E   I have one member of my team, Jack, who's not really pulling his weight. I'm afraid his appearance is sloppy and his social skills are quite poor. I need the full support from management to deal with him. I've spoken to him about it, but, if anything, he's got worse.

D   OK. Maybe we can get someone from HR in to offer you some advice on taking that conversation forward. I'll speak to them right after this and get back to you.

BSA4.2.20

1   We were expecting that to translate into increased sales by the end of the year. It hasn't happened so far, but I'm sure we'll see results next year.

2   With the new delivery system? Well, to be honest, the staff in the delivery room were against the changes from the start. I was hoping that they would cooperate more with this project once it was up and running, but they were very critical, and that didn't really help.

3   I have one member of my team, Jack, who's not really pulling his weight. I'm afraid his appearance is sloppy and his social skills are quite poor.

1.1 Meetings

TASK

Meeting leader

Your task is to open, lead and close the meeting. Welcome the participants and state the meeting aims, timings and rules. Use the agenda to keep the meeting on track. Make sure the final decisions for the architect's brief are summarised clearly.

Observer(s)

Your task is to report on how well the meeting aims are achieved. During the meeting, observe the participants' performance and make brief notes on good meetings' language used. After the meeting, give feedback on this. Use the observer sheet below.

Participant(s)

Your task is to discuss the items on the agenda. Try to use the useful language for taking part in meetings whenever possible.

Observer sheet

As you observe the meeting(s), make notes using the following headings.

Language used	Examples
Asking for opinions	
Giving opinions	
Agreeing	
Disagreeing	
Making suggestions	

Agenda: are participants using it?	
Participation: is everyone contributing?	
Overall: good meeting? Why? / Why not?	

4.2 Interviews

Ⓔ SPEAKING 2

Student A

You are the manager of a chain of clothing stores. You have called an appraisal meeting with Student B, one of your shop assistants. This is the current situation:

- Your worker has had good sales this year and generally has good customer relations.

- The worker was late regularly for a two-month period. This has improved, but only after you spoke to him/her about it.

- All store managers need to attend a training course. To be accepted on the training course, you need to achieve sales growth of five per cent.

2.1 Small talk

D SPEAKING 2

Student A

Position: Sales Director

Company: GYJ INTERNATIONAL

Business: Luggage manufacturer

Founded: 1976

HQ: Stuttgart, Germany

Staff worldwide: 2,500

Student B

Position: Marketing Manager

Company: GYZ Travel

Business: Adventure holidays

Founded: 1999

HQ: Brisbane, Australia

Staff worldwide: 3,300

2.1 Small talk

TASK

Group A

	Student 1	Student 2	Student 3	Student 4
Position	Finance Manager	Sales Manager	Account Manager	IT Manager
Characteristic or body language	Doesn't like personal questions	Never looks people in the eye	Stands too close to people	Pats someone on the back
Unsuitable topics to introduce	Ask about salary.	Ask if they like their boss.	Introduce a comment about politics.	Ask if they are married.

Group B

	Student 1	Student 2	Student 3	Student 4
Position	Marketing Manager	Production Manager	Travel Consultant	IT Manager
Characteristic or body language	Doesn't like small talk; impatient to talk business	Looks around the room all the time and doesn't seem to be listening	Stands very far away from others	Makes direct eye contact all the time
Unsuitable topics to introduce	Ask about their views on the company CEO.	Ask if they like their colleagues.	Ask if they are married.	Introduce a comment about politics.

2.2 Presentations

Ⓐ SPEAKING 1

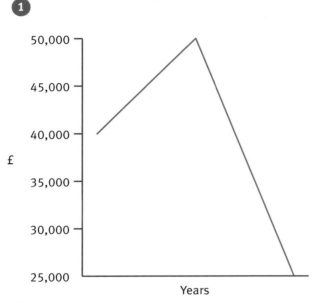

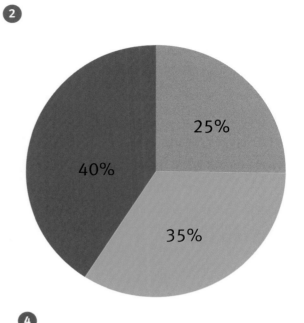

Model	Memory	Weight	Touch screen
X2	2G	40 g	✗
X3	3G	55 g	✓

4.2 Interviews

Ⓔ SPEAKING 2

Student B

You are a sales assistant in a chain of clothing stores. You are going to attend an appraisal meeting with Student A, your manager. This is the current situation:

- You have higher sales than anyone else in your store, and several customers ask for you personally when they come in.

- You had trouble getting in on time for a two-month period, when there were road works on your usual route to work. Everyone in the town suffered, but that's luckily sorted now.

- You have heard that the company has a management training scheme and you want to join.

2.2 Presentations

Ⓓ SPEAKING 2

Student A

1 Look at the chart on the right and consider the following
   background information behind the figures.

   - growing demand in key markets (Europe and US)

   - strong marketing campaign

   - opening new markets (Eastern Europe)

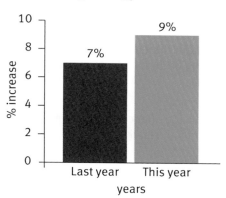

Sales of high energy drinks

2 Plan how you are going to present the information in the
   chart. Remember to:

   1 introduce your visual

   2 describe the numbers confidently

   3 use language to show transitions between information
      (e.g. *As you can see ..., This slide shows ..., Let's look
      in more detail at ..., The first/second reason is ...,
      On a positive note, ...*).

3 Listen to Student B presenting some figures. Take notes
   and be ready to ask questions.

4.1 Presentations

TASK

Students A and B

Company relocation

You represent the Finance Department. You are preparing a
presentation to staff explain why the company wants to relocate its
offices. These are your main reasons:

- You can sell the expensive office building you have in the city
  centre. This will generate revenue. It's of great architectural value
  and could be a hotel.

- You can buy bigger premises in the new industrial estate, 30
  kilometres from the city centre. This will allow for expansion.

- You can integrate offices, production area and warehouse, which
  will improve communication between the different departments.

2.2 Presentations

D SPEAKING 2

Student B

1 Listen to Student A presenting some figures. Take notes and be ready to ask questions.

2 Look at the charts on the right. Consider the following background information behind the figures.

- disappearance of one main competitor from the market
- new deals with smaller retailers
- other companies' failure to invest in online marketing

3 Plan how you are going to present the information in the charts on the right. Remember to:

1 introduce your visual

2 describe the numbers confidently

3 use language to show transitions between information (e.g. *As you can see ..., This slide shows ..., Let's look in more detail at ..., The first/second reason is ..., On a positive note, ...*).

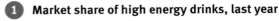

1 Market share of high energy drinks, last year

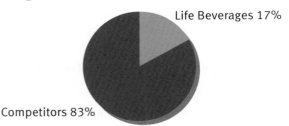

Life Beverages 17%

Competitors 83%

2 Market share of high energy drinks, this year

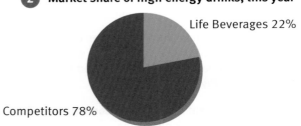

Life Beverages 22%

Competitors 78%

2.2 Presentations

TASK

Storm Technology

The charts show annual figures from Storm Technology which was launched three years ago, manufacturing a range of personal computing devices, such as mobile phones and tablets, and offering internet and mobile data services, such as cloud computing and mobile access. They sell their products through popular retailers, either on the high street or online.

Company information

The company launched a new range of tablets in Year 1.

In Year 2, the company made an agreement to retail their phones directly to the public through a chain of stores. They also bought the rights to offer the service contract for another mobile provider that year.

In Year 3, their competitors launched a rival tablet that was lighter and retailed for a lower price.

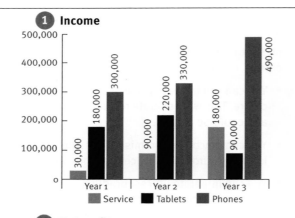

1 Income

Service Tablets Phones

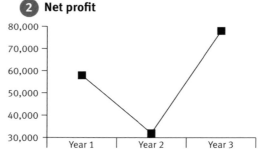

2 Net profit

3.1 Negotiations

TASK

Group A

- You are buyers for your company or organisation. You need to negotiate a deal with your regular supplier. Discuss the kind of T-shirts you need (e.g. low or high quality). You will need to state your negotiating position regarding price, quantity, quality, terms and conditions.

- You are an organisation with a staff of 200: there are 100 warehouse staff, 75 office staff and 25 managers. About 40 per cent of your staff are women. Decide when the staff are going to wear the T-shirts (e.g. every day).

- You would like the T-shirts to have your logo. You don't mind if the supplier brand name is also on the T-shirt, but it must be smaller than your company logo.

- Consider the style, colour(s) and design you would like, (e.g. women in the organisation may want a more fitted style). You are prepared to consider a T-shirt for the winter, but it depends on how staff react to the summer T-shirt.

- You need at least three sizes: small, medium and large.

- You would like the supplier to send you five different samples this week so that your team can vote for the best option.

- You need the T-shirts as soon as possible. 50 per cent of your staff are attending the summer conference in one month's time and you want them to wear the T-shirt at the event.

- Your standard delivery terms and conditions are 90-day credit terms, although you are prepared to pay 60-day credit terms for urgent orders.

Negotiations planning sheet

Stages of the negotiation	Notes
1 Getting started	
2 Stating the purpose	
3 Agenda	
4 Body of the negotiation	
5 Action points	
6 Concluding the meeting	

3.1 Negotiations

TASK

Group B

- You are suppliers at DifrenT Fashions. You need to negotiate a deal with a regular client who wants to order staff T-shirts. Discuss the kinds of products they need and what you can supply. You will need to state your negotiating position regarding price, quantity, quality, terms and conditions.

- You offer a basic range of colours (red, white, black, grey and blue) and a more expensive range of colours (lemon, orange, purple, pink, green, light/dark blue, beige, brown, etc.).

- You supply pure cotton T-shirts, but you can also offer better quality materials (e.g. organic cotton, and lycra/cotton mixed fabrics).

- If the buyer only wants one style of T-shirt, tell them you can offer a wider range (e.g. styles for men and women, a better quality T-shirt for management, a long-sleeved T-shirt for the winter and a short-sleeved T-shirt for the summer). In addition, staff would need two T-shirts during a working week. These considerations will double or quadruple the order!

- You offer five sizes: extra small, small, medium, large and extra large.

- A standard cotton T-shirt with a simple company logo costs about five euros and a more fitted T-shirt in a cotton/lyrca mix with a nice design can cost up to 10 euros.

- Your standard delivery terms and conditions are 90-days credit terms. Your other clients usually offer you 60-day credit terms. You need 30-day credit terms for urgent orders. You want your brand name to appear in large letters on all T-shirts.

- Aim high and establish what you want to achieve by the end of the negotiation.

Negotiations planning sheet

Stages of the negotiation	Notes
1 Getting started	
2 Stating the purpose	
3 Agenda	
4 Body of the negotiation	
5 Action points	
6 Concluding the meeting	

3.2 E-mails

D WRITING

Dear Olivia,

[a] I hope you are well and not too busy!

[b] Please find attached some forecasts for next year [c] as requested in your e-mail of yesterday, with top five products and corporate customers. We haven't had time yet to do a detailed analysis, so the forecasts, [d] just to confirm, are realistic but not totally precise.

You asked for a quick overview of 'special sales activities'. I'm not sure what you mean by this exactly or if you want information on this year or next year. [e] But I have attached a document with highlights from both this year and next, just in case. I hope this helps to clarify things.

[f] The main activities for you to note in these documents are:

Current year

We have just signed contracts with two new clients in the Middle East, which should become a top five by the end [g] of next year. We are working to sign a third by the end of the year; should be confirmed by October.

Next year

We plan to attend the Tech France-Asia trade fair in Paris next year, as part of our strategy to meet clients from Korea (see *Asia strategy* document attached). We haven't confirmed our attendance yet as cost is quite high.

[h] I guess it would be useful for us to chat through the documents briefly so that Richard has a little more background for his presentation. You said you are free in the morning, so shall I give you a call tomorrow at [i] 11.30 your time?

[j] Looking forward to talking tomorrow.

Best regards,
Jean Paul

4.1 Presentations

TASK

Students C and D

Staff training

You represent the Human Resources Department. You are preparing a presentation to staff to explain a new training initiative. You want to replace all face-to-face training with online courses. These are your main reasons:

- The attendance at face-to-face courses is very low. Staff say they are often too busy to attend classes.

- It will be more cost effective than face-to-face classes. You can dedicate this money to more specialised training courses.

- It is a more flexible way to organise training. Staff can connect at anytime from anywhere. Everyone has internet access these days.

4.2 Interviews

TASK

Scenario 1

Appraiser

You are the team leader of the claims department in an insurance company.

The appraisee has been a member of your claims team for the last sixteen months. He/She is a good worker, is helpful and uses his/her initiative. He/She is now in charge of the office supplies for the whole division and three months ago you received an email from the Finance Director praising his/her helpfulness and organisation skills, the only letter he sent this year.

However, he/she has made a number of errors recently. A few claims were paid out before all the documentation was received and he/she sometimes does not return calls to customers. Other members of the team have complained about having to deal with angry customers for him/her. One of the team left six months ago and, because of budget reasons, wasn't replaced. You want him/her to reduce the errors and think of a strategy to make sure that the work is covered. You've heard a rumour that he/she wants to move to the accounts department, but there are no vacancies there at the moment.

Employee

You work as an assistant in the claims department of an insurance company.

You have worked for this company for sixteen months. Since Tim, your colleague, left six months ago and wasn't replaced, you have been under a lot more pressure to do the work of two people. You have regularly worked longer hours and have tried to improve the efficiency of the office, but you don't feel like you get enough support. You have been taking courses at college and would like to move to the accountancy department, where you think you would have more opportunities. The Finance Director noticed your good work and sent an email to your team leader. You hope this is a sign that you might be able to move within the company.

Scenario 2

Appraiser

You are the team leader of the customer services department in a large bank.

Your appraisee has been a member of your team for the last two years. He/She is a good worker, relates well to customers and is particularly good at dealing with complaints. He/She is a popular member of the team and has supported the newest members with training and support well this year. You have received several letters from customers praising his/her work.

Since his/her last appraisal, he/she has worked at reducing the average length of the calls from 7.5 minutes to 6.5. However, this is still short of the 4.2 average for your department. You accept that he/she is popular with customers, but your goals to reduce call time are suffering. You do not think he/she is suitable for a team leaders' role in the company.

Employee

You work as an advisor in the customer services department of a bank.

You have a good relationship with customers and many of them have sent letters praising your work dealing with their problems. You are more often asked to deal with difficult customers and complaints, which you do, but feel that this should be recognised or rewarded more. In your last appraisal, your team leader set you the goal of reducing the amount of time you spend on each call, which you have done, from 7.5 to 6.5 minutes. You feel that the company doesn't really understand the importance of customer relations and focuses too much on speed and keeping the calls short. You recently took on extra responsibilities for training new staff and you feel that the next step in your career is to move into team management.

4.1 Presentations

TASK

Students E and F

Remote working

You represent the new CEO. You are preparing a presentation to staff to explain the new policy on remote working. It has been tradition in the company to allow some staff to work from home one day a week. You want to change that. You want everyone to work from the office all week. These are your main reasons:

- More work will get done if your staff are in the office all week.

- It will mean better communication, make it easier to exchange ideas and lead to quicker decision-making.

- It will build more of a corporate team spirit.

Glossary

- **adjective** *(adj.)* Headwords for adjectives followed by information in square brackets, e.g. *[only before a noun]* and *[not before a noun]*, show any restrictions on where they can be used.
- **noun** *(n.)* The codes *[C]* and *[U]* show whether a noun, or a particular sense of a noun, is countable *(an agenda, two agendas)* or uncountable *(awareness, branding)*.
- **verb** *(v.)* The forms of irregular verbs are given after the headword. The codes *[I]* (intransitive) and *[T]* (transitive) show whether a verb, or a particular sense of a verb, has or does not have an object. Phrasal verbs *(phr.v.)* are shown after the verb they are related to.
- Some entries show information on words that are related to the headword. Adverbs *(adv.)* are often shown in this way after adjectives.
- **Region labels** The codes *AmE* and *BrE* show whether a word or sense of a word is used only in American or British English.

abolish *v.* [T] to officially end a law, a system for doing something, an organisation etc., especially one that has existed for a long time

acquire *v.* [T] if one company acquires another, it buys it

acquisition *n.* [C] when one company buys another one, or part of another one

advertising campaign *n.* [C] an organisation's programme of advertising activities over a particular period of time with specific aims, for example to increase sales of a product

agenda *n.* [C] **1** a list of the subjects to be discussed at a meeting
2 the things that someone considers important or that they are planning to do something about

aggressive *adj.* **1** An *aggressive* plan or action is intended to achieve its result by using direct and forceful methods.
2 An *aggressive* person or organisation is very determined to achieve what they want.

application *n.* [C] **1** a formal, usually written, request for something or for permission to do something
2 a formal request for work
3 a practical use for something
4 a piece of software for a particular use or job

apply *v.* **1** [I] to make a formal, usually written, request for something, especially a job, a place at university or permission to do something
2 [T] to use something, such as a law or an idea, in a particular situation, activity or process
3 [I, T] to have an effect on someone or something; to concern a person, group or situation

appoint *v.* [T] to choose someone for a job or position

appointment *n.* **1** [C] an arrangement to meet someone at a particular time and place
2 [C, U] when someone is chosen to do a job, or the job itself

ASEAN *n.* Association of South-East Asian Nations: a political and economic group of countries formed in 1967 which now has 10 members, including Indonesia, Malaysia, the Philippines, Singapore, Thailand and Vietnam

asset *n.* [C] something belonging to an individual or a business that has value or the power to earn money

assignment *n.* **1** [C] a piece of work that someone is given
2 [U] when someone is given a particular job or task, or sent to work in a particular place or for a particular person

associate *n.* [C] **1** someone who you work with or do business with
2 a member of an organisation who has some but not all the rights of a full member

attend *v.* [I, T] to go to an event, such as a meeting

authority *n.* *(plural* **authorities***)* **1** [C] an official organisation which controls a particular activity and checks that the rules and laws relating to it are being obeyed
local authority [C] a government organisation in Britain that is responsible for providing public services, such as schools, the collection of rubbish, etc. in a particular area
2 the authorities [plural] the organisations that are in charge of a particular country or area or a particular activity
3 [C] the power that a person or organisation has because of their official or legal position

authorise *(also* **authorize** *AmE) v.* [T] to give official or legal permission for something
authorised *(also* **authorized** *AmE) adj.*

automotive *adj.* [only before a noun] relating to cars or the car industry

awareness *n.* [U] knowledge or understanding of a particular subject, situation or thing

award[1] *n.* [C] **1** an amount of money that is given to someone as a result of an official decision or judgement
2 something such as a prize or an amount of money given to a person or company to reward them for something they have done

award[2] *v.* [T] **1** to officially decide that someone should have something, such as an amount of money
2 to officially give a prize or an amount of money to a person or company, to reward them for what they have done

background *n.* **1** [C] someone's past, for example their education, qualifications, and the jobs they have had
2 [C, U] the situation or past events that explain why something happens in the way that it does [+ *to*]

bankrupt *adj.* not having enough money to pay your debts

bankruptcy *n.* *(plural* **bankruptcies***)* [C, U] when someone is judged to be unable to pay their debts by a court of law, and their assets are shared among the people and businesses that they owe money to

banner ad *n.* [C] an advertisement that appears across the top of a page on the Internet
banner advertising *n.* [U]

barrier to trade *n.* (*plural* **barriers to trade**) [C] something that makes trade between two countries more difficult or expensive, for example a tax on imports (= **trade barrier**)

bid *n.* [C] an offer to buy something, for example a company in a takeover; the price offered

bill[1] *n.* [C] **1** a list showing how much you have to pay for services or goods received (= **invoice**)
2 *BrE* a list showing how much you have to pay for food you have eaten in a restaurant (= **check** *AmE*)

bill[2] *v.* [T] to send a bill to someone saying how much they owe (= **invoice**)

billboard *n.* [C] a large sign used for advertising (= **hoarding** *BrE*)

board *n.* [C] (*also* **board of directors**) the group of people who have been elected to manage a company by those holding shares in the company

boardroom *n.* [C] the place in a company where its board of directors meets

bonus *n.* [C] an extra amount of money added to an employee's wages, usually as a reward for doing difficult work or for doing their work well

booking *n.* [C] an arrangement in which a place on a plane, in a hotel, restaurant, etc. is kept for a customer who will arrive later (= **reservation**)

boost *v.* [T] to increase something such as production, sales or prices

bottom line *n.* [C] *informal* **1** the figure showing a company's total profit or loss
2 the end result of something or the most important point about something

branch *n.* [C] an individual bank, shop, office, etc. that is part of a large organisation

branch manager *n.* [C] someone in charge of a particular branch of a bank, shop in a chain of shops, etc.

branch office *n.* [C] a local office of a company, usually in a different town or city to the company's main office

brand *n.* [C] a name given to a product by a company so that the product can easily be recognised by its name or its design

brand image *n.* the collection of ideas and beliefs that people have about a brand

branded *adj. Branded* goods or products have brand names and so can easily be recognised by their name or design.

bribery *n.* [C] dishonestly giving money to someone to persuade them to do something to help you

budget *n.* [C] a detailed plan made by an organisation or a government of how much it will receive as income over a particular period of time, and how much it will spend, what it will spend the money on, etc.
advertising budget an organisation's spending plan for advertising during a particular period of time

bureaucratic *adj.* involving or having a lot of complicated and unnecessary official rules

buzzword *n.* [C] a word or phrase from one special area of knowledge that people suddenly think is important and use a lot

cancel *v.* (**cancelled, cancelling** *BrE*; **canceled, canceling** *AmE*) [T] to arrange that a planned activity or event will not now happen

cancellation *n.* [C, U] a decision or statement that a planned activity will not happen or that an agreement will be ended

carrier *n.* [C] a person or company whose job is to transport goods from one place to another

cashflow (*also* **cash flow**) *n.* **1** [U] the amounts of money coming into and going out of a company, and the timing of these
2 [C, U] profit for a particular period, defined in different ways by different businesses

charity *n.* (*plural* **charities**) [C] an organisation that collects money to help people, for example those who are sick or poor, or to help certain types of activity, such as artistic activity (= **not-for-profit organization; non-profit organization** *AmE*)

chart *n.* [C] a mathematical drawing or list, showing information arranged in a way that is clear and easy to understand

check *v.* [T] to find out whether something is correct, true or safe

check in *phr.v.* [I, T] to go to the desk at a hotel or airport and say that you have arrived

Chief Executive Officer (CEO) *n.* the manager with the most authority in the normal, everyday management of a company. The job of Chief Executive Officer is sometimes combined with other jobs, such as that of president.

claim[1] *n.* [C] a request or demand for money, or the amount of money asked for
expenses claim money that an employee spends on things such as food and travel while they are doing their job, which their employer then pays back to them

claim[2] *v.* [T] to state that something is true, even though it has not been proved

commission *n.* **1** [C, U] an amount of money paid to someone according to the value of goods, shares, bonds, etc. they have sold
2 [C] an official organisation that ensures that the law is obeyed in a particular activity
3 [C] a temporary official organisation looking at problems in a particular area and suggesting changes

commitment *n.* **1** [C, U] a promise to do something or to behave in a particular way
2 [U] the hard work and loyalty that someone gives to an organisation or activity

commodity *n.* (*plural* **commodities**) [C] a product that can be sold to make a profit, especially one in its basic form before it has been used or changed in an industrial process. Examples of commodities are farm products and metals.

compensation *n.* [U] **1** an amount paid to someone because they have been hurt or harmed
2 the total amount of money and other advantages that someone receives as an employee

concept *n.* [C] **1** an idea for a product
2 a rule or idea saying how something should be done

conflict n. [C, U] **1** a state of disagreement between people, groups, countries, etc.
2 a situation in which you have to choose between two or more different needs

consignment n. [C] a quantity of goods delivered at the same time

contract n. [C] a formal, written agreement between two or more people or groups which says what each must do for the other, or must not do

convene v. [I, T] If a group of people convenes, or if someone convenes them, they come together for a formal meeting.

corporate adj. [only before a noun] relating to a company, usually a large one, or business in general

corruption n. [U] **1** the crime of giving or receiving money, gifts, a better job, etc. in exchange for doing something dishonest or illegal
2 when someone who has power or authority uses it in a dishonest or illegal way to get money or an advantage

counter n. [C] the place where you are served in a shop, bank, etc.

counterfeit adj. made to look exactly like something else, in order to deceive people

coverage n. [U] when a subject or event is reported on television or radio, or in newspapers

credit n. [U] an arrangement with a shop, supplier, etc. to buy something now and pay for it later
trade credit [U] when a supplier allows a business customer to pay for goods or services after they are delivered, usually 30, 60 or 90 days later

credit crunch n. [singular] when borrowing money becomes difficult because banks are forced to reduce the amount they lend

crew n. [C] all the people working on a ship or plane

culture n. [C, U] **1** the ideas, beliefs and customs that are shared and accepted by people in a society
2 the attitudes or beliefs that are shared by a particular group of people or in a particular organisation

currency n. (plural **currencies**) [C, U] the system or type of money used in a particular country

customise (also **customize** AmE) v. [T, usually passive] If something is customised for a customer, it is designed, built, etc. specially for that customer, making it different to other things of the same kind.

customs n. [U] **1** the government department responsible for collecting the tax on goods that have been brought into the country and making sure that illegal goods are not imported or exported
2 the place at an airport or port through which people and goods arriving in a country must pass and where any tax owed must be paid

damage¹ n. [U] **1** a bad effect on something that makes it weaker or less successful
2 physical harm caused to something

damage² v. [T] **1** to cause physical harm to something
2 to have a bad effect on something in a way that makes it weaker or less successful

debt n. **1** [C] money that one person, organisation, country, etc. owes to another
2 [U] the state of owing money

3 [U] capital borrowed by a business or government organisation on which it pays interest

decline¹ v. [I] **1** If an industry or country declines, it becomes less profitable, productive, wealthy, etc.
2 If sales, profits, production, etc. decline, they become less.

decline² n. [C, U] **1** when sales, profits, production, etc. become less
2 when an industry or country becomes less profitable, productive, wealthy, etc.

deficit n. [C] **1** an amount of money that a business has lost in a particular period of time
2 an amount by which the money that a government spends is more than it receives in tax in a particular period
trade deficit the amount by which the money going out of a country to pay for imports is more than the amount coming in from exports

delivery n. (plural **deliveries**) [C, U] the act or process of bringing goods, letters, etc. to a particular place or person

demand n. [U] **1** the amount of spending on goods and services by companies and people in a particular economy
2 the total amount of a type of goods or services that people or companies buy in a particular period of time
3 the total amount of a type of goods or services that people or companies would buy if they were available

deposit n. [C] an amount of money paid into a bank account or held in a bank account, especially when it is earning interest

deregulate v. [I, T] to remove or reduce the number of government controls on a particular business activity, done to make companies work more effectively and to increase competition

deregulation n. [U]

derivative n. [C, usually plural] something such as an option (= the right to buy or sell something at a particular price within a particular period) or a future (= a fixed price that you pay now for delivery of something in the future) based on underlying assets such as shares, bonds and currencies

despatch (also **dispatch**) v. [T] to send something or someone to a place

differentiate v. [T] When a company differentiates its products, it shows how they are different from each other and from competing products, for example in its advertising. This is done to show buyers the advantages of one product over another.

dispose of something phr.v. [T] to get rid of something that is no longer needed or wanted

diversify v. (past tense and past participle **diversified**) [I] If a company or economy diversifies, it increases the range of goods or services it produces.
diversification n. [C, U]

dividend n. [C] a part of the profits of a company for a particular period of time that is paid to shareholders for each share that they own

downmarket adv. **1** go/move **downmarket** to start buying or selling cheaper goods or services (= **downscale** AmE)
2 take something **downmarket** to change a product or a service, or people's ideas about it, so that it is cheaper or seems cheaper and more popular (= **downscale** AmE)

downturn *n.* [C, U] the part of the economic cycle when prices or the value of stocks, shares, etc. fall

dump *v.* [T] to sell products cheaply in an export market, perhaps in order to increase your share of the market there

dumping *n.* [U]

durable *adj.* If something is *durable*, it lasts a long time, even if it is used a lot.
durability *n.* [U]

earnings *n.* [plural] **1** the money that a person receives for the work they do in a particular period of time
2 the total amount that people receive for the work they do in a particular industry or economy in a particular period of time
3 the profit that a company makes in a particular period of time, or the total profits that companies make in a particular industry or economy in a particular period of time

emerging *adj.* [only before a noun] *Emerging* nations/countries/economies are countries, especially those in Asia, Africa and South America, that are just starting to have influence or power in trade, finance, etc.

endorse *v.* [T] If a well-known person *endorses* a product, they say in an advertisement how good they think it is. People will buy the product because they like or trust the person.
endorsement *n.* [C, U]

entrepreneur *n.* [C] someone who starts a company, arranges business deals and takes risks in order to make a profit

equity *n.* **1** [U] the capital that a company has from shares rather than from loans
2 equities [plural] trading in companies' shares on a stock market, rather than trading on other types of market

ethical *adj.* **1** connected with principles of what is right and wrong
2 morally good or correct
ethically *adv.*

etiquette *n.* [U] the formal rules for polite behaviour

exceed *v.* [T] to be more than a particular number or amount

exchange¹ *n.* [C, U] when you accept one thing in return for another¹
information exchange [U] when information is passed between people or organisations, by means of computer equipment

exchange² *v.* [T] to give someone something and receive something in return

expand *v.* [I, T] **1** to become larger in size, amount or number, or to make something larger in size, amount or number
2 If an economy, industry or business activity *expands*, it gets bigger or more successful.

expansion *n.* [U] **1** when something increases or is increased in size, amount or number
2 when an economy becomes more successful, and there is increased economic activity, more jobs, etc.

expense *n.* **1** [C, U] an amount of money that a business or organisation has to spend on something
2 expenses [plural] money that an employee spends while doing their job on things such as travel and food, and which their employer then pays back to them

expertise *n.* [U] special skills or knowledge in an area of work or study

facility *n.* (*plural* **facilities**) **1 facilities** [plural] special buildings or equipment that have been provided for a particular use, such as sports activities, shopping or travelling
2 [C] a place or large building that is used to make or provide a particular product or service (= **plant**)
3 [C] an arrangement made by a bank for its customers which lets them use the services the bank offers. These services would include, for example, borrowing or investing money.

fake¹ *adj.* made to look like something valuable or genuine (= **real**) in order to deceive people

fake² *n.* [C] a copy of an original document, valuable object, etc. that is intended to deceive people into believing it is the real document, object, etc.

fake³ *v.* [T] informal to make an exact copy of something, or invent figures or results, in order to deceive people

fall¹ *v.* (*past tense* **fell**; *past participle* **fallen**) [I] to go down to a lower price, level, amount, etc.

fall² *n.* [C] a reduction in the amount, level, price, etc. of something

fare *n.* [C] the price paid to travel by plane, train, etc.

faulty *adj.* If a machine, system, etc. is *faulty*, there is something wrong with it that prevents it from working correctly.

flexible *adj.* **1** A person, plan, etc. that is *flexible* can change or be changed easily to suit any new situation.
2 If arrangements for work are *flexible*, employers can ask workers to do different jobs, work part-time rather than full-time, give them contracts for short periods of time, etc.
flexibility *n.* [U]

flyer *n.* [C] a small sheet of paper that is used to advertise something. *Flyers* are usually handed out in the street or delivered to people's houses (*see also* **frequent flyer**)

focus group *n.* [C] a group of consumers brought together by a company to help it do market research. The consumers are asked to discuss their feelings and opinions about products, advertisements, companies, etc.

forecast¹ *n.* [C] a description of what is likely to happen in the future, based on the information that you have now

forecast² *v.* (*past tense and past participle* **forecast** *or* **forecasted**) [T] to make a statement saying what is likely to happen in the future, based on information that is available now

fraud *n.* [C, U] a method of illegally getting money from a person or organisation, often using clever and complicated methods

frequent flyer *n.* [C] someone who flies with a particular airline a lot and is often offered special advantages, such as free flights or a better seat

futures *n.* [plural] buying and selling futures contracts (= a contract for a fixed amount of a commodity or security to be delivered at a fixed price on a fixed date in the future; futures are traded on financial markets)

generate *v.* [T] **1** to produce energy or power
2 to do something that will produce or increase sales, income, profit, etc.

global *adj.* **1** including and considering all the parts of a situation together, rather than the individual parts separately

2 affecting or involving the whole world
3 go global If a company or industry *goes global*, it starts doing business all over the world.
globally *adv.*

grow *v.* (*past tense* **grew**; *past participle* **grown**) **1** [T] to increase in amount, size or degree
2 [T] If you *grow* a business activity, you make it bigger.

growth *n.* [U] an increase in size, amount or degree
economic growth an increase in the value of goods and services produced in a country or area

headquarters *n.* [plural] the head office or main building of an organisation

hedge fund *n.* [C] a fund that makes investments that are unlikely to fall in value, as well as those that go up or down in value, to reduce the risk of losing a lot of money

hire *v.* [T] **1** to employ a person or an organisation for a short time to do a particular job for you
2 to agree to give someone a permanent job
3 *BrE* to pay money to use something for a period of time (= **rent** *AmE*)

hoarding *n.* [C] *BrE* a large sign used for advertising (= **billboard** *AmE*)

host country *n.* [C] a country where a company that is based in another country has business activities

human resources (HR) *n.* [plural] the department in an organisation that deals with employing, training and helping employees (= **personnel**)

impact *n.* [C] the effect or influence that an event, situation, etc. has on someone or something

import¹ *n.* **1** [C, usually plural] something that is made in one country and brought into another, usually to be sold
2 [C, usually plural; U] the activity of bringing goods into a country
3 imports [plural] the amount or value of the goods brought into a country over a particular period of time

import² *v.* [T] to bring something into a country from abroad, usually in order to sell it

incentive *n.* [C] something which is used to encourage people to do something, especially to make them work harder, produce more or spend more money
tax incentive an offer to pay less tax, given to people who do something that the government is trying to encourage

income *n.* [C, U] money that you earn from your job or that you receive from investments

innovate *v.* [I] to design and develop new and original products

innovation *n.* **1** [C] a new idea, method or invention
2 [U] the introduction of new ideas or methods
product innovation [C, U] when new or better products are designed and developed, or the new or better product itself

innovative *adj.* **1** An *innovative* product, method, process, etc. is new, different and better than those that existed before.
2 using or developing new and original ideas and methods

interest *n.* [U] an amount paid by a borrower to a lender, for example to a bank by someone borrowing money for a loan or by a bank to a depositor (= someone keeping money in an account there)

interest rate *n.* [C] the percentage rate used for calculating interest over a particular period of time, usually one year

interim *adj.* [only before a noun] **1** intended to be used or accepted for a short time only, until something final can be made
2 prepared after only part of a full financial year has been completed, often after half a year

introductory *adj.* [only before a noun] An *introductory* offer, price, etc. is a special low price that is charged for a new product for a limited period of time.

invest *v.* [I, T] **1** to buy shares, bonds, property, etc. in order to make a profit
2 to save money in a high-interest bank account or to buy an insurance policy that pays bonuses
3 to spend money on things that will make a business more successful and profitable

investment *n.* **1** [C, U] when money is put into a business in order to make it more successful and profitable, or the money that is put into a business
Return on investment (ROI) or return on capital (ROC) is the amount of profit received on an investment in relation to the amount of money invested.
2 [C] something you buy, such as shares, bonds or property, in order to make a profit
3 [C] an amount of money that you invest
4 [U] when you buy shares, bonds, property, etc. in order to make a profit

invoice *n.* [C] a document sent by a seller to a customer with details of goods or services that have been provided, their price and the payment date

jobseeker (*also* **job seeker**) *n.* [C] someone who is looking for a job (= **job hunter**)

labor union *AmE* (= **trade union** *BrE*) *n.* [C] an organisation representing people working in a particular industry or profession that protects their rights

launch¹ *v.* [I, T] **1** to show or make a new product available for sale for the first time
2 to start a new company
3 to start a new activity or profession, usually after planning it carefully

launch² *n.* [C] **1** an occasion at which a new product is shown or made available for sale or use for the first time
2 the start of a new activity or plan

launder money/profits *v.* [T] to put money which has been obtained illegally into legal businesses and bank accounts in order to hide where it was obtained
laundering *n.* [U]

level¹ *n.* [C] **1** the measured amount of something that exists at a particular time or in a particular place
2 all the people or jobs within an organisation, industry, etc. that have similar importance and responsibility

level² *v.* (**levelled, levelling** *BrE*; **leveled, leveling** *AmE*) **level off/out** *phr.v.* [I] to stop increasing or growing and become steady or continue at a fixed level

level playing field *n.* [singular] *informal* a situation in which different companies, countries, etc. can all compete fairly with each other because no one has special advantages

liberalise (*also* **liberalize** *AmE*) *v.* [T] to make rules or controls on something less strict
liberalisation (*also* **liberalization** *AmE*) *n.* [U]

loan n. [C] money borrowed from a bank, financial institution, person, etc. on which interest is usually paid to the lender until the loan is repaid

logo n. [C] a design or way of writing its name that a company or organisation uses as its official sign on its products, advertising, etc.

lose v. (*past tense and past participle* **lost**; *present participle* **losing**) [T] **1** to stop having something any more, or to have less of it
2 to have less money than you had before or to spend more money than you are receiving
3 to fall to a lower figure or price
lose out phr.v. [I] to not get something good, when someone else does get it

loss n. **1** [C, U] the fact of no longer having something that you used to have, or having less of it
job loss [C, U] when people lose their jobs
2 [C] when a business spends more money than it receives in a particular period of time, or loses money in some other way

loyal adj. If customers are *loyal* to a particular product, they continue to buy it and do not change to other products.
loyalty n. [U]

margin n. [C, U] the difference between the price that something is sold for and the cost of producing or buying it. A margin is usually calculated as a percentage of the price that something is sold for.
profit margin [C, U] the difference between the price of a product or service and the cost of producing it, or between the cost of producing all of a company's products or services and the total sum they are sold for

market¹ n. **1** [C] the activity of buying and selling goods or services, or the value of the goods or services sold
2 [C] a particular country, area or group of people to which a company sells or hopes to sell its goods or services
3 [singular] the number of people who want to buy something
4 [C] (*also* **financial market**) the buying and selling of shares, bonds, commodities, etc.; a place where this happens. Some *markets* are in a particular building, while trading on others takes place on computers and over the telephone, with no central building.

market² v. [T] **1** to sell something or make it available for sale, especially in a particular way
2 to sell something by considering what customers want or need when buying a product or service, for example how much they are willing to pay, where they will buy it, etc.

marketing n. [U] activities to design and sell a product or service by considering buyers' wants or needs, for example where and how they will buy it, how much they will be willing to pay, etc.

meet v. (*past tense and past participle* **met**) [I, T] **1** to get together with another person to discuss something
2 meet a debt/cost/payment/expense to pay a debt or payment
3 meet a target/expectation/projection/standard to achieve a level that has been set or expected
4 meet a demand to produce enough goods to satisfy the demand for them
5 meet a deadline to finish something at or before the time it was meant to be finished

6 meet a requirement/condition/obligation to succeed in doing something that you have to do

merge v. [I, T] If two or more companies, organisations, etc. *merge*, or if they are *merged*, they join together.

merger n. [C] an occasion when two or more companies, organisations, etc. join together to form a larger company, etc.

model n. [C] **1** a particular type or design of a vehicle or machine
2 a simple description or structure that is used to help people understand similar systems or structures
3 the way in which something is done by a particular country, person, etc. that can be copied by others who want similar results

morale n. [U] the level of confidence and positive feelings among a group of people who work together

motivate v. [T] to encourage someone and make them want to work hard

motivated adj. very keen to do something or achieve something, especially because you find it interesting or exciting

outlet n. [C] a shop, company or organisation through which products are sold

outsource v. [T] If a company, organisation, etc. outsources its work, it employs another company to do it (= **subcontract**)
outsourcing n. [U]

overtime n. [U] **1** time that you spend working in your job in addition to your normal working hours
2 the money that you are paid for working more hours than usual

ownership n. [U] the state of owning something

packaging n. [U] **1** material, boxes, etc. used for wrapping goods to protect them, for example because they are being taken somewhere (= **packing**)
2 the process of wrapping or packing goods so they are ready to be sent somewhere (= **packing**)

panel n. [C] a group of people chosen to give advice or decide something

parent company n. [C] If one company is the *parent* of another, it owns at least half the shares in the other company, and has control over it.

partner n. [C] **1** a company that works with another company in a particular activity, or invests in the same activity
2 someone who starts a new business with someone else by investing in it
3 a member of certain types of business or professional groups, for example partnerships of lawyers, architects, etc.

4 economic partner, trade partner, trading partner a country that invests in another or is invested in by another or that trades with another

partnership n. **1** [C] a relationship between two people, organisations or countries that work together
2 [U] the situation of working together in business
3 [C] a business organisation made up of a group of accountants, lawyers, etc. who work together, or of a group of investors

patent *n.* [C] a legal document giving a person or company the right to make or sell a new invention, product or method of doing something and stating that no other person or company is allowed to do this

peak¹ *n.* [C] the time when prices, shares, etc. have reached their highest point or level

peak² *adj.* **1 peak level/price/rate, etc.** the highest level, etc. something reaches
2 peak time/period/hours/season the time when the greatest number of people in a country are doing the same thing, using the same service, etc.

peak³ *v.* [I] to reach the highest point or level

perk *n.* [C] something in addition to money that you get for doing your job, such as a car

personnel *n.* **1** [plural] the people who work for a company or organisation
2 [U] the department in an organisation that deals with employing, training and helping employees (= **human resources**)

pitch *n.* [C] **1 sales pitch** *informal* what a sales person says about a product to persuade people to buy it
2 an attempt by an advertising agency to persuade a company to use its services to advertise a product

poverty *n.* [U] **1** the situation or experience of being poor
2 the poverty line the income below which people are officially considered to be very poor and needing help

predict *v.* [T] to say what you think will happen
prediction *n.* [C]

pricing *n.* [U] the prices of a company's products or services in relation to each other and in relation to those of their competitors, and the activity of setting them

produce *v.* **1** [I, T] to make or grow something in large quantities to be sold
2 [T] to make something happen or to have a particular result or effect

producer *n.* [C] **1** a person or organisation that manages and finds the finance for films, plays, etc.
2 a company or country that makes goods or grows foods

product *n.* **1** [C] something useful and intended to be sold that comes from nature or is made in a factory
2 milk/steel/tobacco/wood, etc. products products made from milk, etc.
3 [C] a service

production *n.* **1** [U] the process of making or growing things to be sold as products, usually in large quantities
2 [U] an amount of something that is produced

profile *n.* [C] **1** a short description of someone or something, giving the most important details about them
2 used to talk about how much things are noticed and the degree to which they are given attention

promote *v.* [T] **1** to help something develop, grow, become more successful, etc. or encourage something to happen
2 to try hard to sell a product or service by advertising it widely, reducing its price, etc.
3 to give someone a better-paid, more responsible job in a company or organisation

promotion *n.* [C, U] **1** a move to a more important job or position in a company or organisation
2 sales promotion an activity such as special advertisements or free gifts intended to sell a product or service

property *n.* [U] **1** all the things that someone owns
2 land and buildings, and the activity of buying, selling and renting them (= **real estate**)

proposal *n.* [C] a plan or idea which is suggested formally to an official person, or when this is done

propose *v.* [T] **1** to suggest something such as a plan or course of action
proposed *adj.* [only before a noun]
2 to formally suggest a course of action at a meeting and ask people to vote on it

protect *v.* [T] **1** to keep someone or something safe from harm, damage, bad influences, etc.
2 to try to help an industry in your own country by taxing foreign goods that are competing with it, so limiting the number that can be imported

protectionism *n.* [U] when a government tries to help industry, farming, etc. in its own country by taxing foreign goods that compete with it, so limiting the number that can be imported

prototype *n.* [C] the first form that a newly designed car, machine, etc. has

purchase¹ *n.* **1** [U] the act of buying something
2 make a purchase to buy something
3 [C] something that has been bought

purchase² *v.* [T] *formal* to buy something, especially something big or expensive

qualification *n.* **1** [C, usually plural] an examination that you have passed at school, university or in your profession
2 [C] a skill, personal quality or type of experience that makes you suitable for a particular job

quarter *n.* [C] **1** one of four equal parts into which something can be divided
2 a period of three months, especially in connection with bills, payments and income

quarterly *adv.* happening or produced once every three months

quota *n.* [C] an amount of something that is officially allowed or expected in a particular period of time

quote *v.* [T] to tell a customer the price you will charge them for a service or product

R and D (*also* **R&D**) *n.* [U] **1** research and development; the part of a business concerned with studying new ideas and planning new products
2 research and development; the department in a company responsible for developing new products, improving existing products, etc.

rate *n.* [C] **1** a charge or payment fixed according to a standard scale
2 the number of examples of something or the number of times something happens, often expressed as a percentage
3 the speed at which something happens
4 interest rate the percentage charged for borrowing money or a percentage you receive when you put money in a bank, make an investment, etc.

real estate *n. AmE* [U] **1** land or buildings
2 the business of selling land or buildings

receipt *n.* **1** [U] the act of receiving something
2 [C] a written statement showing that you have received money, goods or services
3 receipts [plural] money that has been received

recession *n.* [C, U] a period of time when an economy or industry is doing badly, and business activity and employment decrease. Many economists consider that there is a *recession* when industrial production falls for six months in a row.

recommend *v.* [T] **1** to advise someone to do something, especially because you have special knowledge of a situation or subject
2 to say that something or someone would be a good thing or person to choose

recommendation *n.* [C, U] **1** official advice given to someone about what to do
2 a suggestion that someone should choose a particular thing or person because they are very good or suitable

recover *v.* **1** [I] to increase or improve after falling in value or getting worse
2 [T] to get back money that you have spent or lost
3 [T] to get back something that was stolen, lost or almost destroyed

recovery *n.* (*plural* **recoveries**) **1** [C, U] when prices increase, or when the economy grows again after a period of difficulty
2 [U] the act of getting something back, such as money that you are owed

recruit *v.* [I, T] to find new people to work for an organisation, do a job, etc.

recruitment *n.* **1** [U] the process or the business of recruiting new people
2 [C] an occasion when someone is recruited

redundancy *n.* (*plural* **redundancies**) [C, U] *especially BrE* when someone loses their job in a company because the job is no longer needed

redundant *adj. especially BrE* If you are made *redundant*, you lose your job because your employer no longer has a job for you.

reference *n.* [C] **1** a letter written by someone who knows you well, usually to a new employer, giving information about your character, abilities or qualifications
2 a person who provides information about your character, abilities or qualifications when you are trying to get a job (= **referee**)

reliable *adj.* Someone or something that is *reliable* can be trusted or depended on.
reliability *n.* [U]

relocate *v.* [I, T] If a company or workers *relocate* or are *relocated*, they move to a different place.

relocation *n.* [C, U]

requirement *n.* [C] **1** something that an official organisation says a company or person must have or do
2 something that someone needs or wants

reschedule *v.* [T] to arrange a new time or date for a meeting or event

resignation *n.* [C, U] when someone officially states that they want to leave their job, position, etc.

respond *v.* [I] **1** to react to something that has happened
2 to reply to a letter, telephone call, etc.

restriction *n.* [C] an official rule that limits or controls what people can do or what is allowed to happen

restructure *v.* [I, T] If a company *restructures*, or someone *restructures* it, it changes the way it is organised or financed.

retail *n.* [U] **1** the sale of goods to customers for their own use, rather than to shops, etc.
2 retail trade/market/business, etc. the selling of goods or services to members of the public, or companies involved in this
3 retail shop/outlet/store, etc. a shop, etc. that is open to members of the public

retailer *n.* [C] **1** a business that sells goods to members of the public, rather than to shops, etc.
2 someone who owns or runs a shop selling goods to members of the public

return¹ *v.* [T] to take a product back to the shop you bought it from to get your money back, or to get other goods in exchange for it

return² *n.* [C, U] the amount of profit made from an investment

revenue *n.* [C] (*also* **revenues**) money that a business or organisation receives over a period of time, especially from selling goods or services

reward¹ *n.* **1** [C] something that you receive because you have done something good or helpful
2 [C, U] money that you earn for doing a job or providing a service
3 [C, U] money earned by an investment
4 [C] an amount of money offered to someone in return for some information about something

reward² *v.* [T] to give someone something such as money because they have done something good or helpful

rise¹ *v.* (*past tense* **rose**; *past participle* **risen**) [I] to increase in number, amount or value

rise² *n.* **1** [C] an increase in number, amount or value
2 [C] *BrE* an increase in salary or wages (= **raise** *AmE*)
3 [singular] the process of becoming more important, successful or powerful

sale *n.* **1** [C, U] the act of selling someone property, food or other goods
2 sales [plural] the total number of products that a company sells during a particular period of time
3 sales [U] the part of a company that deals with selling products

sample *n.* [C] a small amount of a product that people can use or look at in order to find out what it is like

saving *n.* **1** [U] the act of keeping money to use later rather than spending it
2 [C, usually singular] an amount of something that you have not used or spent, especially compared with a larger amount that you could have used or spent
3 savings [plural] money that is kept in a bank to be used later or invested, rather than spent

security n. (plural **securities**) **1** [U] actions to keep someone or something safe from being damaged, stolen, etc.
2 [U] a feeling of being safe and free from worry about what might happen
3 [U] property or other assets that you promise to give someone if you cannot pay back the money that you owe them
4 [C] a financial investment such as a bond or share, or the related certificate showing who owns it

segment n. [C] **1** a part of the economy of a country or a company's work
2 market segment a group of customers that share similar characteristics, such as age, income, interests and social class
3 market segment the products in a particular part of the market

seniority n. [U] **1** the fact of being older or higher in rank than someone else
2 the official advantage someone has because they have worked for an organisation for a long time

share n. [C] one of the parts into which ownership of a company is divided

shareholder n. [C] someone who owns shares in a company

shipment n. **1** [C] a load of goods sent by sea, road, train or air
2 [U] the act of sending a load of goods by sea, road, train or air

shortlist¹ n. [C] BrE a list of the most suitable people for a job or a prize, chosen from all the people who were first considered

shortlist² v. [T, usually passive] BrE to put someone on a shortlist for a job or a prize

skill n. [C, U] an ability to do something well, especially because you have learned and practised it

slowdown n. [C, usually singular] when something gets slower

specification n. [C, usually plural] a detailed description of how something should be designed or made

sponsor¹ v. [T] to give money to pay for a television programme, a sports or arts event, training, etc. in exchange for advertising or to get public attention

sponsor² n. [C] a person or company that pays for a television programme, a sports or arts event, training, etc. in exchange for advertising or to get public attention

stake n. [C, usually singular] money risked or invested in a business

standard n. [C, U] a level of quality, skill, ability or achievement by which someone or something is judged, and that is considered good enough to be acceptable

standard of living n. (plural **standards of living**) [C, usually singular] the amount of wealth or comfort that a person, group or country has

statement n. [C] **1** something you say or write publicly or officially to let people know your intentions or opinions, or to record facts
mission statement a short written statement made by an organization, intended to communicate its aims to customers, employees, shareholders, etc.
2 a list showing amounts of money paid, received, owing, etc. and their total

bank statement a statement sent regularly by a bank to a customer, showing the money that has gone into and out of their account over a particular period of time

stock n. [C, U] **1** especially AmE one of the shares into which ownership of a company is divided, or these shares considered together
2 stocks a supply of a commodity (= oil, metal, farm product, etc.) that has been produced and is kept to be used when needed
3 especially BrE a supply of raw materials or parts before they are used in production, or a supply of finished goods (= **inventory** AmE)
4 a supply of goods, kept for sale by a shop or other retailer

strategic adj. done as part of a plan to gain an advantage or achieve a particular purpose
strategically adv.

strategy n. (plural **strategies**) **1** [C] a plan or series of plans for achieving an aim, especially success in business or the best way for an organisation to develop in the future
2 [U] the process of skilful planning in general

strengthen v. **1** [I, T] If a currency strengthens, or something strengthens it, the currency increases in value.
2 [T] to improve the financial situation of a country, company, etc.

stunt n. [C] something that is done to attract people's attention to a product or company

subsidiary n. (plural **subsidiaries**) [C] a company that is at least half-owned by another company

subsidise (also **subsidize** AmE) v. [T] If a government or organisation subsidises a company, activity, etc., it pays part of the cost.
subsidised adj. [only before a noun]

subsidy n. (plural **subsidies**) [C] money that is paid by a government or organisation to make something such as a particular food or product cheaper to buy, use or produce

supplier n. [C] a company that provides a particular type of product

supply¹ v. (past tense and past participle **supplied**) [T] **1** to provide goods or services to customers, especially regularly and over a long period of time
2 to give someone something they want or need

supply² n. (plural **supplies**) [C] an amount of something that is available to be sold, bought, used, etc.

supply chain (also **distribution chain, chain of distribution**) the series of organisations that are involved in passing products from manufacturers to the public

surplus n. [C, U] an amount of something that is more than what is wanted, needed or used
trade surplus (also **balance of trade surplus**) [C, U] a surplus related to imports and exports, rather than other payments

sustain v. [T] to manage to make something continue to exist over a long period of time
sustained adj.

survey n. [C] a set of questions given to a group of people to find out about their opinions or behaviour
market survey a study of the state of a particular market, showing competitors' sales, buyers' intentions, etc.

take on phr.v. (past tense **took on**; past participle **taken on**) [T] **1 take somebody on** to start to employ someone

2 take something on: to agree to do some work or to be responsible for something

take over *phr.v.* (*past tense* **took over**; *past participle* **taken over**) [T] to take control of a company by buying more than 50% of its shares
takeover *n.* [C]

target¹ *n.* [C] **1** an organisation, industry, government, etc. that is deliberately chosen to have something done to it
2 a result such as a total, an amount or a time which you aim to achieve
3 target customer/group/area, etc. a limited group of people or area that a plan, idea, etc. is aimed at

target² *v.* [T] **1** to aim products, programmes of work, etc. at a particular area or group of people
2 to choose someone or something for a particular type of treatment
targeted *adj.* [only before a noun]

tariff *n.* [C, usually plural] a tax on goods coming into a country or going out of it

teaser *n.* [C] an advertisement intended to get people's attention for advertisements that will come later or products that will be available later

tip *n.* [C] **1** a piece of advice about what is likely to happen, for example about which shares are likely to go up or down in value
2 a small amount of additional money that you give to someone such as a waiter in order to thank them for their services

track record *n.* [C, usually singular] all the things that a person or organisation has done in the past, which shows how good they are at doing their job, dealing with problems, etc.

transaction *n.* [C] **1** a payment, or the process of making one
2 a business deal

trend *n.* [C] the general way in which a particular situation is changing or developing

trial *n.* **1** [C] a legal process in which a court of law examines a case to decide whether someone is guilty of a crime
2 [C, usually plural] a process of testing a product to see whether it is safe, effective, etc.
trial *v.* [T], **trialling** *n.* [U]

turnaround (*also* **turnround** *BrE*) *n.* [C, usually singular] **1** the time between receiving an order for goods, dealing with it and sending the goods to the customer
2 a complete change from a bad situation to a good one
3 a complete change in someone's opinion or ideas

turnover *n.* [singular] **1** *BrE* the amount of business done in a particular period, measured by the amount of money obtained from customers for goods or services that have been sold
2 the rate at which workers leave an organisation and are replaced by others
3 the rate at which goods are sold

tycoon *n.* [C] someone who is successful in business and industry and has a lot of money and power

unfair *adj.* **1** not right or fair
2 not giving a fair opportunity to everyone

unique selling point (USP) *n.* [C] a feature of a product that no other similar products have, used in advertising, etc. to try to persuade people to buy it

upgrade¹ *v.* [I, T] **1** to make a computer, machine, program, etc. better and able to do more things
2 to get a better seat on a plane, a better rented car, etc. than the one you paid for

upgrade² *n.* [C] **1** the act of improving a product or service, or one that has been improved
2 an occasion when someone is given a better seat on a plane, or a better rented car, than the one they paid for

upmarket¹ (*also* **upscale** *AmE*) *adj.* involving goods and services that are expensive and perhaps of good quality compared to other goods, etc. of the same type, or the people that buy them

upmarket² (*also* **upscale** *AmE*) *adv.* **1 go/move upmarket/upscale** to start buying or selling more expensive goods or services
2 take something upmarket/upscale to change a product or a service, or people's ideas about it, so that it is or seems to be more expensive and of better quality

upturn *n.* [C] an increase or improvement in the level of something

vacancy *n.* (*plural* **vacancies**) [C] a job that is available for someone to start doing

value *n.* **1** [C, U] the amount of money something is worth
good/excellent, etc. value (for money) If something is *good/excellent, etc. value,* it is of good quality, considering its price or you get a large amount for the price.
2 values [plural] the principles and practices that a business or organisation thinks are important and which it tries to follow

voice mail (*also* **voicemail**) *n.* [U] an electronic system on your telephone that lets you leave messages for people who phone you when you are not available, and lets them leave messages for you

volatile *adj.* A *volatile* market, situation, etc. changes quickly and suddenly, for example rising and falling without much warning.
volatility *n.* [U]

volume *n.* [C, U] **1** the amount of space that a substance or object contains or fills
2 the total amount of something

wage *n.* [C] (*also* **wages**) money that someone earns according to the number of hours, days or weeks that they work, especially money that is paid each week
minimum wage [singular] the lowest amount of money that can legally be paid per hour to a worker

warehouse *n.* [C] a large building used for storing goods in large quantities

wealth *n.* [U] a large amount of money or valuable possessions
wealthy *adj.*

withdraw *v.* (*past tense* **withdrew**; *past participle* **withdrawn**) [T] **1** to take money out of a bank account
2 If a company *withdraws* a product or service, it stops making it available, either for a period of time or permanently.

workforce *n.* [singular] all the people who work in a particular country, industry or factory

Pearson Education Limited

Edinburgh Gate, Harlow, Essex CM20 2JE, England
and Associated Companies throughout the world.

www.pearsonelt.com

© Pearson Education Limited 2021

First Edition first published 2000
Fourth impression 2023

Third Edition first published 2010
Third Edition Extra first published 2016

Third Edition Extra Premium Digital edition first published 2021

ISBN: 978-1-292-36113-0

Set in Meta OT 9.5/12pt

Printed in Slovakia by Neografia

Acknowledgements

The publishers would like to thank the following authors for writing the Business Skills lessons: Margaret O'Keefe, Clare Walsh, Iwona Dubicka, Lizzie Wright, Bob Dignan, Sara Helm and Fiona Scott-Barrett.

The authors would like to thank the following for their invaluable help during the project: Melanie Bryant, Peter Falvey, Sarah Falvey, Gisele Cotton, Mark Cotton, Jason Hewitt, Richard Falvey, Darrell Mercer and all the former staff and students of the English Language Centre, London Metropolitan University. Thanks also to John Rogers for writing the Review units and Glossary.

The authors and publishers are very grateful to the following people who agreed to be interviewed for the recorded material in this book: Chris Cleaver, Anne Deering, David Hillyard, Elizabeth Jackson, Darrell Mercer, Carys Owen, Richard Rawlinson, Marco Rimini, Andy Simmons, Sholto Smith, Rory Taylor, Jeff Toms. Special thanks from the authors to Chris Hartley for his great help with the interviews.

The publishers and authors are very grateful to the following advisers and teachers who commented on earlier versions of this material and contributed to the initial research: Aukjen Bosma, Michael Bundy, Higor Cavalcante, Ian Duncan, Roberto Dutra, Rosana Goncalves, Judy Nandall, Nancy Pietragalla Dorfman, Dr Petra Pointner, Steven Pragnell, Malgorzata Rzeznik, Robert McLarty, David Kadas, Hans Leijenaar, Sabine Prochel, Ulrich Schuh.

We are grateful to the following for permission to reproduce copyright material:

Text

Photos